Social Media Campaigning in Europe

Studies of election campaigns have shown an increased employment of websites, weblog tools, email, and social media by political campaigners, as well as the use of similar platforms by citizens to find information, communicate about elections or engage more generally in political issues. This comprehensive volume explores the ways in which social media is used on the one hand as a campaigning tool, and on the other, by local citizens. It aims to develop a more holistic and Eurocentric research agenda by capturing both supply and demand practices at the European level. The authors employ both single and multi-nation case studies, furthering debates on *how* political actors and voters embrace the new information and communication environment, in what ways, and for what purposes. The book offers new perspectives on social media campaigning within European democracies, thereby contributing to a more global and comprehensive understanding of how campaigning is affected, and might be enhanced, by developing an interactive digital strategy.

This book will be of great interest to students of both politics and media studies. It was originally published as a special issue of the *Journal of Information Technology & Politics.*

Darren G. Lilleker is Associate Professor in Political Communication in the Faculty of Media and Communication at Bournemouth University, UK. His research focuses on the nexus between political campaigns and voter engagement, trust, and self-efficacy as conceptualized in his book *Political Communication and Cognition* (2014).

Karolina Koc-Michalska is Associate Professor at Audencia Business School and Associated Researcher at CEVIPOF Sciences-Po Paris, France. Her research focuses on the strategies of political actors in the online environment and citizens' political engagement, where she employs comparative approach focusing on the U.S. and European countries.

Ralph Negrine is Emeritus Professor of Political Communication in the Department of Journalism Studies at the University of Sheffield, UK. His publications include *The Transformation of Political Communication* (2008) and *The Political Communication Reader* (with James Stanyer, 2007).

Rachel Gibson is Professor of Politics at the University of Manchester, UK. Her research focuses on how digital technologies are changing the way in which election campaigns are fought and won. She is interested in comparative research and has a particular focus on developments in the UK, the U.S., Australia, and France.

Thierry Vedel is a CNRS Senior Research Fellow with the Center for Political Research at Sciences-Po Paris, France.

Sylvie Strudel is Professor of the Political Sciences (Professeur des Universités) at Pantheon-Assas University, France, and Associated Researcher at Centre Marc Bloch de Berlin, Germany, and CEVIPOF Sciences-Po Paris, France.

Social Media Campaigning in Europe

Social Media Campaigning in Europe

Edited by
Darren G. Lilleker, Karolina Koc-Michalska, Ralph Negrine, Rachel Gibson, Thierry Vedel, and Sylvie Strudel

Routledge
Taylor & Francis Group
LONDON AND NEW YORK

First published 2019
by Routledge
2 Park Square, Milton Park, Abingdon, Oxon, OX14 4RN

and by Routledge
52 Vanderbilt Avenue, New York, NY 10017

Routledge is an imprint of the Taylor & Francis Group, an informa business

British Library Cataloguing in Publication Data
A catalogue record for this book is available from the British Library

ISBN 13: 978-0-367-18566-4

Typeset in Minion Pro
by RefineCatch Limited, Bungay, Suffolk

Publisher's Note
The publisher accepts responsibility for any inconsistencies that may have arisen during the conversion of this book from journal articles to book chapters, namely the possible inclusion of journal terminology.

Contents

Citation Information

The chapters in this book were originally published in the *Journal of Information Technology & Politics*, volume 14, issue 4 (December 2017). When citing this material, please use the original page numbering for each article, as follows:

Chapter 1
Social media campaigning in Europe: Mapping the terrain
Darren G. Lilleker, Karolina Koc-Michalska, Ralph Negrine, Rachel Gibson, Thierry Vedel, and Sylvie Strudel
Journal of Information Technology & Politics, volume 14, issue 4 (December 2017), pp. 293–298

Chapter 2
"Beer is more efficient than social media"—Political parties and strategic communication in Austrian and Swiss national elections
Ulrike Klinger and Uta Russmann
Journal of Information Technology & Politics, volume 14, issue 4 (December 2017), pp. 299–313

Chapter 3
The role of gender in online campaigning: Swedish candidates' motives and use of social media during the European election 2014
Linn A. C. Sandberg and Patrik Öhberg
Journal of Information Technology & Politics, volume 14, issue 4 (December 2017), pp. 314–333

Chapter 4
From hybrid media system to hybrid-media politicians: Danish politicians and their cross-media presence in the 2015 national election campaign
Mark Blach-Ørsten, Mads Kæmsgaard Eberholst, and Rasmus Burkal
Journal of Information Technology & Politics, volume 14, issue 4 (December 2017), pp. 334–347

Chapter 5
Brute force effects of mass media presence and social media activity on electoral outcome
Marko Kovic, Adrian Rauchfleisch, Julia Metag, Christian Caspar, and Julian Szenogrady
Journal of Information Technology & Politics, volume 14, issue 4 (December 2017), pp. 348–371

Chapter 6
When David and Goliath campaign online: The effects of digital media use during electoral campaigns on vote for small parties
Carol Galais and Ana Sofía Cardenal
Journal of Information Technology & Politics, volume 14, issue 4 (December 2017), pp. 372–386

Chapter 7
Sharing Is Caring! Investigating Viral Posts on Politicians' Facebook Pages During the 2014 General Election Campaign in Hungary
Marton Bene
Journal of Information Technology & Politics, volume 14, issue 4 (December 2017), pp. 387–402

Chapter 8

Personalization of Politics Between Television and the Internet: Leader Effects in the 2013 Italian Parliamentary Election
Diego Garzia
Journal of Information Technology & Politics, volume 14, issue 4 (December 2017), pp. 403–416

Notes on Contributors

Marton Bene is a Junior Research Fellow at the Centre for Social Sciences at the Hungarian Academy of Sciences, Hungary, and a PhD student in the Department of Political Science at Corvinus University of Budapest, Hungary.

Mark Blach-Ørsten is Professor of Journalism in the Department of Communication and Art at Roskilde University, Denmark. His research interests are in political communication, journalism ethics and credibility, and media use and media systems.

Rasmus Burkal is a PhD student in the Department of Communication and Art at Roskilde University, Denmark. His research interests are in political and public communication.

Ana Sofía Cardenal is Professor of Political Science at the Universitat Oberta de Catalunya, Spain. Her research fields include comparative politics and political behaviour. Her recent research interests include electoral politics, public agenda, political mobilisation, political parties, and uses of the Internet.

Christian Caspar is a PhD student in the Department of Political Science at the University of Zurich, Switzerland, and a board member of ZIPAR. His research interests are in democracy, public sphere, and power.

Carol Galais is a Postdoctoral Fellow in the Department of Political Science and Law at the Universitat Oberta de Catalunya, Spain. Her research interests include the psychological factors that lead to participation, the civic duty to vote, the role of digital media in public opinion, and the political socialization process.

Diego Garzia is Senior Researcher and Lecturer in the Department of Political Science at the University of Lucerne, Switzerland.

Rachel Gibson is Professor of Politics at the University of Manchester, UK. Her research focuses on how digital technologies are changing the way in which election campaigns are fought and won. She is interested in comparative research and has a particular focus on developments in the UK, the U.S., Australia, and France.

Mads Kæmsgaard Eberholst is a PhD student and Journalism Lecturer in the Department of Communication and Art at Roskilde University, Denmark. His research is concerned with cross-border reporting, data journalism, digital trends, social media, and news production. He has previously worked as a broadcast television reporter.

Ulrike Klinger is Assistant Professor at the Institute of Journalism and Communication Science at the Freie Universität Berlin, Germany. She works on workplace digital communication considering gender aspects.

Karolina Koc-Michalska is Associate Professor at Audencia Business School, and Associated Researcher at CEVIPOF Sciences-Po Paris, France. Her research focuses on the strategies of political actors in the online environment and citizens' political engagement, where she employs a comparative approach focusing on the U.S. and European countries.

Marko Kovic is co-Founder and President of the Zurich Institute of Public Affairs Research, Switzerland. His research interests include decision-making, ethics, political theory, and existential risks.

Darren G. Lilleker is Associate Professor in Political Communication in the Faculty of Media and Communication at Bournemouth University, UK. His research focuses on the nexus between political campaigns and voter engagement, trust and self-efficacy as conceptualized in his book *Political Communication and Cognition* (2014).

Julia Metag is Professor in the Department of Communication and Media Research at the University of Fribourg, Switzerland. Her research interests include political communication, science communication, and media effects.

Ralph Negrine is Emeritus Professor of Political Communication in the Department of Journalism Studies at the University of Sheffield, UK. His publications include *The Transformation of Political Communication* (2008) and *The Political Communication Reader* (with James Stanyer, 2007).

Patrik Öhberg is Associate Professor of Political Science at the University of Gothenburg, Sweden. He has a wide research interest in theories and practices of representative democracy. His specific interests include the perceptions and behaviours of political and administrative elites.

Adrian Rauchfleisch is co-Founder of the Zurich Institute of Public Affairs Research, Switzerland, and Assistant Professor at the Graduate Institute of Journalism at the National Taiwan University, Taiwan. His research interests include political communication, online communication, and public sphere theory.

Uta Russmann is Professor in the Department of Communication, Marketing and Sales at the FHWien of WKW University of Applied Sciences for Management and Communication, Austria. Her research interests include online communication, visual social media, public relations, strategic communication, political communication, and media and elections.

Linn A. C. Sandberg is a PhD student in the Department of Media and Communication at the University of Oslo, Norway. She is conducting research on how digitalization and the growth of social media affect representative democracy and the democratic values that are traditionally viewed as providing legitimacy to political decisions.

Sylvie Strudel is Professor of the Political Sciences (Professeur des Universités) at Pantheon-Assas University, France, and Associated Researcher at Centre Marc Bloch de Berlin, Germany, and CEVIPOF Sciences-Po Paris, France.

Julian Szenogrady is a graduate in Media and Communication Science of the University of Zurich, Switzerland. He is a Junior Transition Specialist at UBS, Switzerland. His research interests include social media, science communication, and marketing.

Thierry Vedel is a CNRS Senior Research Fellow with the Center for Political Research at Sciences-Po Paris, France.

Social media campaigning in Europe: Mapping the terrain

Darren G. Lilleker, Karolina Koc-Michalska, Ralph Negrine, Rachel Gibson, Thierry Vedel, and Sylvie Strudel

The evolution of political communication as a practice has seen political actors constantly adapting to communication technologies. Scammell (1994) documents how, as a gubernatorial candidate, Theodore Roosevelt exploited the potential of embedded pictures in print news, and how UK prime minister Stanley Baldwin employed actors to help him develop the appropriate tone of voice for radio to match the news he was imparting. Later, Ronald Reagan pioneered the televisual performance, while in the UK Margaret Thatcher was redefining prime ministerial media management. While mainstream political figures innovated with traditional media the pioneers of Internet campaigning were largely outsiders—challengers to the U.S. two-party system. When former wrestler Jesse Ventura crowdsourced support for his 1998 insurgent campaign that won him the governorship of Minnesota, he demonstrated how an outsider could challenge the establishment using digital technology. The unsuccessful but groundbreaking campaign of Democrat candidate Howard Dean in 2003 demonstrated the utility of an online crowdfunding strategy. It was Dean's innovative style that would inform the Obama campaign of 2007–8, which would harness the full potential of social media to reach out to voters, earn donations, and build a campaign infrastructure across the United States by harnessing the enthusiasm of his young support base (Lilleker & Jackson, 2011) as well as an established progressive online activist network (Karpf, 2012; Kreiss, 2012). Although the history of innovative use of technology has a U.S.-centric flavor, one should not underestimate the impact of these developments across Western democracies. Campaign strategists travel the world learning how to campaign and what innovations work, shopping around to learn the latest tactical advantages (Plasser & Plasser, 2002) and then adapting them for competitive advantage in their home nations (Lees-Marshment & Lilleker, 2012). The developments have largely seen digital technology employed to further the objectives of the campaign, not create interactive spaces where citizens and politicians can meet or where political issues of the day are debated (Lilleker & Vedel, 2013). Hence, technology is employed to meet the requirements of a campaign with minimal adaptation to the content of political communication. The communication forms appropriate to technologies, such as Twitter and Facebook as was formerly the case with radio and television, become incorporated into the toolboxes and repertoires of political campaigners.

In turn, as digital technologies increasingly become embedded in political communication, research has burgeoned with works exploring the way in which e-mail, Web sites and more recently the plethora of social media platforms are employed and impact the implementation of election campaigns. Studies have charted the increased use of Web sites, Weblog tools, e-mail, and most recently social media by political campaigns (Gibson & Ward, 2009), as well as the use of similar platforms by citizens to communicate about elections and political issues more generally (Loader, Vromen, & Xenos, 2014). As political participation develops an online dimension, so political parties, in particular during elections, seek to exploit the affordances of digital technologies to harness supporters and garner support (Tencher et al., 2016). The questions are how and with what effect?

Apart from the innovations of outsider candidates such as Ventura, the early days of Internet campaigning involved the development of something akin to an online shop front. The Web site provided a means by which citizens could learn more about a candidate or party, and be persuaded that the platform they offered was an attractive and viable alternative to their competitors. Web sites have evolved from being static, information-heavy spaces to stripped down, functional campaigning hubs. When entering a party Web site, visitors are more likely to face invitations to sign up, join, and donate than a campaign slogan. These developments reflect the recognition by strategists that visitors are likely to have already formed an interest and possibly be supportive prior to their visiting. The idea that a Web site will gain accidental visitors in the days of search results being determined by complex and personalized algorithms and search engine optimization strategies is moribund.

Although a Web site has become a standard campaign tool for the postmodern campaigner, the new election battleground is increasingly found on social media. Political actors at all levels, from presidents to neighborhood campaigners, are increasingly likely to use platforms such as Facebook and Twitter as their primary means of communication. Such tools clearly mark a significant step forward in the technical and practical know-how needed to run and maintain a viable digital campaign. Their introduction brings a more multimodal, cross-referencing, and interactive style to the political communication genre. They also offer a myriad of new ways for citizens to connect with politicians: *likes*, *shares*, *retweets*, and *follows* have all now become standard terms in the campaign lexicon. Each action has the potential to make the campaign more visible to a wider audience, getting the message out while also drawing in visitors (Gerodimos & Justinussen, 2015). The social media pages created for a campaign can then direct followers to other sites and video content, drawing them closer to the campaign.

Beyond the expanded and enriched voter interface they offer there is also a richer organizational legacy that flows from campaigns' adaptation to the Facebook era. Through social networking sites it now becomes possible for parties, big and small, to engage in new forms of community building and to open their boundaries beyond formal membership (Gibson, 2015; Gibson et al. 2016). Through Facebook groups, meet-up software, hashtags, and dissemination of mobile apps, parties are increasingly able to mobilize and "weaponize" members—and more crucially, nonmembers—to take action on their behalf during and between elections (Karpf, 2012; Kreiss, 2012; Warren, Sulaiman, & Jaafar, 2015). The new resources that such tools generate clearly offer a considerable boost to parties' capacity to fight and win elections and may even provide a way to regenerate Europe's faltering "mass" party model. However, the inevitable dilution of elite control and party discipline that this more devolved and "outsourced" model of organization causes could also act as a barrier to their full exploitation. Whether this tension will be resolved through a shift toward more personalized and candidate-centered politics and a further weakening of traditional party models is thus an open question.

However, the wider tectonic plates of party systems may shift in response to the new technology. It is a given that political candidates and parties will continue to compete for attention via digital media. Beyond signing-up helpers, the Internet and particularly social media have a range of affordances that can help campaigners persuade voters into the polling booth on election day. Campaigns utilize the full hypermedia environment to disseminate content that combines slogans and images which can gain accelerated reach through peer-to-peer sharing within online networks. Although the traditional media forms of television and newspapers remain the main priorities during election campaigns, digital communications and social media in particular do not lag far behind (Lilleker, Tenscher, & Štětka, 2015).

Success can be measured in election outcomes, but it remains challenging to determine what impact digital technologies really have in securing votes. The recent surprise success of leftist insurgent movements in the UK during the 2017 general election and on the right in the United States with the Trump "takeover" of the Republican party are widely credited to their leaders' and followers' savvy use of Twitter and the unique instantaneous sharing facilities of social media. Isolating any communication medium from others, however, is complex and challenging, especially when attempting to isolate the effects of a medium on the attitudes and behaviors of an audience. Experimental research has developed understandings of the role that mass media plays, in particular Graber's work on television (Graber & Dunaway, 2014), in exposing audiences to political ideas as well as influencing voter choices. Similarly research has also given insights into the power of Web sites, Weblogs, and social media to increase engagement in politics, heightening the propensity to seek information and take part in a range of acts of political participation (Gil de Zúñiga, Veenstra, Vraga, & Shah, 2010). Therefore, arguably, political science has laid the groundwork for understanding that media can have an impact on voter choices and that such impacts can be measured. Yet the hybrid media environment mapped by Chadwick (2017) remains somewhat enigmatic in terms of its impact upon voter attitudes, interest, engagement, participation and voter choices and the links between each of these components. The digital environment affords visibility to a range of political information outlets, legacy media, and insurgent online-only news sites as well as the platforms created by campaigners. These may offer genuine facts, biased reports, loaded arguments, or even fake news but all are part of the digital communication environment. Due to the difficulty in charting how citizens navigate the online world, it remains equally difficult to determine the relationship between the visibility afforded parties or candidates by having a presence across digital platforms and their vote share. Presence is also only one of myriad variables that might determine whether a party or candidate wins attention, engagement, and support. Parties and candidates can use social media platforms in a variety of ways, often simply due to their personal perspectives on the efficacy of pursuing a given strategy. Differential usage of digital platforms can be found in the type of content posted or the levels of interactivity offered, for example, but do such variances matter? Variances in communication strategy have been found to have an impact upon the receivers' levels of engagement and their propensity to seek further information, and determine their propensity to participate (Xenos & Moy, 2007). Yet isolating these factors remains a challenge for strategists and researchers alike. Although the ceteris paribus principle can provide indications (Koc-Michalska, Lilleker, Surowiec, & Baranowski, 2014), it remains impossible to isolate any one factor when studying the vibrant atmosphere that is an election campaign. The evidence suggests that independent of scientific evidence for a digital campaign effect, campaign strategists see these technologies as being able to offer significant gains. In the UK, social media campaigning by the Conservatives in 2015 was argued to be pivotal in persuading floating voters in marginal constituencies (Moore, 2016), while the Labour-supportive Momentum infrastructure was designed to leverage younger disaffected citizens (Klug, Rees, & Schneider, 2016). The belief thus predominates that although traditional media remain a key battleground, innovations within the digital environments can make a real difference in winning over voters (Lilleker et al., 2015).

This special edition collects seven papers that add theoretically and empirically to an academic understanding of how candidates and parties view and so use digital technologies to communicate with voters and explores the effect of usage on the attitudes and behaviors of citizens within the context of elections in Europe (national, regional, or European Parliament). Recognizing the United States as the locus of innovation in this area, we wish to explore how digital technologies are employed in systems where resources are less plentiful and where the political culture is less polarized and expressive. We cannot aspire to provide a definitive response to the very complex questions of effects; rather we seek to contribute to those wider debates. Our papers map onto debates regarding how politicians view the potential of social media as a campaigning tool, as well as how they embrace the hybrid media environment. Papers test the validity of claims of an "Internet effect," exploring whether political and media-related variables impact upon any suggested effect due to social media campaigning. The contributors also explore the demand side, testing how citizens use the online environment to gain information and with what effect as well as what communication they are most likely to share, the suggestion being what they engage with is what they like. Cumulatively, we offer new perspectives on social media campaigning within European democracies, thereby contributing a more global and holistic understanding of how campaigning is effected by—and might be enhanced and given greater utility by—developing a digital strategy.

This special edited collection includes research that adopts quantitative and qualitative methodologies in order to contribute to knowledge and debates from a number of perspectives. We begin with candidate and practitioner studies (Klinger & Russmann, 2017; Sandberg & Öhberg, 2017), traditional and/or social media content analysis (Bene, 2017; Blach-Ørsten, Eberholst, & Burkal, 2017; Rauchfleisch, Kovic, Metag, Caspar, & Szenogrady, 2017), and the survey-based studies of citizens (Galais & Cardenal, 2017; Garzia, 2017). Cumulatively, these contributions aid in understanding the role and motivation of political actors using social media; they also examine the consequences of social media communication, as well as testing the potential impact of traditional and digital media presence on the propensity to vote. The issue includes studies based on single-country data (Denmark, Hungary, Italy, or Sweden) as well as comparative research (Austria and Switzerland, France, Germany, Spain and Canada).

Klinger and Russmann (2017) define the motives, goals, strategies, and tactics of social media use within the media planning of Swiss and Austrian parties during electoral campaigns. A social media presence seems to be a "must-have" and part of the all-media presence rather than a conscious strategic vision of how new media communication could be employed to enhance the scope of campaigning. The campaigners claim direct interactivity as the main reasoning for having a social media presence. Regardless of the country context, the strategy chosen (e.g., controlled vs. general access, time employment, etc.) depends mainly on parties' resources. Still, among communication strategists, social media remains the secondary channel of communication—since "beer (on the market square) is more effective"—with deep skepticism concerning the real gains that social media may bring to campaign effectiveness.

Sandberg and Öhberg (2017) study the motivations, meaning, and possible gains from social media usage by candidates in the Swedish 2014 European Parliament election, with special focus on gender variance. The results indicate a distinction along campaign types, with social media emerging as a separate factor. Gender differences are important in understanding differences in approaches to using campaigning tools, with female candidates evaluating the value of social media higher, especially Facebook, followed by Twitter. Women candidates, however, seem to use social media as a partisan promotional tool rather than for personal advertising.

Blach-Ørsten et al. (2017) employ the hybridization hypothesis to describe politicians' multimedia campaigning during the Danish 2015 general election. Subsequently, they compare the traditional and new media (Twitter) appearance of those candidates by counting the recognition they receive from online or traditional media outlets. Little evidence is found to suggest a hybrid communication strategy is embedded in Danish election campaigns; rather, if used, it is by young candidates standing in large cities. The authors find traditional media still focusing on the most prominent candidates, with a relatively small number of politicians receiving attention from both traditional and new media outlets. No clear evidence is found for a relationship between electoral success and social media performance.

Rauchfleisch and collegues (2017), in the context of Swiss elections, discuss the role of "brute force" effects, the term they employ to identify the possible impact of having high visibility within traditional and social media on electoral outcomes in Swiss elections. The authors find a minimal effect from both media outlets on electoral victory (with incumbency playing the crucial role for being elected). Yet, more granular analysis (using the number of votes obtained) illustrates the positive role of the traditional media and a substantial effect from having a Facebook presence. Surprisingly, the Facebook effect does not originate from the activity of the candidates themselves but rather from the community's resonance. Overall, the possible brute force effect from traditional media, especially newspaper, remains stronger than any impact from social media campaigning.

Galais and Cardenal (2017) discuss the potential effect of Internet use by voters on their propensity to acknowledge and possibly vote for the more marginal parties. Based on a study in four nations (France, Germany, Switzerland, and Canada), the authors find that traditional media usage lowers the voter's chance to preserve or switch their vote decision toward small parties. On the contrary, Internet use, especially browsing party Web sites, encourages greater consideration of voting for smaller parties, particularly when there are high levels of voter uncertainty. Therefore, party Web site browsing can increase the propensity to vote for marginal parties. Nevertheless, the authors remain skeptical when estimating the potential of digital technology use in changing voter decisions.

In his research, Garzia (2017) points toward the role of the evaluation of the leaders' personality by voters in shaping their voting patterns. He compares the possible impact of a personalization effect among voters consuming mostly traditional media versus online resources within the 2013 Italian elections. Garzia finds the effect of leaders' personality evaluation on voting behavior stronger for those heavily exposed to television; those active on the Internet pay significantly less attention to leaders' personality evaluations. Nonetheless, the effect of personality evaluation remains strong for those active on the Internet and increases the propensity to vote for the Five Star Movement.

Bene (2017) focuses on the most viral Facebook posts during the 2014 general election in Hungary. He studies the logic of the most viral posts and compares them to those that did not receive high virality. Additionally he follows those posts' life after being shared. In the Hungarian context, the posts by oppositional left-wing parties received the most extended shares. The virality does not depend on the structure or timing of the post, but on its emotionally negative character and more personal commentary rather than provision of general information. Further, Bene finds that once shared, the posts have a very short life, with minimal echo among the users, with one exception: if a post is shared by a prominent Facebook user, another politician, or important opinion leader, it receives significantly greater resonance and a longer social media life.

References

Bene, M. (2017). Sharing is caring! Investigating viral posts on politicians' Facebook pages during the 2014 general election campaign in hungary. *Journal of Information Technology & Politics, 14*(4). 1–16. doi:10.1080/19331681.2017.1367348

Blach-Ørsten, M., Eberholst, M., & Burkal, R. (2017). From hybrid media system to hybrid media politicians: Danish politicians and their cross-media presence in the 2015 national election campaign. *Journal of Information Technology & Politics, 14*(4). 1–14. doi:10.1080/19331681.2017.1369917

Chadwick, A. (2017). *The hybrid media system: Politics and power*. Oxford, England: Oxford University Press.

Galais, C., & Cardenal, A. (2017). When David and Goliath campaign online: The effects of digital media use during electoral campaigns on vote for small parties. *Journal of Information Technology & Politics*, 1–15. doi:10.1080/19331681.2017.1367347

Garzia, D. (2017). Personalization of politics between television and the Internet: Leader effects in the 2013 Italian parliamentary election. *Journal of Information, Technology and Politics, 14*(4). doi:10.1080/19331681.2017.1365265

Gerodimos, R., & Justinussen, J. (2015). Obama's 2012 Facebook campaign: Political communication in the age of the like button. *Journal of Information Technology & Politics, 12*(2), 113–132. doi:10.1080/19331681.2014.982266

Gibson, R. K. (2015). Party change, social media and the rise of 'citizen-initiated' campaigning. *Party politics, 21*(2), pp. 183–197.

Gibson, R., & Ward, S. (2009). Parties in the digital age—A review article. *Representation, 45*(1), 87–100. doi:10.1080/00344890802710888

Gibson, R. K., Aldrich, J. H., & Cantijoch, M. (2016). Voter mobilisation in context: Special issue editors' introduction. *Party Politics, 22*(2), 145–148.

Gil de Zúñiga, H., Veenstra, A., Vraga, E., & Shah, D. (2010). Digital democracy: Reimagining pathways to political participation. *Journal of Information Technology & Politics, 7*(1), 36–51. doi:10.1080/19331680903316742

Graber, D. A., & Dunaway, J. (2014). *Mass media and American politics*. New York, NY: CQ Press.

Karpf, D. (2012). *The move on effect: The unexpected transformation of American political advocacy*. Oxford, England: Oxford University Press.

Klinger, U., & Russmann, U. (2017). "Beer is more effective than social media"—Political parties and strategic communication in Austrian and Swiss national elections. *Journal of Information, Technology and Politics, 14*(4). doi:10.1080/19331681.2017.1369919

Klug, A., Rees, E., & Schneider, J. (2016). Momentum: A new kind of politics. *Renewal: A Journal of Labour Politics, 24*(2), 36.

Koc-Michalska, K., Lilleker, D. G., Surowiec, P., & Baranowski, P. (2014). Poland's 2011 online election campaign: New tools, new professionalism, new ways to win votes. *Journal of Information Technology & Politics, 11*(2), 186–205. doi:10.1080/19331681.2014.899176

Kreiss, D. (2012). *Taking our country back: The crafting of networked politics from Howard Dean to Barack Obama*. Oxford, England: Oxford University Press.

Lees-Marshment, J., & Lilleker, D. G. (2012). Knowledge sharing and lesson learning: Consultants' perspectives on the international sharing of political marketing strategy. *Contemporary Politics, 18*(3), 343–354. doi:10.1080/13569775.2012.702976

Lilleker, D., & Jackson, N. (2011). *Political campaigning, elections and the Internet: Comparing the US, UK, France and Germany*. London, England: Routledge.

Lilleker, D. G., Tenscher, J., & Štětka, V. (2015). Towards hypermedia campaigning? Perceptions of new media's importance for campaigning by party strategists in comparative perspective. *Information, Communication & Society, 18*(7), 747–765. doi:10.1080/1369118X.2014.993679

Lilleker, D. G., & Vedel, T. (2013). The Internet in campaigns and elections. In W. Dutton (Ed.), *The Oxford handbook of Internet studies* (pp. 401–420). London, England: Routledge.

Loader, B. D., Vromen, A., & Xenos, M. (Eds.). (2014). *The networked young citizen: Social media, political participation and civic engagement*. London, England: Routledge.

Moore, M. (2016). Facebook, the Conservatives and the risk to fair and open elections in the UK. *The Political Quarterly, 87* (3), 424–430. doi:10.1111/poqu.2016.87.issue-3

Plasser, F., & Plasser, G. (2002). *Global political campaigning: A worldwide analysis of campaign professionals and their practices*. New York, NY: Greenwood Publishing Group.

Rauchfleisch, A., Kovic, M., Metag, J., Caspar, C., & Szenogrady, J. (2017). Brute force effects of mass media presence and social media activity on electoral outcome. *Journal of Information, Technology and Politics*.

Sandberg, L., & Öhberg, P. (2017). The role of gender in online campaigning: Swedish candidate's motives and use of social media during the European election 2014. *Journal of Information Technology & Politics*, *14*(4), 1–20. doi:10.1080/19331681.2017.1369918

Scammell, M. (1995). Designer politics: How elections are won. Basingstoke: Macmillan.

Tenscher, J., Koc-Michalska, K., Lilleker, D. G., Mykkänen, J., Walter, A. S., Findor, A., & Róka, J. (2016). The professionals speak: Practitioners' perspectives on professional election campaigning. *European Journal of Communication*, *31*(2), 95–119. doi:10.1177/0267323115612212

Warren, A. M., Sulaiman, A., & Jaafar, N. I. (2015). Understanding civic engagement behaviour on Facebook from a social capital theory perspective. *Behaviour & Information Technology*, *34*(2), 163–175. doi:10.1080/0144929X.2014.934290

Xenos, M., & Moy, P. (2007). Direct and differential effects of the Internet on political and civic engagement. *Journal of Communication*, *57*(4), 704–718. doi:10.1111/jcom.2007.57.issue-4

"Beer is more efficient than social media"—Political parties and strategic communication in Austrian and Swiss national elections

Ulrike Klinger and Uta Russmann

ABSTRACT
We investigate political parties' social media strategies, their perceived effectiveness, and how social media campaigns are internally organized. Our study focuses on Austria and Switzerland, countries with consociational political systems with less competitive elections and less personalization. The paper is based on semistructured interviews with all parties in Austrian and Swiss parliaments after the national elections in 2011 and 2013, when, for the first time, all parties employed social media in their campaigns. Our findings support a skeptical perspective regarding social media's perceived significance and effects.

Introduction and theoretical background

The main goal of political parties and candidates in democratic election campaigns is to communicate purposefully and deliberately their objectives, ideas, and activities in order to gain legitimacy, and hence persuade the electorate to say yes and vote for them. The primary focus of parties, when applying strategic communication practices, is on how they present and promote themselves through intentional communication and activities of their top candidates, their politicians, supporters, etc. (e.g., Hallahan, Holtzhausen, Van Ruler, Verčič, & Sriramesh, 2007). Strategic communication is "intentional and objectives-driven" (Kiousis & Strömbäck, 2015, p. 384) and this separates it from other types of communication.

Strategic communication "establishes the battleground issues [agenda-building/agenda-setting], orchestrates consistent key themes and images [framing]" (Norris, 2000, p. 10) and identifies the vulnerabilities of the parties' targets. Specifically with the process of professionalization of political communication in general and digitalization of political campaigning in particular, strategic communication emphasizes the use of polls, focus groups, and market research into target audiences, their needs, wants, and drives. It focuses more on advertising and personalization as well as technical and media experts, political consultants, and spin doctors (e.g., Kiousis & Strömbäck, 2015; Norris, 2000; Strömbäck & Kiousis, 2014).

Fundamental aims of strategic political communication are to develop and maintain beneficial relationships between political parties and their key stakeholders, foster stakeholder engagement, and build a dependable reputation (Bennett & Manheim, 2001; Kiousis & Strömbäck, 2015; Norris, 2000). The essence of strategic communication is to engage people in deliberative communication practice and in how meaning is shaped and co-created (Hallahan et al., 2007). Specifically social media may provide platforms to enable citizens to take part in politics and to communicate with the mass media.

Strategic communication "lays out the framework within which campaign communications operate" (Norris, 2000, p. 10): it "sets out party objectives," "prioritizes organizational and financial resources" (Norris, 2000, p. 10), plans, and coordinates campaign activities. Strategic communication is characterized by identifying target voters and supporters. Specifically during election campaigns, political parties increasingly aim at exploiting the affordances of digital communication technologies to attract and bind supporters and potentially new voters.

Both authors have contributed equally and are listed in alphabetical order.

Today, technology, technocrats, and techniques (Farrel, 1996) increasingly characterize strategic political communication and, especially during campaigns, political parties are becoming "communication machines" (Mancini, 1999, p. 242). Several authors have presented models of evolving phases in strategic political communication (e.g., Blumler, 2013; Strömbäck & Kiousis, 2014). Linking styles of campaigning to temporally defined phases, however, ignores largely asynchronous developments in different countries (particularly beyond the U.S. context) and serves to understand long-term transformations rather than immediate strategies and effects of newly implemented communication technologies. For this reason, we opt to connect our study with the model of four ideal types of campaigning (rather than phases) that are differentiated by four specific target audiences (Magin, Podschuweit, Haßler, & Russmann, 2017): partisan-centered campaigns, mass-centered campaigns, target group-centered campaigns, and individual-centered campaigns.

As outlined in Table 1 and described by Magin et al. (2017), partisan-centered campaigns address core party members and partisans, and social media are not a central campaign tool. This is also the case for mass-centered campaigns, when parties aim to reach disperse masses by using one-way communication channels. When parties started to use tailored messages to address the increasingly fluid electorate, target group-centered campaigns developed. Besides traditional communication channels, here, the Internet and with it party and candidate Web sites, banner ads, and direct mailing by e-mail, started to gain in importance. In individual-centered campaigns, social media plays a great role. Parties use the different social media platforms to individualize campaign content to small groups of voters or even tailor campaign messages to single voters. However, concerning micro-targeting, it is important to notice that the use of data on users' habits and preferences for tailoring party messages to single voters is a major issue of public concern in Austria and Switzerland, and, in both countries, it is against the law to send direct marketing e-mail messages without the prior consent of recipients (opt-in) (DLP Piper, 2014; Russmann, 2016).

Against this background, our study aims to understand how Swiss and Austrian parties make sense of social media and operate in a new campaign environment. How do they perceive the efficiency of social media as campaign tools in general, and more specifically, their impact on voters? This study seeks to contribute to our knowledge about social media's role as a campaign tool and communication channel in Swiss and Austrian election campaigns from an organizational perspective. One goal of our paper is to identify and systemize primary strategies and challenges that political parties face when communicating via social media. It approaches this topic by means of qualitative interviews with party web strategists and heads of communication of Swiss and Austrian political parties after national elections. This approach allows us to get a broad perspective on the motives, goals, strategies, and tactics of

Table 1. Four ideal types of campaigning.

	Partisan-centered	Mass-centered	Target group-centered	Individual-centered
Mode of political communication system	Party-dominated	Television-centered	Multiple channels and multimedia	Data based
Dominant style of political communication	Messages along party lines to supporters	Sound bites to mass audience	Tailored messages to target groups	Personalized messages and social media ads to individual voters
Dominant media	Partisan press, newspaper ads, radio broadcasts	Television	Television narrow casting, direct e-mails, Web sites	Social media, voter mining
Campaign coordination	Party leaders and party staff	Party campaign managers, advertising and survey experts	Special party campaign units and consultants	Special party campaign units and data scientists
Dominant campaign paradigm	Party logic	Media logic	Marketing logic	Data logic
Campaign preparation	Short-term, ad hoc	Longer term campaigning	Permanent campaigning	Permanent campaigning

Based on Strömbäck and Kiousis (2014, p. 177) and Magin et al. (2017, pp. 1700–1701)

Table 2. Comparing political communication in Austria and Switzerland.

	AUSTRIA	SWITZERLAND
MEDIA SYSTEMS		
Internet adoption	High	High
Press circulation	High	High
Strength of PSM	High	High
Commercial broadcasting	Low	Low
Giant-Next-Door effect	High	High
POLITICAL SYSTEMS		
Role of elections	High	Low
Citizen participation in decision-making	Low	High
Consociational tradition	Medium	High
Personalization of politics	High	Low
Strength of opposition	High	Low
Voter turnout	High	Low

political parties' social media use. It provides insights into parties′ expectations when using social media and the perceived effects. We also focus on the internal organization of communication on social media (e.g., the number of employees, responsibilities, guidelines, and policies for social media communication). The study focuses on these research questions:

RQ1: What are the main strategies and challenges for communication via social media in election campaigns from a party perspective?

RQ2: What effects do parties expect of social media campaigning and do they monitor their performance?

RQ3: How do parties implement and deal with this new form of communication (in their organization)?

After briefly discussing the existing literature in this area of research and the comparative perspective on Austria and Switzerland, we present our method and results. In the discussion section we will return to the four ideal types of campaigning to outline cross-national differences and longitudinal developments in both countries. Thus, our results are first presented along the categories that emerged in the inductive research process, then discussed from both a deductive angle based on the model of four ideal types of campaigning and from a comparative perspective.

Literature review: Perceptions about social media in election campaigns

Particularly since the 2008 Obama campaign, political campaigns around the world have been using social media to improve their communication with electorates. Therefore it is key to empirically examine the adoption of the new communication medium, because of its potential to change communication between citizens and politicians. However, so far only a few studies have examined the perceptions of political parties about social media.

Tenscher and colleagues (2015) conducted a survey among top-ranked party secretaries and campaign managers from 68 parties in 12 European countries (including Austria) to acquire their perceptions of professional election campaigning. They note that

> parties have shifted from predominantly mobilizing adherents to persuading undecided voters at each contest. Furthermore, technological innovations have transformed the media environment, with multi-platform digital entertainment delivering a fragmented, hard to reach audience. The new media environment requires new campaign strategies and techniques. Cumulatively, these trends, affecting all developed nations, have led political parties to initiate substantial changes, both in their organizational structure and in their communicative strategy“ (Tenscher et al., 2015, p. 98).

Based on the same data, Lilleker, Tenscher and Štětka (“Lilleker, Tenscher and Štětka 2015”, p. 747), found that the adoption of hypermedia campaigning, integrating both old and new media, is “becoming a standard feature of professional campaigning strategy in Europe.” Facebook is perceived as the most important social media platform and as a catch-all medium. Moreover, strategists working within newer parties perceive Facebook and YouTube as more important than their counterparts in more established parties do. However, no differences were found between oppositional and governmental parties.

Bor (2013) examined the implementation of social networking sites during the 2012 U.S. election. Qualitative interviews were conducted with campaign staff of political campaigns of candidates running in Utah’s Fourth District. Concerning campaign communication with citizens, the study shows that social network sites were primarily used for

> disseminating mass messages [to audiences], maintaining a positive presence, promoting engagement among their audiences, and removing certain citizens' comments. Additionally, it was found that the campaigns did not engage in dialogue with citizens; nor did they respond to individual messages unless they contained questions about how to volunteer or donate money to the campaign. (Bor, 2013, p. 10)

Social network sites were integrated into the campaigns' broader communication strategies. The new media helped to control candidates' campaign messages, to show a more personal side of a candidate, to assess message effectiveness and reception, to promote messages on other communications platforms, and to generate campaign contributions in the form of volunteer efforts and donations (Bor, 2013). The collection of donations and the organization of volunteers through social network sites has already been highlighted by Gueorguieva (2008) in a study on MySpace and YouTube in the 2006 U.S. election campaign. On the basis of interviews with 31 consultants and operatives involved in the 2008 U.S. presidential elections, Vaccari (2013, p. 114) notes that "the Internet's main campaign functions are opinion reinforcement and supporter mobilization." Furthermore, the utilization of social media fosters indirect persuasion through interpersonal communication, as highly involved voters who are using social media reach out to less aware voters.

In the case of Norway, Kalnes (2009) points out that political parties knew very little about social media's efficiency for political networking and were skeptical of it. The national party organizations "had a hesitant approach" (p. 264) to this new communication toolset. Especially the relatively strong organization of Norwegian parties seemed to have been a primary reason why parties were "less reliant on ad hoc networking" (p. 264). A few years later, a study comparing political parties' social media strategies and practices on Facebook during the following Norwegian national election campaign found different results. It shows that Facebook had in the meantime been integrated in parties' campaign communication (Kalsnes, 2016). When it comes to interaction on Facebook, the interviewed heads of communication highlighted three strategic advantages: (a) dialogue with voters, (b) feedback, and (c) to bypass mass media, and three challenges: (a) offensive online behavior, (b) negative media attention, and (c) limited resources. However, the study also shows that reality does not always live up to the goals mentioned.

In short, previous studies show that political parties hope that the utilization of social media may foster interaction and dialogue with citizens; may support the mobilizing and organizing of supporters; may disseminate positive messages and reinforce the political message online and offline; may assess message effectiveness; may reinforce opinions; may generate campaign donations; and may "humanize" a candidate. However, numerous empirical studies have shown that political actors tend to underexploit (Cardenal, 2013) social media and that "politicians report higher and more idealistic motivations for democratic dialogue for their social media use than they actually manage to manoeuvre in practice" (Enli & Skogerbø, 2013, p. 770). That political actors broadcast rather than dialogue on social media has been repeatedly found in studies from various countries (Graham, Broersma, Hazelhoff, & Van 'T Haar, 2013; Grant, Moon, & Busby Grant, 2010; Larsson, 2015; Svensson & Larsson, 2016; Vergeer, Herman, & Sams, 2011).

At the same time, it still seems unclear *why* political actors only reluctantly adopt and mostly broadcast on social media platforms. Lassen and Brown (2011) concluded that mere structural indicators cannot explain this, and that it proved difficult to discern patterns of individual motivation to use Twitter. Also, it remains unclear if and how many additional votes could be generated by online mobilization. One could argue that political parties have goals other than maximizing votes, such as office-seeking and policymaking. However, as there is only an uncertain spillover effect from online communication to offline participation and voting behavior (Vissers & Stolle, 2014), reluctance to mobilize support on social media platforms may not be a passing phenomenon, but may be grounded in very rational considerations. Another reason that might undermine the purpose of mobilizing support online is the notion of "preaching to the converted"—broadcasting to and dialoguing with citizens who are politically active and already supporting a party, instead of reaching out to new potential voters, members, or supporters (Skovsgaard & Van Dalen, 2013).

Comparing Austria and Switzerland

A comparison of Austria and Switzerland seems particularly fruitful when trying to find out how political parties make sense of social media and why they include it in their communication strategies, because the two countries have similar media systems and political systems (institutional structure, party systems, etc). However, their political systems also feature strong differences that might affect how parties approach campaigning (see Table 2). Because political communication and electoral communication strategies are shaped by media and political contexts, this comparative perspective allows us to discuss how political parties perceive social media against varying backgrounds.

The media systems in Austria and Switzerland are similar: Both are counted among the democratic corporatist model (Hallin & Mancini, 2004, p. 67), characterized by high newspaper circulation and an early emergence of mass-circulation press. Free daily newspapers have hit the market in both countries and their traditionally biased party press has developed into a (more or less) neutral commercial press (see Udris & Lucht, 2014 for a comparison of Switzerland and Austria, pp. 117 & 121). We find strong professionalization in the media sector, strong public service broadcasting as well as weak commercial broadcasting owing to the strong presence of commercial programs from same-language neighboring countries with larger media markets (Germany, and for Switzerland, also France and Italy; Hallin & Mancini, 2004). As shown in Table 3, the Internet adoption took a similar pace and pattern in both countries.

The political systems in Austria and Switzerland are both similar and quite different: Although both countries have multiparty systems, two-chamber parliaments, and government coalitions, Switzerland has a more consociational tradition than Austria. In Switzerland, government includes parties from opposite sides of the party spectrum and works according to the consensus principle. As the composition of the government coalition remained stable over decades, Swiss citizens cannot vote out their government, and traditionally there are no opposition parties. This structural feature is checked and balanced by direct democratic elements, by which Swiss citizens, parties, or interest groups can participate in decision-making. Furthermore, Swiss politicians are compensated on a volunteer basis ("militia system"), so that political

Table 3. Internet use in Austria (A) and Switzerland (CH) in %.

	CH 2011	A 2013	CH 2015
Internet users	77[a]	80[c]	88[a]
Facebook	42[a]	51[d]	52[a]
Twitter	11[b]	3[d]	17[e]
Video portals (YouTube)	65[b]	65[d]	62[e]

[a]http://www.mediachange.ch/media//pdf/publications/Verbreitung_und_Bruchlinien_2015.pdf
[b]http://www.mediachange.ch/media/pdf/publications/Anwendungen_Nutzung.pdf (2011)
[c]http://www.integral.co.at/downloads/Internet/2014/02/AIM-Consumer_-_Q4_2013.pdf
[d]INTEGRAL, AIM (Austrian Internet Monitor) (Internet users 14 years and older) and http://socialmediaradar.at
[e]http://www.mediachange.ch/media//pdf/publications/Anwendungen_Nutzung_2015.pdf

Table 4. Overview of sample (political parties).

	Party	Votes (%) in 2013 national elections	Votes (%) in 2008 national elections	Political position
AUSTRIA	SPÖ*	26.8	29.3	Center-left
	ÖVP*	24.0	26.0	Center-right
	FPÖ	20.5	17.5	Right-wing
	Green Party	12.4	10.4	Center-left
	NEOS	5.0	—	Center
	Pirate Party	0.8	—	Left
		Votes (%) in 2011 national elections	Votes (%) in 2007 national elections	Political position
SWITZERLAND	SVP*	26.6	28.9	Right-wing
	SP*	18.7	19.5	Left-wing
	FDP*	15.1	15.8	Center-right
	CVP*	12.3	14.5	Center
	GPS	8.4	9.8	Left-wing
	BDP*	5.4	—	Center right
	GLP	5.4	1.4	Center
	EVP	2.0	2.4	Center

* Parties in government coalition.

office is never their primary source of income. Thus, elections play a less important role in Switzerland than in Austria or other European countries. In Austria, citizens hardly participate in decision-making, as direct involvement is basically limited to elections, hence, elections play a major role. For the most part of the Second Republic (since 1945) Austria has been ruled by coalition governments, with the exception of 1966 to 1983 (Bundesministerium für Inneres, 2017). For most of this time, the social democratic SPÖ and the Conservative ÖVP have governed as part of a "grand coalition" and even between 1966 and 1983 the parties worked closely together in the context of the institutionalized cooperation between the representations of employers and labor in Austria (*Sozialpartnerschaft*), which renders domestic continuity (Gehler, 2006). However, since the mid-1980s, Austria has a strong opposition whose power is growing with each election (Bundesministerium für Inneres, 2017).

With the trend of decreasing voter turnout, growing lack of trust and faith in parties, and declining partisanship (Dalton, 2000; Eurobarometer, 2016), Swiss and Austrian parties are looking for new ways to directly communicate with (potential) voters. Turnout in Austrian parliamentary elections had decreased from 78.8% in 2008 to an all-time low of 74.9% in 2013 (Bundesministerium für Inneres, 2017; Wahlbeteiligung, 2016), but is still high in international comparison. In Switzerland, the voter turnout in the national parliamentary elections in both 2011 and 2015 was 48.5%, only slightly higher (0.3%) than in 2007 (The Swiss Federal Statistical Office, 2016). Voter turnout in Switzerland is traditionally low (<50% since 1975), and while turnout is influenced by many variables (Blais, 2006), the lack of competitiveness of Swiss elections certainly plays a role here. In both countries, Internet penetration is higher than voter turnout: about 80% of the Swiss and Austrian populations aged 14 and older regularly use the Internet (Latzer, Just, Metreveli, & Saurwein, 2012; The Swiss Federal Statistical Office, 2016).

The 2011 Swiss national elections and the 2013 Austrian national elections were the first national elections in both countries in which all political parties used social media as a campaign tool. Facebook, Twitter, and YouTube were the major (and sometimes only) platforms on which political parties and their (top) candidates were present. Social media adoption has steadily increased over the past few years in Austria and Switzerland, and both countries display similar Internet use patterns, as shown in Table 3. However, social media use differs greatly among the many platforms. Taking a closer look at the most often used platforms, YouTube, Facebook, and Twitter, YouTube is the social media site with the largest number of users.

Campaign Web sites have become a standard communication tool in both countries, and parties have adapted to the emergence of a social media platform's network media logic to supplement the mass media logic of traditional media outlets (see Klinger & Svensson, 2015). However, compared to other countries with similar media or political systems and comparable Internet access and use, Austrian parties started using social media to communicate and connect to the public very late. Although social media became very popular in Austria between 2006 and 2008, particularly among the young, the Austrian regional election campaign in Vienna in autumn 2010 was the first election campaign in which all major and minor political parties in the federal state government used Facebook to gain support. In Switzerland, social media were not a standard communication tool in the electoral campaign of 2007, but YouTube already played an important role. Fraefel (2012) presents similar results on the regional level, where Swiss parties only rarely used social media and, even if so, often did not promote it on their web sites in cantonal election campaigns. Quantitative data on Switzerland's 2011 election campaign showed that political parties used social media largely for broadcasting, as an additional channel to spread information or link mass media references, and only to a marginal degree for participation and dialogue with voters (Klinger, 2013).

Method

To generate an in-depth understanding of political parties' utilization of social media as a campaign instrument in Switzerland and Austria, we conducted personal semistructured qualitative interviews with the heads of communication or the web party strategists of all major and minor parties in parliament (see Table 4) following the Swiss national elections on October 23, 2011 (eight interviews held from December 6, 2011, to June 21, 2012) and the Austrian national elections on September 29, 2013 (six interviews held from October 9 to October 28, 2013), with the exception of the new Austrian party Team Stronach. According to the party, an external agency was in charge of their web campaign; it was not available for an interview. Fourteen interviews might be considered a small database, but they encompass the entire political spectrum represented in both parliaments. The ongoing transcriptions and analyses of interviews indicated data saturation—that is, more interviews would have led to more repetition but not new information.

Qualitative research allows us to investigate and discover new processes of political communication. Qualitative interviews help us answer the *how* and *why* questions that must be addressed in order to advance our understanding of political parties' use of new communication technologies and their campaign work (Karpf, Kreiss, Nielson, & Powers, 2015). However, when conducting qualitative interviews, researchers have to consider that qualitative interviews ascertain the individual perspective of the interviewed person (Karpf et al., 2015). Answers may be edited, based on what he/she recalls about the campaign and chooses to share. Therefore, it is important to interview the "right" person. To identify interviewees we took a positional approach: we identified the relevant actors based on their formal position in the party organization (and not based on their reputation or their power resources). Our interviewees are the party employees who were in charge of the party's social media campaigns during the studied election periods, in most cases the heads of communication. In the Swiss case, interviewees were granted anonymity, so that we do not connect the party name with quotes later in the results section.

In both countries, interviews lasted between 30 and 60 minutes and were conducted in person at the parties' headquarters or coffeehouses. The interviews were recorded, transcribed in full, and qualitatively analyzed. Rather than counting predefined deductive variables, qualitative content analyses allow categories to emerge inductively—these categories are the heart and centerpiece of qualitative content analyses (Schreier, 2014). More than just close and critical reading, qualitative content analyses are a structured, systematic, category-oriented, and intersubjective way to identify and conceptualize relevant content by reducing, summarizing, and organizing text (Mayring, 1991; Nawratil & Schönhagen, 2009). The analytical reduction process revealed major categories, along which we present the findings.

Results

All parties had implemented social media into their broader web campaigns. Facebook, Twitter, and YouTube were the primary platforms; almost all party web sites contained a direct link to them. Other social media such as Google+ or Instagram were only rarely used and hardly integrated into the campaign. Hence, the presented results generally refer to the question of why and how campaigns were implementing and using Facebook, Twitter, and YouTube.

Internal organization of social media

Although all parties in Austria and Switzerland centered their social media campaigns on the same three platforms—Facebook, Twitter, and YouTube—the analysis of the interview data reveals differences in parties' operational habits. Parties either opted for centralized organisation, which limited loss of control, or decentralized organisation, which reduced the costs. Parties varied concerning external support and outsourcing social media campaigns. Differences between approaches to internal organization of social media activities did not run along ideological lines. Party size did matter in Austria—with the exception of the Pirate Party, but not in Switzerland.

A centralized approach to online campaigning means that a small team of party employees, most often based in the party headquarters, posts and comments on social media. In Switzerland, this was the predominant pattern. In most cases, Swiss parties have very few employees, and many work on a part-time basis. They tend to build small teams, and treat online campaigning as only one part of their workload. Almost all parties dedicated only very small amounts of work time to social media. To keep control of the messages (according to the party line), the web strategists or heads of communication using this pattern of organization allowed only a few employees to post: "I must have control. In the end, it must remain in the hands of the boss. I would need someone in my department who can do this from morning to evening, and who will ask me again and again what he can post and what he can comment. . . . It is all about conforming with the party line." Austria's Pirate Party took a similar approach. Although the party is managed in a direct democratic process (*liquid democracy*), most campaign communication is operated by the party's board, a team of five to six people.

A decentralized approach to online campaigning means that employees or supporters from various parts of the organization post and comment on social media, largely without control from web strategists or heads of communication. The rationale behind this form of operation is lower costs (fewer staff resources) and benefiting from all media-savvy employees. Austria's Green Party was running its social media campaign with a social media team of 150 people from different parts of the organization. The team was posting on Facebook, YouTube, Twitter, and in online newspaper forums. The party claims to lack the financial resources to employ people "who sit in the main campaign office and only work for our social media campaign." The communication head office "tried to mobilise people, to get them interested in the social media campaign, and provided them with background information to be able to take part in citizens' discussions." Similarly, Austria's NEOS managed its social media by means of a bigger team. About 40 people either posted in the party's name, used their own profiles to post on the party's sites, or posted on their own accounts in the party's name. During the campaign's "hot phase," most of the postings on the party's official Facebook page came from the top candidate and party leader, Matthias Strolz, who also ran a personal Twitter account. In Switzerland, one party experimented with strong decentralization and allowed media-savvy supporters to run the party's Twitter feed, a controversial decision: "Some people (in the party organization) were very upset when we discussed to let two or three people who were not employed at headquarters run the Twitter feed. . . . For some, it is almost unthinkable that we let them emit official messages although they are not employees or elected functionaries."

Concerning external support and outsourcing, we found that Swiss parties, and to some extent also Austrian parties, rely on professional agencies for their online campaigning in general (web sites), but keep social media activities an internal activity. An exception is Austria's SPÖ: Most of the posts and comments on SPÖ's main (campaign) on Facebook, Twitter, and YouTube accounts were published by an external agency. The SPÖ was the only party in the 2013 election campaign that hired an external agency to plan and support its social media campaign.

Planning of social media campaigns

In Switzerland, campaign planning is very similar across all interviewed parties. It takes place over months, sometimes years. For instance, one web strategist stated: "The planning of social media campaigns started about two and a half years before Election Day—the day when voters' interest in social media is the greatest." Although in most cases one or two functionaries are responsible for online communication as part of their regular workload, Swiss parties tend to hire extra staff for campaigns (elections, initiatives, referenda).

The interviews with Austrian political parties revealed great differences concerning the process of planning across the six parties. The conservative ÖVP started to plan its Facebook and Twitter presences for the campaign about a year before the elections in early autumn 2012. The other major Austrian party, the Social Democrats, started to plan their social media campaign only in April 2013, half a year before the elections—and then mainly outsourced it to an external agency. The Green Party and the FPÖ both describe their social media campaigns as a dynamic process, which developed from when their social media presences started about two to three years earlier. The planning of the social media campaign of the new party, NEOS, was part of the organizational process of its overall campaign. It started in April 2012, about six months before the party went public in October 2012. The "Internet party," the Pirate Party, started to publish campaign information on their social media sites only three months before Election Day. They waited with the planning of their campaign until they had secured the 2,600 statements of support necessary to run in the general election.

Most Swiss parties have social media guidelines, or at least some basic pamphlet, while their Austrian counterparts relied on "netiquette," but none of the

Austrian parties had official social media guidelines and/or policies for the internal organization (i.e., concerning operation of social media communication). To facilitate a homogenous presence on social media, parties in Austria and Switzerland organized workshops for party employees, regional and local party groups, and candidates without exerting control or force to comply with fixed rules or designs.

Primary motives and goals of social media use

Faced with partisan dealignment and a decrease in voter turnout, party strategists agreed that their primary motive for using social media was to interact directly with voters and to increase audience interest and engagement to secure votes. All parties highlighted social media's dialogue and mobilization potentials, as well as the possibility to broadcast information. In the "run for voter attention" (as expressed by Austrian Social Democrats), all parties sought to foster dialogue with citizens, to get more people involved in their campaigns than in previous elections. Austria's NEOS emphasized that direct contact with the public was essential to it as a new party, because the mass media gave them little attention (cf. Lilleker & Jackson, 2011). A new party in Switzerland also confirmed the important role of social media for a young party, but also mentioned the problem of loss of control: not to become a catch-all for various niche voices. Another motif mentioned by several parties was the low costs involved with social media. Posting information instead of sending letters by post to supporters and potential voters saves time, labor, and resources. A Swiss party claimed to have implemented social media "for fun," but soon realized the serious aspects: It started its social media campaign to avoid "dozens of non-official party sites springing up like mushrooms." Although most parties claimed to start social media campaigns for dialogue and two-way communication with voters, an often-mentioned motif referred to the normative force of the factual: party strategists do not expect much gain from social media, but perceive them as part of "modern" campaigns. They feel they must implement social media, because "everyone is doing it" and the public expected it, fearing negative media coverage on a campaign without social media. In sum, in Austria and Switzerland we found a large degree of trial and error while facing insecurity about costs and benefits of social media. However, the perceived normative force of implementation superimposed the uncertain cost–benefits ratio.

Strategies of and challenges to social media use

Less social media is more: Taking a close look at different social media sites, Facebook, Twitter, and YouTube were the most often used platforms and were primarily utilized for disseminating campaign messages as well as reinforcing the party's political message. Parties often give the impression of being active only on those platforms they consider unavoidable. Overall, their social media activities are fairly conformist, rather than innovation-oriented. Strategists agreed that being active on only a few platforms ensures optimum and more effective performance.

Facebook ranked top among implemented social media in both countries (cf. Lilleker, Tenscher, & Štětka, 2015). All political parties had at least a party site on Facebook, and some also a site for the top candidate. Facebook was mainly used to disseminate mass messages and to generate a dialogue between the party and the citizens as well as between citizens. Twitter was more a secondary medium, used to communicate with opinion leaders, journalists, and (in some cases) spin doctors. For instance, Austria's conservatives pointed out that Twitter was used to push (or weaken) messages. YouTube was mainly used as an additional communication instrument for distributing information, and provided the parties with a different channel to explain their messages in greater detail. For example, Austria's ÖVP published "explanation" videos that gave simple explanations of their campaign messages. For Swiss parties, YouTube is an attractive low-cost platform: "Instead of investing large sums of money in campaign posters, we did a funny movie about the party." In Switzerland, electoral law does not allow parties to broadcast campaign spots on radio or TV. Therefore, video platforms provide a stage for campaign tools that did not exist in their traditional form, enabling Swiss parties to circumvent the no-spots rule.

Interviewees also mentioned the use of Google+, Flickr, Instagram, Pinterest, Tumblr, and Vine, but only for smaller, specific actions. These platforms were hardly used by the population at that point in time. In cases where parties were active on these sites, it was to run small campaigns to attract young voters.

Personalization strategy

In the context of campaigns' broader communication strategies, Austria's parties FPÖ and NEOS, and to some extent also the Green Party, used social media to personalize their campaigns. Particularly the right-wing populist party centered its social media campaign on its top candidate, HC Strache. For instance, the party's official Facebook site was that of HC Strache. Facebook was also used to show a more personal side of the candidates: HC Strache was pictured in his swimming trunks at a lake trip on the weekend, or he was posting pictures of his dog. Similarly, the new party, the NEOS, as well as the Greens, used Facebook to "humanize" its top candidates. The primary goal of the strategy of "humanizing" provided content was to build a more personal community, hoping to enhance dialogue within voters and supporters. This fact is highlighted by the interviewed Swiss parties: They repeatedly argued that they cannot benefit fully from social media's potential, because they communicate as organizations, not as natural persons. In their perceptions, social media platforms are made for "faces," for individuals rather than groups or organizations, for mainly two reasons: First, individuals can share private information and personal interest content that are interesting for a larger number of people. Second, organizations cannot post whatever they want, but must act within certain limits and regulations. Thus, parties are limited in what content they can post; as a result, this leads to lower resonance. In addition, the Swiss political system and political culture is not very personalized, and politicians' popularity broadly varies geographically. It was even mentioned that some candidates deliberately abstained from social media because their voters would "not appreciate" it.

Feedback

Assessing message effectiveness: Overall, interviewees highlighted social media's feedback function. The feedback gives them an opportunity to assess the effectiveness of their campaign messages, at least to some extent. However, parties in both countries do not report any professional monitoring of their messages' effectiveness. When asked about satisfaction with their performance and the feedback to their posts, they reported contentment—particularly the smaller parties. They all expect social media to play a more important role in the next electoral campaign and its significance in political communication to grow, but they are not systematically assessing their performance. It is more "getting used" to social media than initializing structured learning processes. They also do not assess whether they reach their target groups; in most cases, they do not have a clear target group.

Responding as well as removing comments

Besides the challenge of responding to individual messages, inappropriate user comments are considered a problem. Participants agreed that comments by citizens who discriminate against or insult other people (e.g., sexist or homophobic comments) must be removed from discussions. However, to maintain transparency, parties often had to deal with these people in individual messages or even by means of an open discussion about the removal of such comments. A Swiss party strategist underlined that in discussion threads with many inappropriate user comments, one of the biggest challenges was the lack of personal resources to swiftly deal with such situations. Overall, the analysis of interview data revealed that the number of inappropriate comments was manageable.

Loss of control

All Austrian parties mentioned the loss of control over political messages on social media as a primary challenge in their online campaigns. For instance, ÖVP stated: "Today, we must face the fact that, at every public event, there will be someone with a mobile phone with a camera who is documenting everything and will distribute it online immediately." In addition, an increasing amount of discussions between politicians and journalists are public, as they are taking place on Twitter and not face-to-face. Swiss parties seem to take a more dispassionate stance; as one strategist explained: "Openness to interactivity always involves that Facebook users of other parties will also comment on our Facebook profile and write that our party is the worst party, gets everything wrong, and that we are all bank lobbyists. That happens." However, some parties admitted to actively censoring racist and other inappropriate comments.

Social media in the broader campaign context

Major, minor, traditional, and new parties sought to coordinate their social media campaigns with their off-line campaigns. For instance, the ÖVP and the Greens in Austria noted that people involved in the social media campaigns took part in the daily campaign meetings. The three minor parties in Austria integrated social media to a greater extent into their offline campaigns than the two major parties. The FPÖ claimed that its offline and online campaigns were geared to each other. For instance, all newspaper ads and posters showed a link to Facebook and QR codes (Quick Response code) linking to additional information. The FPÖ web strategist stated: "We think of online and offline as one." Furthermore, highlighting the feedback function of social media, the FPÖ and NEOS noted that issues they received positive response to on social media or that were often liked on Facebook, retweeted on Twitter, or that provoked vibrant online discussions were also integrated into or boosted in the off-line campaign, for instance, advertising additional newspaper ads on these particular issues or pushing them in the TV debates. In Switzerland, web strategists underlined synergies between mass media and social media. In many cases, they would just recycle press information by posting press releases on social media or linking to newspaper articles. Many web strategists appreciated social media for the opportunity to have a link between traditional press relations and campaigning on the street. They sought to produce "sexy and scoopy" postings and to experiment with interactive formats (such as quizzes), but largely relied on broadcasting ready-made information.

Interviewees from the two major Austrian parties mentioned that certain groups within the parties still do not know how to handle social media communication and that this is why social media are not fully incorporated in their broader campaign. Mostly, this is due to them being older. To them, social media means more work and can hardly be controlled. Yet, in comparison to minor parties, this group of older functionaries in the major parties has strong standings in the party organizations, mainly owing to traditional party structures. This way of thinking may be one reason for different approaches between the major and minor parties (cf. Kalnes, 2009).

Political parties in Austria and Switzerland were generally largely skeptical about the benefits of social media. Traditional relationships to mass media and journalists, which are considered a key factor for campaign success, take place outside social media. Face-to-face contact and interpersonal communication with voters remained a very important element of election campaigns in both countries. As a head of communication in Switzerland put it: "We have small electoral districts. Today, I would argue, it is still more interesting for a politician to go to the marketplace with brochures every Saturday. If someone there offers free beer, this is more efficient than a social media strategy." In short, at least some social media have been implemented in parties' broader communication strategies to some extent. Nonetheless, all interviewed Web strategists and heads of communications pointed out that they aim for greater integration of social media in their next campaigns.

Discussion

In the following section, we will discuss our inductively gained results from a deductive angle: What does this all mean in the context of the four evolving ideal types of campaigning outlined in the theoretical part (see Magin et al., 2017)? How do the different political structures affect social media campaigns in both countries?

Concerning our first research question on Austrian and Swiss parties' main strategies and challenges for communication via social media, the results show that no discernable social media strategies have yet emerged in the two countries. Moreover, in both countries, the advent of social media has not (yet) fundamentally changed campaign practices: although the parties′ heads of communications appreciated some aspects of target-group-centered and individual-centered campaign styles, much of mass-centered and even partisan-centered campaigning remains. The mode of the political communication system is in both countries largely target-group-centered and based on multiple channels and multimedia. Television and radio play only a minor role in parties' strategies, as the broadcasting of campaign spots is (for the most part) illegal. Still, YouTube is not seen as an alternative outlet to reach out to a mass audience with campaign videos. We also raised the question how parties implement and deal with social media communication; and here, besides similarities, small differences between the two countries emerged: campaign coordination lies in the hands of party campaign managers in Switzerland, while their Austrian counterparts have begun to form larger campaign units, also specializing in social media activities. Although external consultants and experts play a role in coming up with a general strategy and in maintaining the Web sites, social media remains an in-house campaign activity in most parties. One the one hand, this might be connected with the fear of losing control of the message on social media, which was widely voiced in the interviews. For instance, Austrian and Swiss campaigns did not engage in dialogue, and hence are no different from campaigns in the United States (Bor, 2013), Australia (Grant et al., 2010), the UK (Graham et al., 2013), and Norway (Enli & Skogerbø, 2013; Kalsnes, 2016). On the other hand, political parties in both countries tended to spend few resources on social media campaigning. Campaign paradigms remain rooted in party logic and, to some extent, also marketing logic. This is also displayed in the planning process of the social media campaigns. Overall, the results suggest that there is still much trial and error when it comes to social media campaigning.

Parties primarily expect their social media campaigns to mobilize specific target groups, which they mostly find among their supporters. Here, our findings are in line with previous studies showing that campaigning parties and politicians hope that the utilization of social media may support the mobilization and organization of supporters (Bor, 2013; Gueorguieva, 2008; Tenscher et al., 2015; Vaccari, 2013). Research question 2 also asked whether Austrian and Swiss parties monitor their social media performances or message effectiveness, which they did not do.

Overall, we find only few differences between the two countries studied here, as most differences occur between parties—validating the results from previous comparative studies of online campaigning. Some of the differences are clearly linked to political structures: we find much larger teams working on social media campaigns in Austria, reflecting that elections matter more in the Austrian political system. In Austria, the party size influenced how social media campaigns were internally organized, while in Switzerland there was hardly any variation among the parties. This can also be linked to the fact that there is not much to be gained for parties in election campaigns due to the consociational structure of governments in the Swiss case. Social media as platforms for personalization played a larger role in the Austrian parties' strategizing. Personalization is less important in Switzerland, due to small electoral districts and strong federalism ("Kantönligeist"), so that few candidates appeal to voters beyond one district. Swiss parties find it difficult to fully exploit social media's potential as organizations, and cannot promote individual candidates, because it does not make sense in the political system's setting. Thus, with regards to "why," there are fewer incentives to use social media in election campaigns in Switzerland than in Austria. In Switzerland we see, even more than in Austria, a party-centered and mass-centered ideal type of campaigning. Although parties use multiple channels and platforms, the logic behind it remains party-driven, party-centered, and anchored in internal organization. Austrian parties have moved more to specialized campaign teams including external actors, to permanent campaigning and a marketing logic of voter-group targeting. Austrian parties invest more in social media campaigning, because they can also win more in elections.

However, when it comes to "how," we see a lot of trial and error in both countries: parties are experimenting with new communication technologies, and they test various ways to implement social media within their strategic campaign communication. The organizational patterns still remain transient and volatile, while strongly connected to established campaign styles: canvassing (with beer or without) and messages along party lines remain more important than data-mining and personalized targeting of individual voters. In Austria and Switzerland, parties have not (yet) entered the data-based "fourth age of political communication"; established ideal types of campaigning prevail.

Conclusion

In a general perspective on social media in online political communication, our findings support a skeptical perspective regarding social media's perceived significance. In line with the emergence of hybrid media systems (Chadwick, 2013), political parties in Austria and Switzerland do not discriminate between offline and online political communication strategies, but perceive social media as a fairly marginal part of their online activities within a broader integrated campaign strategy. Although they feel normative pressures to implement these new tools as part of "modern" campaigning, they expect low impact from it and, as a result, invest few resources into social media. These perceptions are in line with and even hold some explanatory potential for the empirical findings of quantitative studies (Graham et al., 2013) that reported more broadcasting than mobilization and an under-exploitation of social media's potentials in party communication in various countries. However, all parties expect social media to become more important in the future, and we cannot predict social media's roles in upcoming campaigns. The perceptions of political actors about new technology are an important data access point when assessing how they try on new roles, adopt new media, and react to changing expectations of political communication.

As with all studies, our analysis has its limitations: we only included two countries, two election campaigns, and the perspectives of the parties' heads of communication. Particularly because of the transient state of social media in electoral campaigns in both countries, we can expect that future campaigns will differ from what we have learned. Rather than laying a basis for broad generalization, our results document the status quo of social media in two consociational democracies in the first decade of social media availability. We hope it can be useful for future research with a longitudinal perspective.

References

Bennett, W. L., & Manheim, J. B. (2001). The Big Spin: Strategic communication and the transformation of pluralist democracy. In W. L. Bennett & R. M. Entman (Eds.), *Mediated politics. Communication in the future of democracy* (pp. 279–298). Cambridge, UK: Cambridge University Press.

Blais, A. (2006). What affects voter turnout? *Annual Review of Political Science, 9*, 111–125. doi:10.1146/annurev.polisci.9.070204.105121

Blumler, J. G. (2013). The fourth age of political communication. Retrieved from http://www.fgpk.de/2013/gastbeitrag-von-jay-g-blumler-the-fourth-age-of-political-communication-2/(20.02.2017).

Bor, S. E. (2013). Using social network sites to improve communication between political campaigns and citizens in the 2012 election. *American Behavioral Scientist, 58*(9), 1195–1213. doi:10.1177/0002764213490698

Bundesministerium für Inneres (2017). Wahlen [elections]. Retrieved from http://www.bmi.gv.at/cms/BMI_wahlen/nationalrat/start.aspx

Cardenal, A. S. (2013). Why mobilize support online? The paradox of party behaviour online. *Party Politics, 19*(1), 83–103. doi:10.1177/1354068810395059

Chadwick, A. (2013). *The hybrid media system: Politics and power*. Oxford, UK: Oxford University Press.

Dalton, R. J. (2000). The decline of party identification. In R. J. Dalton & M. P. Wattenberg (Eds.), *Parties without partisans: Political change in advanced industrial societies* (pp. 19–36). Oxford, UK: Oxford University Press.

Enli, G. S., & Skogerbø, E. (2013). Personalized campaigns in party-centered politics: Twitter and Facebook as arenas for political communication. *Information, Communication & Society, 16*(5), 757–774. doi:10.1080/1369118X.2013.782330

Eurobarometer (2016, Spring). *Standard Eurobarometer 85—Spring 2016*. Retrieved from: http://ec.europa.eu/COMMFrontOffice/PublicOpinion

Farrel, D. M. (1996). Campaign strategies and tactics. In L. LeDuc, R. G. Niemi, & P. Norris (Eds.), *Comparing democracies: Elections and voting in comparative perspective* (pp. 160–183). Thousand Oaks, CA: Sage.

Fraefel, M. (2012). Mobilizing effects of online campaigning. In *CeDEM 12 Proceedings: Conference for E-Democracy and Open Government* (pp. 205–217). Krems, Austria: Edition-Donau-Univ. Krems.

Gehler, M. (2006). Die Zweite Republik—zwischen Konsens und Konflikt. Historischer Überblick (1945–2005) [Second Republic]. In H. Dachs, P. Gerlich, H. Gottweis, H. Kramer, V. Lauber, W. C. Müller, & E. Talos (Eds.), *Politik in Österreich. Das Handbuch* [Politics in Austria] (pp. 35–51). Vienna, Austria: Manz.

Graham, T., Broersma, M., Hazelhoff, K., & Van 'T Haar, G. (2013). Between broadcasting political messages and interacting with voters: The use of Twitter during the 2010 UK general election. *Information, Communication & Society, 16*(5), 692–716. doi:10.1080/1369118X.2013.785581

Grant, W. J., Moon, B., & Busby Grant, J. (2010). Digital dialogue? Australian politicians' use of the social network tool Twitter. *Australian Journal of Political Science, 45*(4), 579–604. doi:10.1080/10361146.2010.517176

Gueorguieva, V. (2008). Voters, Myspace, and YouTube: The impact of alternative communication channels on the 2006 election cycle and beyond. *Social Science Computer Review, 26*(3), 288–300. doi:10.1177/0894439307305636

Hallahan, K., Holtzhausen, D., Van Ruler, B., Verčič, D., & Sriramesh, K. (2007). Defining strategic communication. *International Journal of Strategic Communication, 1*(1), 3–35. doi:10.1080/15531180701285244

Hallin, D. C., & Mancini, P. (2004). *Comparing media systems. Three models of media and politics.* Cambridge: Cambridge University Press.

Kalnes, Ø. (2009). Norwegian Parties and Web 2.0. *Journal of Information Technology & Politics, 6*(3), 251–266. doi:10.1080/19331680903041845

Kalsnes, B. (2016). The social media paradox explained: Comparing political parties' Facebook strategy versus practice. *Social Media & Society, 2*(2). doi:10.1177/2056305116644616

Karpf, D., Kreiss, D., Nielson, R. K., & Powers, M. (2015). The role of qualitative methods in political communication research: Past, present, and future. *International Journal of Communication, 9*, 1888–1906.

Kiousis, S., & Strömbäck, J. (2015). The strategic context of political communication. In D. Holtzhausen & A. Zerfass (Eds.), *The Routledge handbook of strategic communication* (pp. 383–395). New York, NY: Routledge.

Klinger, U. (2013). Mastering the art of social media: Swiss parties, the 2011 national election and digital challenges. *Information, Communication & Society, 16*(5), 717–736. doi:10.1080/1369118X.2013.782329

Klinger, U., & Svensson, J. (2015). The emergence of network media logic in political communication: A theoretical approach. *New Media & Society, 17*(8), 1241–1257. doi:10.1177/1461444814522952

Larsson, A. O. (2015). Green light for interaction: Party use of social media during the 2014 Swedish election year. *First Monday, 20*, 12. doi:10.5210/fm.v20i12.5966

Lassen, D. S., & Brown, A. R. (2011). Twitter: The electoral connection? *Social Science Computer Review, 29*(4), 419–436. doi:10.1177/0894439310382749

Latzer, M., Just, N., Metreveli, S., & Saurwein, F. (2012). *Internet-Anwendungen und deren Nutzung in der Schweiz. Themenbericht aus dem World Internet Project—Switzerland 2011.* Retrieved from www.mediachange.ch/media/pdf/publications/Anwendungen_Nutzung.pdf

Lilleker, D. G., & Jackson, N. A. (2011). *Political campaigning, elections and the Internet.* New York, NY: Routledge.

Lilleker, D. G., Tenscher, J., & Štětka, V. (2015). Towards hypermedia campaigning? Perceptions of new media's importance for campaigning by party strategists in comparative perspective. *Information, Communication & Society, 18* (7), 747–765. doi:10.1080/1369118X.2014.993679

Magin, M., Podschuweit, N., Haßler, J., & Russmann, U. (2017). Campaigning in the fourth age of political communication: A multi-method study on the use of Facebook by German and Austrian parties in the 2013 national election campaigns. *Information, Communication & Society, 20*(11), 1698–1719. doi:10.1080/1369118X.2016.1254269

Mancini, P. (1999). New frontiers in political professionalism. *Political Communication, 16*(3), 231–245. doi:10.1080/105846099198604

Mayring, P. (1991). Qualitative Inhaltsanalyse. In U. Flick, E. V. Kardoff, H. Keupp, L. V. Rosenstiel, & S. Wolff (Eds.), *Handbuch qualitative Forschung: Grundlagen, Konzepte, Methoden und Anwendungen* (pp. 209–212). Weinheim, Germany: Beltz, Psychologie-Verlag-Union

Nawratil, U., & Schönhagen, P. (2009). Die qualitative Inhaltsanalyse: Rekonstruktion der Kommunikationswirklichkeit. In H. Wagner (Ed.), *Qualitative Methoden in der Kommunikationswissenschaft. Ein Lehr- und Studienbuch* (pp. 333–346). Baden-Baden, Germany: Nomos.

Norris, P. (2000). *A virtuous circle: Political communications in postindustrial societies.* Cambridge, UK: Cambridge University Press.

Piper, D. L. P. (2014). Data protection laws of the world handbook. Retrieved from https://www.dlapiper.com/

Russmann, U. (2016). Voter targeting online in comparative perspectives: Political party websites in the 2008/2009 and 2013 Austrian and German election campaigns. *Journal of Political Marketing.* Advance online publication. 1–24. doi:10.1080/15377857.2016.1179241

Schreier, M. (2014). Varianten qualitativer Inhaltsanalyse: Ein Wegweiser im Dickicht der Begrifflichkeiten. *Forum Qualitative Sozialforschung/Forum: Qualitative Social Research, 15*(1), 27.

Skovsgaard, M., & Van Dalen, A. (2013). Dodging the gatekeepers? Social media in the campaign mix during the 2011 Danish elections. *Information, Communication & Society, 16* (5), 737–756. doi:10.1080/1369118X.2013.783876

Strömbäck, J., & Kiousis, S. (2014). Strategic political communication in election campaigns. In C. Reinemann (Ed.),

Political Communication (pp. 109–128). Berlin, Germany: Mouton de Gruyter.

Svensson, J., & Larsson, A. O. (2016). Interacting with whom? Swedish parliamentarians on Twitter during the 2014 elections. *International Journal of E-Politics (IJEP)*, *7*(1), 1–15. doi:10.4018/IJEP

The Swiss Federal Statistical Office (2016). Nationalratswahlen: Wahlbeteiligung and Internetnutzung in der Schweiz. Retrieved from http://www.bfs.admin.ch

Tenscher, J., Koc-Michalska, K., Lilleker, D. G., Mykkänen, J., Walter, A. S., Findor, A., … Róka, J. (2015). The professionals speak: Practioners' perspectives on professional election campaigning. *European Journal of Communication*, *31* (2), 95–119. doi:10.1177/0267323115612212

Udris, L., & Lucht, J. (2014). Mediatization on the structural level: Independence from politics, dependence on the market. In F. Esser & J. Strömbäck (Eds.), *Mediatization of Politics* (pp. 114–136). Houndmills, England: Palgrave Macmillan.

Vaccari, C. (2013). From echo chamber to persuasive device? Rethinking the role of the Internet in campaigns. *New Media & Society*, *15*(1), 109–127.

Vergeer, M., Herman, L., & Sams, S. (2011). Online social networks and micro-blogging in political campaigning: The exploration of a new campaign tool and a new campaign style. *Party Politics*, *19*(3), 477–501. doi:10.1177/1354068811407580

Vissers, S., & Stolle, D. (2014). Spill-over effects between Facebook and on/offline political participation? Evidence from a two-wave panel study. *Journal of Information Technology & Politics*, *11*(3), 259–275. doi:10.1080/19331681.2014.888383

Wahlbeteiligung (2016). *Wahlbeteiligung bei den Nationalratswahlen*. Retrieved from http://www.wahlbeteiligung.at/nationalratswahlen.html

The role of gender in online campaigning: Swedish candidates' motives and use of social media during the European election 2014

Linn A. C. Sandberg and Patrik Öhberg

ABSTRACT

This study addresses politician's motives and use of social media platforms for campaigning purposes from a gender perspective. The role of gender is tested using survey data on Swedish candidates and behavioral data from Twitter before, during, and after the 2014 European election. Our findings show gender-related patterns in how candidates assess the usefulness of social media as a campaign tool. Female candidates tend to value social media to a greater extent and evaluate social media use more positively than male candidates. We also find that the election campaign affects how male and female candidates interact with their followers.

Introduction

Social media can provide candidates with better control over their self-images and public narratives. As a result, candidates have altered their campaign tactics to avoid the filtered interpretation of campaign messages released through traditional media outlets (Gainous & Wagner, 2013). Even as social media is increasingly integrated into election campaigning, the question of what it signifies for politicians to be active online remains largely unanswered. This is especially true for female candidates.

Because individual candidates can influence public perception through strategic use of social media, such media might be a particularly useful tool with which women candidates can counteract masculine communication norms in politics (Meeks, 2013). The possibility of direct communication and interaction with voters and followers may also be particularly compelling to women who wish to avoid the images given to them by traditional media, which is generally less favorable to female candidates (Heith, 2003; Jalalzai, 2006; Kahn, 1996). In this regard, social media could provide a means to strengthen women candidates by presenting new opportunities to reach out, mobilize voters, and target particular groups, such as young women. There are, however, very few studies that explicitly explore gender-based differences in social media use, rather than simply including gender as a control variable in the uptake of online campaign tools. We therefore know very little about the contours of gendered differences, both in terms of motives and actual use. Moreover, most of the studies concerning online campaigning have been conducted in Anglo-American contexts (Hermans & Vergeer, 2012; Jungherr, 2014), where the political systems are more candidate-oriented and female politicians are quite few.

In this study, we test the relationship between gender and candidate approaches to social media campaigning by exploring a party-oriented system with a strong presence of female politicians, namely Sweden. Women have been present in politics and parliament for a long time in Sweden, and gender-equal political representation is the norm rather than an unachievable ideal. Exploring gendered campaign strategies and practices in this relatively gender-equal political setting allows us to test whether there is a difference between the motives behind and use of social media platforms for campaigning purposes by male and female candidates, even in a seemingly gender-equal context. Moreover, Sweden provides an interesting case for examining candidates' use of social media in general, since Swedish parties and candidates stand out as early adopters and the most extensive users of Web technologies (Vergeer, Hermans, & Cunha, 2013).

Additionally, most studies concerning the factors driving Web campaigning do not account for individual attitudes and subjective assessments of the value of online platforms as campaign tools. Previous research findings have also confirmed a discrepancy between the intention to use Web campaigning and the actual adoption (Marcinkowski & Metag, 2014; Segaard & Nielsen, 2013). By combining survey data with data regarding how candidates actually use social media, we expected to gain a deeper insight into the factors that drive the use of social media for election campaigning. When considering types of activity on Twitter, we also used three time periods to capture the candidates' behavior during noncampaign periods, whereas most studies have concentrated only on the campaign period surrounding elections when assessing the online behavior of politicians (Larsson, 2015a).

The paper will proceed as follows. First, we discuss candidates' use of social media during election campaigns and the possible impact of this use. Second, we discuss research concerning gendered campaigning practices, emphasizing the online environment. Thereafter, we discuss Sweden as a case for studying gender and online campaign practices together with data and design. Finally, we discuss our results and their implications.

Social media and personalized campaigning

The mediatization of politics and the arrival of social media coincide with a development toward individualized campaigning, in which a more personal communication style has become advantageous (see Bimber & Davis, 2003; Strömbäck, 2008; Vergeer & Hermans, 2013). The characteristics of social media provide individual politicians with new opportunities for personal campaigning and political communication. The individual politician can easily adopt social media as a campaign tool and the opportunities for more personalized campaigning through social media can be expected to increase even within party-centered systems (Enli & Skogerbø, 2013; Karlsen, 2011), such as Sweden.

In addition to bypassing media filters and journalistic frames, advantages for individual politicians include opportunities to make statements about different events, add interpretations, or make comments (Gainous & Wagner, 2013). Furthermore, politicians might have other advantages in addition to accessibility through social media for individual campaigning; experimental research has shown that engagement with voters online also leads to positive evaluations of politicians (e.g., Grant, Moon, & Grant, 2010; Utz, 2009; Vergeer & Hermans, 2013). Politicians who use a more interactive communication strategy can additionally obtain a larger number of followers (Lilleker & Koc-Michalska, 2013), which in turn can redistribute content. The effects of social media interactivity in political campaigns, such as exposure to comments, can conversely shape both positive and negative perceptions of candidates (Brewer et al., 2015), suggesting that it is important for politicians to control the content on their social media profiles.

Because it gives control over messages and strategies, social media may work particularly well for female candidates, who are often unelected or have junior status and, therefore, are less likely to be constrained by having to conform to the party message (European Parliament, 2013). For female candidates in particular, social media can also allow the contradiction of pertinent gender stereotypes, such as negative appraisals of issue competencies, in voter evaluations (Dolan, 2010). The potential benefits will be discussed further in the next section, along with previous research concerning gender and campaigning, as well as previous studies on candidates' use of social media.

Gender representation as a function of the equalization perspective

The arrival and amplified use of social media as an interactive, open, and transparent platform has raised questions of its democratizing potential. A main issue to be addressed is whether new technologies can improve democratic processes by allowing interaction among candidates, parties, and voters, or by organizing election campaigns in less costly and more direct ways (Gainous & Wagner, 2013). According to the equalization theory (Barber, 2001), the use of the Internet helps remove barriers that favor some groups and individuals in the electorate, and in this view, online platforms can provide a means by which people and politicians gain more opportunities for interaction (Barber, 2003; Hagen & Mayer, 2000). In contrast, research has shown that use of the Internet and new technology is being normalized into the current electoral paradigm to be used as a part of the conventional political structure (Bimber & Davis, 2003; Hindman, 2008; Ward, Gibson, & Lusoli, 2003). Normalization theory states that actors who already have the most influence will be most likely to benefit from new online campaign methods (Margolis & Resnick, 2000). Parties that have more resources would, in this view, afford more professional campaigns, and social media would be used as just another channel, causing no disruption to traditional patterns in off-line politics (Lilleker et al., 2011).

Overall, the literature suggests that different functions of normalization apply for patterns of Web site adoption as compared to social media, which offers some evidence to refute normalization (Southern, 2015). Minor parties, for instance, appear to be more effective in gaining votes through social media than through the adoption of personal Web sites (Gibson & McAllister, 2015). It is possible that given time, the differences in social media use compared to other Web platforms will even out. It could be argued, however, that specific attributes of social media would be more beneficial for minor parties or lesser known candidates. One difference, and perhaps advantage, would be the interactive attributes of social media and the possibilities of actively building a personal platform through which candidates could more efficiently reach out to voters and media, as opposed to Web pages and similar platforms.

Although the definition of normalization as a concept tends to lack specificity (Southern, 2015), party size, campaign budget, and incumbency often serve as measures to indicate whether potentially weaker parties or candidates can gain favor through Web-based campaigning (Vaccari, 2013). Lusoli (2005) suggested that the influences of Internet use on women candidates' chances of electoral success, or lack thereof, should also be thought of as functions of normalization. The same logic applies to social media use by underrepresented or politically marginalized groups, such as women and ethnic minorities (Jacobs & Spierings, 2016).

As the term "equalization" in this context often refers to social media giving opportunities to minor parties or lesser known candidates, the new opportunities it could provide to female candidates would, in a similar way, be an indication that social media upsets traditional campaign dynamics or breaks traditional patterns of gender representation. Thus, gender representation can also be thought of as a function of equalization. Flowing from the same line of reasoning, differences in Internet-based campaigning that show male advantages and overrepresentation would subsequently indicate a normalized pattern. Perceived male bias during elections would, from this perspective, result in women candidates using the platform over which they have the most control. If women are perceived as being portrayed disadvantageously by editorial media, this would also speak in favor of using alternative campaign strategies. In a relatively gender-equal context such as Sweden, equalization in terms of new campaign possibilities for women candidates can be seen as a way for women to avoid gendered perceptions that continue to persist. A lack of difference in social media use would, in this context, suggest that men and women are campaigning under relatively similar terms.

Research on Web-based campaigning and candidates' use of social media has, to a very limited extent, examined the role or function of gender. The literature concerning gender and representation has likewise not examined whether and how gender has an impact on online practices and strategies. This article provides a first attempt to test the perseverance for gendered campaign strategies online by studying a context where the conditions for campaigning are relatively equal between male and female candidates. Below, we will develop our discussion of Sweden as a case, in the context of the European elections. Prior to that, the literature on gender and campaigning will be discussed, as well as literature concerning candidates' use of online platforms and social media in particular.

Gender and campaign practices

There remain substantial gender differences in modern democracies pertaining to representation, although women generally perform as well as their male counterparts in similar types of electoral races (Darcy, Welch, & Clark, 1994). Recent research has found little evidence to support previous claims that voters employ gender stereotypes when they evaluate women candidates (Dolan & Lynch, 2016). Furthermore, no financial disadvantages appear to constrain women candidates in particular (Hogan, 2007; Werner, 1997). A great issue involved in increasing the positions of women to elected office remains the significant lack of female candidates. In general, gender affects the decisions of women and men to run for office based on their personal perceptions of capability. In the United States, for instance, women are more likely to doubt their abilities to engage in the campaign process (Fox & Lawless, 2011). Although research has shown that women are equally supported in elections when they run, this is not necessarily because they are treated equitably by the electorate. Instead, it could depend on their political quality; that is, women who do run must be even better candidates to be equally competitive with male contenders (Fulton, 2012; Pearson & McGhee, 2013).

Gender differences related to campaign behavior, in particular, have largely focused on the different issues addressed during the campaign. In previous studies, candidates' genders were, to some extent, related to the issues on which they focused (e.g., Dabelko & Herrnson, 1997; Larson, 2001). Later research does not, however, offer any support that female candidates would focus on different issues than would male candidates, or that a particular set of gender-stereotyped issues, such as social issues, exists (Dolan, 2005). There appear to be few gender differences persistent in overall campaign behavior and the use of varying campaigning tools. For example, similarities tended to outweigh the differences between male and female candidates in the way they are presented in television advertisements (Sapiro, Walsh, Strach, & Hennings, 2011). Much less is known, however, concerning the extent to which male and female candidates use different communication strategies during their campaign or differ in motives for using those strategies. Nonetheless, it is during the campaign that candidates can choose how to present themselves and their political agenda, as well as how to communicate with voters, which later forms the basis of their representation.

For the overall uptake of online campaigning by candidates, important factors include party size, competitiveness, challenger versus incumbent position, and age (Gulati & Williams, 2013; Larsson & Kalsnes, 2014; Lassen & Brown, 2011; Strandberg, 2013; Vergeer, Hermans, & Sams, 2011). Existing research indicates that younger candidates belonging to minor parties and coming from challenger positions are more likely to use social media.

Some studies conducted in the early years of online campaigning using Web sites indicated that gender would generate similar campaign approaches online (e.g., Carlson, 2007), whereas others did not. Women candidates have, for instance, been found to be more likely to use blogs in their campaign and also to utilize a broader range of blogging practices, such as interactive features (Carlson, Djupsund, & Strandberg, 2014). The role of gender in relation to uptake of social media in particular has proven to be important in some studies. Gender had an impact in a study by Jackson and Lilleker (2011), which found that female British MPs were overrepresented on Twitter, compared to their numbers in Parliament. A study of Twitter use by the House candidates in the 2012 campaign also found that women were more likely to use Twitter (Evans, Cordova, & Sipole, 2014). In contrast, gender has proven to be a statistically nonsignificant factor for online presence and adoption by candidates running in the European Parliament elections or by the members of European Parliament (Larsson, 2015a; Vergeer et al., 2013).

Few studies look beyond activity level to variation in actual use, but there are some exceptions. Research conducted in the United States shows that female politicians use Twitter more intensely than do male politicians, have significantly more followers, and differ in their manners of using social media, in terms of content of messages and issues covered. Women were more likely to use "attack tweets," and used campaign issues or mobilization tweets more often. Male candidates were slightly more likely to use personal tweets. Overall, the findings suggest that women use Twitter more actively as a campaign tool (Evans et al., 2014). In contrast to these findings, Just and Crigler (2014) reported a lack of gender difference in relation to some of the above measures. Candidates tended to be as active, focus on similar topics, and use similar tone. They did, however, find significant gender differences in the social aspects of social media use, in the way that women connected more positively with followers. In an analysis of state legislators on Twitter, party and gender effects interacted; specifically, non-Republican women mentioned family somewhat more often than did non-Republican men, but within the group of Republican legislators, women were much less likely to talk about family (Cook, 2016).

Although research concerning the effect of candidate gender is inconclusive, gender does appear to be an important variable in politicians' use of social media platforms. It would be premature to declare that gender is irrelevant in newer forms of online campaigning, but it is also a demanding task to study becausw social media, such as Twitter, is a moving target, and observed patterns in one election could look very different in the next. Furthermore, the different national electoral systems matter for representatives' social media use in Europe (Obholzer & Daniel, 2016). Below, we will discuss the European elections as a particular case for studying online campaigning, as compared to national elections.

European parliament elections

Previous research controlling for gender when measuring uptake and level of activity on social media has mainly looked at politicians who were already holding office. The outcome may be different for challenger candidates, particularly in European elections, in which fewer established candidates run compared to national elections. Women are in general more successful in the European election compared to national elections, because national political parties view these elections as having less at stake and thus are willing to nominate more women or other, less traditional candidates (Freedman, 2002; Harrison, 2005).

The logic of political competition varies across national and European elections, with the latter often referred to as second-order national elections (Schmitt, 2009). Although the positive effects of this second-order setting for small parties are well known, the implications for independent candidates have rarely been discussed (for an exception, see Ehin & Solvak, 2012). There are a number of reasons, however, why independent or nonincumbent candidates may benefit from running in European Parliament elections. For example, in this electoral context, the individual candidates' campaigns are less dependent on the party and the campaign organization. This can be especially rewarding for less-established (female) candidates. The European (second-order) election may therefore provide more variation in personal campaign strategies across parties and candidates than do (first-order) national elections, where individual candidates' campaigns are more dependent on party organization. Lesser known candidates would also struggle more to gain traditional media attention.

Sweden as a case

In this study, we see Sweden as a critical case because female politicians are nearly as prevalent as male politicians in representative assemblies. For more than 20 years, female politicians have made up at least 40% of all three elected levels of representative assemblies (local, regional, and national). In government, there has been equal representation of men and women since 1994 (Krook, 2006). The importance of gender-related issues is also salient in the Swedish debate (Wängnerud, 2015). In a comparative European perspective, Sweden has an equal distribution of representatives in the European Parliament (out of 20 seats, 11 went to female legislators). Moreover, in the 2014 election, a pronounced feminist party, Feminist Initiative, made it into the European Parliament with one seat.

Sweden has a fairly typical party-centered European political structure, in which the members of local and national assemblies are loyal party representatives (Gilljam, Karlsson, & Sundell, 2010). Sweden uses a list system, whereby candidates are placed on the list according to party selectors, and the higher they are on the list, the greater their chances of being elected (Pierre, 2015). The candidates do have an incentive to cultivate personal votes, however, as a candidate who receives 5% of the party's votes can "break" the list. Nonetheless, this semi-open list system does not change much. For example, in the 2014 election, only one candidate became an MP due to personal votes (Berg & Oscarsson, 2015). The political parties are therefore central actors in the success of an aspiring candidate. We know from previous research that in strong party systems, the party leadership stands a better chance of ensuring that their representatives share the party's preferences than they do in more candidate-oriented systems (Müller, 2000). The leeway for individual candidates to cultivate their own relationships with voters is therefore more restricted.

Taken together, the high numbers of women politicians in the Swedish system and their activities within a strong party system, in which individual candidates' actions are centered on party interests, make gendered findings less plausible. Nonetheless, gendered perceptions can be expected to be preserved even when representation is equal in numbers. For instance, women in the legislature tend to speak less on "harder" policy issues than do men in Sweden (Bäck, Debus, & Müller, 2014). Furthermore, a recent study on Swedish municipal politicians revealed that gender inequalities continue to obstruct women from political power, due to the so-called "glass ceiling effect" (Folke & Rickne, 2016). The gender-related patterns we may discover in this study should be relevant in contexts where female politicians are less common and where individual politicians have more pronounced roles to play during the election campaign. Women should, according to this argument, be even more motivated to use social media in other modern democracies with less female representation.

Studying gender-based differences in campaign behavior in Sweden can improve our understanding of whether increased gender equality in representation cultivates new behavior, to the extent that male and female politicians behave fairly similarly, or if gendered campaigning is something more fundamental, and typical male and female behavior among political candidates continues to exist even in gender-equal contexts. Against the backdrop of a development toward personalized campaigning and the interactive features brought forward by social media, we address the following three questions:

(1) Do women candidates consider social media to be a more important campaign tool than do male candidates?
(2) Are female politicians more likely to use Twitter to enhance the political messages of their party or their personal agendas?
(3) Will women politicians behave differently than male politicians on Twitter by being more active and communicating more interactively?

Data material and methods

This study used the Swedish candidate survey of candidates running for the 2014 European election. The survey contained questions regarding the importance of different campaign activities, motives for Twitter use, and evaluation of the candidates' use of Twitter. Previous research has found two main styles of social media campaigning: a party-centered and an individualized style (Karlsen & Enjolras, 2016). Female politicians in general are more concerned about representing the party than representing themselves, when compared to men (Scully & Farrell, 2003). In the survey, we therefore asked questions concerning the dimension of a personal versus party-centered communication style. The questions on motives also covered other aspects of uses for political purposes, such as whether the primary audience consisted of media, politicians, or voters. In the survey, we asked how important Twitter was in terms of the following: communicating the politician's individual daily activities, sharing information about the party's daily activities, displaying a more personal side, contacting voters personally, highlighting personal views, highlighting the party's position, debating with political opponents, criticizing political opponents, reaching as many voters as possible, and making an impact in traditional media (see questionnaire in Appendix 4).

In terms of gender and online campaigning, social media can potentially offer both opportunities and challenges for female candidates. Because women are more likely to be exposed to the risk of online harassment and trolling (Megarry, 2014), this could, for instance, hamper the use of social media platforms for female candidates. We therefore also asked the candidates why they did not use social media, and if the risk of harassment would be one reason not to do so.

To analyze the candidates' actual Twitter use, we collected data on Twitter activity during three time periods for candidates with Twitter accounts. These time periods included the campaign period

(April–May 2014), a pre-campaign period (February 2013) and a period after the election (January–March 2015). From the Twitter accounts, we collected the number of tweets sent, number of @ mentions, retweets, number of tweets with hashtags (#), and number of tweets containing links.

The questionnaire, a Web survey, was sent out directly after the 2014 election to all 315 candidates from the main political parties. The response rate was 46% (see Appendix 3 for response rate per party, age group, and gender in the survey). In the models, we controlled for age, incumbency, placement on the party list, political party, and seniority (whether or not they had been members of the national parliament). These variables had all proved to be important in various previous studies, although their importance was not entirely consistent throughout the different contexts. For social media uptake and use, age was the one factor that stood out as being most significant (Larsson, 2015a; Lassen & Brown, 2011; Vergeer & Hermans, 2013). Electoral vulnerability had no effect on uptake according to Lassen and Brown (2011), and Strandberg (2013) reported incumbency to be positively correlated with social media use. In many other cases, challenger candidates employed social media to a larger extent (Druckman, Kifer, & Parkin, 2007; Gibson, Lusoli, & Ward, 2008; Jackson & Lilleker, 2009). According to a later study of the European 2014 election by Obholzer and Daniel (2016), MEPs at risk of losing their seats are more active on Twitter. Moreover, previous studies have shown that seniority has an impact on activity on Twitter. Senior MPs are in general more active users (Jackson & Lilleker, 2011).

Party size is sometimes used as a measure of how resources influence uptake of social media; the larger the party, the more resources are available. For example, Lilleker and Koc-Michalska (2013) found that MEPs from minor national parties perform better for different categories of online campaigning. In addition to party size, the ideological nature of the parties must be considered if we want to explain uptake and use of social media. Party ideology was unrelated to adoption of Twitter as a campaign tool according to Vergeer and Hermans (2013); however, in a more recent study of candidates in the EU elections of 2014, party belonging was important. There was a higher likelihood that candidates belonging to mainstream parties would use Twitter as opposed to more extreme party candidates, on an economic left–right scale (Nulty, Theocharis, Popa, Parnet, & Benoit, 2016). The more extreme candidates are on the Green-Alternative-Libertarian vs Traditional-Authoritarian-Nationalist (GAL/TAN) dimension, however, the more often they use Twitter (Obholzer & Daniel, 2016). In Sweden, the Feminist Initiative party and the Sweden Democrats are on the opposite ends of the GAL/TAN scale. Based on a study of the parties' official social media accounts, the Feminist Initiative party was among the most active, whereas the Sweden Democrats, on the contrary, were among the least active (Larsson, 2015b). For this reason, we also controlled for party affiliation.

Dimensions in campaign activities

The empirical section begins with a description of how the candidates assessed the importance of social media platforms, such as Facebook and Twitter, in relation to other campaign activities. The survey covered 18 campaign activities, and the candidates ranked these from unimportant to very important on a 5-point, Likert-type scale. Respondents ranked Facebook as the third most important activity; 84% of the candidates used it, 67% of which indicated that it was of importance to their campaign (Figure 1). Respondents ranked Twitter as the sixth most important, with 65% of candidates using it, 38% of which reported it to be important. Other Web-related activities, such as individual blogs and Web pages, were seen as less important compared to social media channels. All in all, although social media platforms were not the most important campaign aspects, Facebook and Twitter were within the upper third of the most important campaign activities.

To study the relationship between the importance of social media and gender, we employed a factor analysis (principal-component). The results yielded five dimensions of campaign activities (see Appendix 1). Web campaign (i.e., Twitter, Facebook, blogs, and Web pages) emerged as a distinct factor (Cronbach's alpha = 0.73). These activities were all related to the candidates' online presences. Other factors were related to what we termed either *traditional*

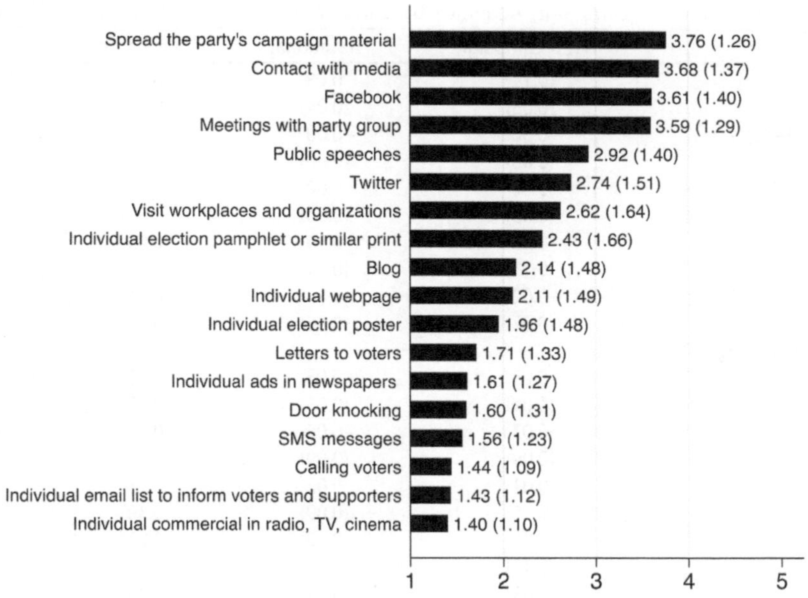

Figure 1. Mean importance of campaign activities to candidates in the 2014 European election.
Note. The scale runs from 1 (unimportant) to 5 (very important). Standard deviation within parentheses.

campaign activities (spreading the party's campaign material, meeting with party groups, contacting media, and making public speeches; Cronbach's alpha = 0.70), *outreaching activities* (calling voters, visiting workplaces and organizations, or communicating through individual e-mail lists or SMS; Cronbach's alpha = 0.67), *personal activities* (visiting door-to-door, putting up individual election posters, or sending letters to voters; Cronbach's alpha = 0.65) and *media activities* (releasing individual advertisements in newspapers, radio, and television channels; cinemas; or individual election pamphlets; Cronbach's alpha = 0.67).

When analyzing these dimensions and their relationships to gender, we found that women candidates overall tended to place greater value on all campaign activities than did male candidates (Table 1). Out of five different campaign categories, female candidates assessed three as significantly more important than did men. Among these were activities on the Web (mean for female candidates was 0.47, mean for men was 0.36).[1] It is of interest that female candidates assessed more activities as important. One of the reasons why female candidates see more activities as important may be related to the fact that women think that more activities are necessary to pursue a political career (Fox & Lawless, 2011). This tendency to stress that more things are important, even in a gender-equal context, could partly explain why women in less equal contexts are reluctant to step forward as candidates; in other words, female candidates assess that an electoral campaign demands more of them than it does of men.

Among the individual control variables, we cannot see that there exists the same type of consistent pattern as there was between male and female candidates, with the exception of age. Younger candidates see Web campaigning as more important than do their older colleagues, whereas the opposite is true when it comes to traditional campaigning, where older candidates stress its importance. It is worth mentioning that Web campaigning is the only thing that the incumbents assessed as more important than did the other candidates, which is in line with Strandberg's results. Strandberg (2013) suggested that a reason for this could be that journalists' use of social media as a news source would favor more established candidates.

If we study the importance of party affiliation and the candidates' assessments, it is evident that Sweden Democrat candidates assessed *all* campaign activities as less important than did candidates from other parties. We cannot offer a solid explanation for this finding. The Sweden Democrats had their best election results ever, so it would be natural to assume that they would be very optimistic about the usefulness of their activities, but that is not the case. It remains plausible

Table 1. Assessment of the Importance of Campaign Activities by Candidates in the 2014 European Election.

	Web campaign	Traditional	Outreach	Personal	Media
Sex (women)	0.11**	0.08*	−0.06	0.09**	0.07
	(0.05)	(0.04)	(0.13)	(0.04)	(0.04)
Placement on the party list (1–43)	−0.00	−0.00***	−0.01	−0.00	−0.00
	(0.00)	(0.00)	(0.01)	(0.00)	(0.00)
Age (22–83)	−0.00**	0.00**	0.00	−0.00	−0.00
	(0.00)	(0.00)	(0.00)	(0.00)	(0.00)
Incumbent	0.22**	−0.03	−0.03	0.12	0.02
	(0.11)	(0.11)	(0.31)	(0.09)	(0.10)
Experience as MP	−0.02	−0.08	−0.04	−0.04	−0.07
	(0.07)	(0.06)	(0.20)	(0.06)	(0.07)
Party (Social Democrats are ref. category)					
Center Party	0.03	−0.05	−0.39***	−0.44***	−0.08
	(0.09)	(0.08)	(0.25)	(0.07)	(0.08)
Christian Democrats	0.03	−0.05	−0.33	−0.43***	−0.13
	(0.09)	(0.09)	(0.25)	(0.07)	(0.08)
Conservative Party	−0.01	0.02	−0.21	−0.06	0.00
	(0.10)	(0.09)	(0.30)	(0.09)	(0.09)
Feminist Party	−0.01	−0.30**	−0.81*	−0.66***	−0.35***
	(0.15)	(0.13)	(0.41)	(0.12)	(0.13)
Green Party	0.03	−0.12	−0.43*	−0.51***	−0.22***
	(0.08)	(0.08)	(0.24)	(0.07)	(0.08)
Left Party	−0.18**	−0.06	−0.86***	−0.53***	−0.36***
	(0.09)	(0.08)	(0.25)	(0.07)	(0.08)
Liberal Party	0.12	−0.03	−0.26	−0.39***	0.05
	(0.10)	(0.09)	(0.28)	(0.08)	(0.09)
Pirate Party	−0.02	−0.21**	−0.87***	−0.53***	−0.30***
	(0.11)	(0.10)	(0.30)	(0.09)	(0.10)
Sweden Democrats	−0.38***	−0.38***	−1.14***	−0.55***	−0.36***
	(0.11)	(0.11)	(0.33)	(0.10)	(0.11)
Intercept	0.57***	0.63***	1.18***	0.65***	0.39***
	(0.10)	(0.10)	(0.30)	(0.09)	(0.09)
R^2	0.24	0.26	0.18	0.49	0.29
N	142	142	137	143	144

Notes. Linear regression (OLS). All dependent variables run between 0–1. Standard errors in parentheses.
***$p < 0.01$. **$p < 0.05$. *$p < 0.1$.

that the attitude stems from their status as an antiestablishment party, and that the candidates feel stigmatized by the editorial mainstream media and the parliament's current cordon sanitaire around the party. This appears to also affect how they view social media, something we will discuss further below.

In looking at each of the activities related to social media and Web-based campaigning, there was a significant gender difference for Twitter, where women assessed Twitter as more important than did men (Table 2.). Nearly half of the women (49%) assessed Twitter as "rather important" or "very important," whereas among the men, the corresponding number was only 28%. We can also see the same pattern emerging as in Table 1. The tendency for female candidates to assess all activities as more important than did men is present (if we collapse the four variables into one, there is a significant gender difference). The only other significant gender difference was found for Facebook, which was in fact even more important for women; 76% of the female candidates saw Facebook as rather or very important, whereas 58% of male candidates felt the same.

For the control variables, list placement had no effect on any campaign activity. Age was significant for Twitter use (as supported by previous research); older candidates were less optimistic about its usefulness. Incumbents assessed Twitter as more valuable than did the other candidates. Among the party variables, the two most interesting significant and nonsignificant results were from the Sweden Democrats and the Feminist Initiative. During the election campaign, the Sweden Democrat candidates and their activities on social media were scrutinized by the media. Some of these candidates even had to resign as a result of this public scrutiny. It is therefore interesting to note that candidates from the Sweden Democrats were slightly more skeptical about the usefulness of social media. In contrast, the Feminist Initiative candidates based their campaigns to a large extent on social media (Blombäck & De Fine Licht, 2015) and were the most active on various social media platforms. The Feminist Initiative party also had more followers than any of the other parties, but Feminist Initiative respondents did not assess Twitter and Facebook as crucial tools for their success. The results here do not support previous research in which candidates from more extreme parties on the GAL/TAN scale used social media more extensively.

It has been theorized that social media not only allow disadvantaged parties and candidates to bypass traditional media, but may also serve populist parties as they strive to appeal to "common people" by offering direct contact opportunities for this aim (Jacobs & Spierings, 2016). Conversely, populist radical right parties such as the Sweden Democrats are often organized around strong leaders who personify the party and seek to control the party as a whole. As these parties are more centralized, this control decreases as a result of social media (Jacobs & Spierings, 2016). The less motivated candidates in the Sweden Democrats could therefore, in addition to being affected by tough media coverage, also be the result of a more centralized control over candidate behavior.[2]

In summary, the results shown in Table 1 and Table 2 help us to answer our first question, suggesting that women candidates consider social media to be a more important campaign tool than do male candidates. There is a tendency, however, for women candidates in general to assess all campaign activities as more important.

Table 2. Assessment of the Importance of Web Campaign Activities by Candidates in the 2014 European Election.

	Twitter	Facebook	Blog	Home page
Sex (women)	0.14**	0.11**	0.08	0.09
	(0.06)	(0.05)	(0.06)	(0.06)
Placement on the party list (1–43)	−0.00	−0.00	0.00	−0.00
	(0.00)	(0.00)	(0.00)	(0.00)
Age (22–83)	−0.01***	−0.00	−0.00	−0.00
	(0.00)	(0.00)	(0.00)	(0.00)
Incumbent	0.42***	−0.05	0.26	0.28*
	(0.15)	(0.13)	(0.16)	(0.16)
Experience as MP	0.04	−0.16*	−0.07	0.06
	(0.10)	(0.08)	(0.10)	(0.10)
Party (Social Democrats are ref. category)				
Center Party	0.04	−0.19*	0.14	0.09
	(0.12)	(0.11)	(0.13)	(0.12)
Christian Democrats	−0.05	−0.05	0.17	0.02
	(0.12)	(0.10)	(0.13)	(0.12)
Conservative Party	0.06	−0.16	0.07	−0.01
	(0.14)	(0.12)	(0.15)	(0.15)
Feminist Party	0.10	−0.03	−0.19	0.07
	(0.20)	(0.18)	(0.21)	(0.21)
Green Party	−0.04	−0.21**	0.21	0.16
	(0.13)	(0.10)	(0.12)	(0.12)
Left Party	−0.15	−0.40***	0.02	−0.20
	(0.12)	(0.10)	(0.12)	(0.12)
Liberal Party	0.15	−0.05	0.29*	0.21
	(0.13)	(0.12)	(0.14)	(0.14)
Pirate Party	−0.08	−0.35**	0.26*	0.09
	(0.14)	(0.13)	(0.15)	(0.15)
Sweden Democrats	−0.36**	−0.79***	−0.11	−0.23
	(0.16)	(0.14)	(0.17)	(0.17)
Intercept	0.81***	0.97	0.20	0.30**
	(0.14)	(0.12)	(0.15)	(0.14)
R^2	0.25	0.32	0.12	0.17
N	144	148	147	147

Notes. Linear regression (OLS). All dependent variables run between 0–1. Standard errors in parentheses.
$***p < 0.01$. $**p < 0.05$. $*p < 0.1$.

Motives for Twitter use and evaluation

In the survey, we asked whether the candidates prioritized using Twitter for individual or party-centered purposes. To measure Twitter's usefulness for individual campaigning practices, we constructed an index based on three questions that asked the candidates to assess the importance of using Twitter for the purposes of (a) displaying a relatable personal side of themselves, (b) getting in personal contact with voters and (c) making their personal views visible (Cronbach's alpha = 0.85). To measure Twitter's usefulness to party-centered campaign approaches, the candidates were asked about the extent to which their Twitter usage was important for (a) spreading information about the party's daily activities and (b) making the party's views visible (Cronbach's alpha = 0.81). The different sets of questions were merged into party-centered and personal-centered categories. In the questionnaire, the scale runs from 1 "to a very small extent" to 7 "to a very large extent"; in the analyses, however, the items are merged into two indices that range between 0 "to a very small extent" and 1 "to a very large extent."

Table 3. Assessment of the Importance of Twitter for Personal or Party-Centered Purposes and Evaluation of the Use of Twitter for These Purposes in the Candidates' Campaign.

	Twitter motivation		Twitter evaluation	
	Personal	Party	Personal	Party
Sex (women)	0.12**	0.18***	0.05	0.13*
	(0.06)	(0.06)	(0.06)	(0.07)
Placement on the party list (1–43)	−0.00	−0.00	−0.00	0.00
	(0.00)	(0.00)	(0.00)	(0.00)
Age (22–83)	−0.00	0.00	−0.00	−0.00
	(0.00)	(0.00)	(0.00)	(0.00)
Incumbent	0.10	−0.11	0.20	0.10
	(0.13)	(0.14)	(0.13)	(0.15)
Experience as MP	−0.08	−0.19*	0.07	−0.03
	(0.13)	(0.10)	(0.10)	(0.11)
Party (Social Democrats are ref. category)				
Center Party	0.18	0.02	0.16	−0.03
	(0.12)	(0.13)	(0.13)	(0.13)
Christian Democrats	0.14	0.15	0.16	0.06
	(0.12)	(0.13)	(0.13)	(0.14)
Conservative Party	0.07	0.01	0.03	−0.18
	(0.12)	(0.13)	(0.13)	(0.14)
Feminist Party	−0.01	0.02	0.14	0.20
	(0.18)	(0.20)	(0.19)	(0.20)
Green Party	0.02	−0.02	0.04	−0.21
	(0.11)	(0.12)	(0.12)	(0.12)
Left Party	−0.28**	0.05	−0.19	−0.22
	(0.11)	(0.12)	(0.13)	(0.13)
Liberal Party	0.12	−0.03	−0.04	−0.19
	(0.12)	(0.13)	(0.13)	(0.14)
Pirate Party	−0.16	−0.03	−0.19	−0.20
	(0.13)	(0.15)	(0.14)	(0.15)
Sweden Democrats	−0.06	0.01	0.08	−0.04
	(0.21)	(0.23)	(0.22)	(0.24)
Intercept	0.58***	0.54***	0.52***	0.53***
	(0.14)	(0.15)	(0.15)	(0.16)
Observations	92	91	88	88
R-squared	0.28	0.19	0.24	0.22

Notes. All dependent variables run between 0–1. Standard errors in parentheses.
***$p < 0.01$. **$p < 0.05$. *$p < 0.1$.

There was, in fact, a significant difference between male and female candidates in terms of motivations for using Twitter to expose themselves as candidates (Table 3). The mean for women candidates was 0.63 and 0.51 for men. At the same time, more female than male candidates stated that they used Twitter to draw attention to their parties (mean for women was 0.68, mean for men was 0.50). This result is again in line with what we found earlier. Women candidates stress more aspects as being important in their campaign than do men, and as a consequence, Twitter is more important for women, both personally and also for their party-oriented purpose. The control variables did not offer much variation. In fact, gender was the only consistent pattern for the party-centered model.

When women candidates evaluated their party-centered uses of Twitter, they were also more positive than male candidates (Table 3). The results indicate that women candidates use Twitter as a professional campaign tool more often than do men, and these findings strengthen the picture that emerged above: women candidates value Twitter as more important in their campaign efforts than do male candidates, as a way to reach out to voters with the party message (mean for women was 0.53, mean for men was 0.40). In their evaluation of how well they performed with their personal usage of Twitter, however, women were not significantly more satisfied than were men (mean for women was 0.45, mean for men was 0.40). Because the number of respondents was limited, it is difficult to further investigate the difference between how male and female candidates evaluate their success in bringing forward their personalized campaign. We can only observe that the difference between male and female candidates' motivations for using Twitter was 0.12, whereas when they assessed their success of forwarding their personalized campaign, the difference remained at 0.5. This could be another indication that women put more pressure on themselves on the campaign trail.

To answer our second question of whether or not female politicians are more likely to use Twitter to enhance the political messages of their party or their personal agenda, we have seen that female candidates actually work harder than men to promote both themselves and their parties. We understand this tendency to be an indication of gendered campaigning.

The presence of incivility can have hampering effects for online political discourse (Gervais, 2015), yet it was not an issue reported by the candidates in our survey. When we asked the respondents who did not use Twitter about their reasons for refraining from doing so, only one male and one female candidate stated that they do not use Twitter because they "do not want to be exposed to personal harassment."

To evaluate the candidates' actual usage of Twitter (see Table 4), we collected tweets from all the Swedish candidates active on Twitter during the 2014 election campaign (between March 25 and May 25). To detect any special campaigning effects, we also collected tweets from the candidates one

Table 4. Activity on Twitter During and After the Election Campaign (NBREG).

	2014 Number of tweets	2014 Twitter interactions	2014 Twitter information	2015 Number of tweets	2015 Twitter interactions	2015 Twitter information
Sex (women)	0.15	0.13	0.22	0.47**	0.46**	0.26
	(0.18)	(0.21)	(0.19)	(0.20)	(0.23)	(0.21)
Placement on the party list (1–43)	−0.02*	−0.02*	−0.01*	−0.02*	−0.02	−0.01
	(0.01)	(0.01)	(0.01)	(0.01)	(0.01)	(0.01)
Age (22–83)	−0.02**	−0.02**	−0.01*	−0.03***	−0.03***	−0.02**
	(0.01)	(0.01)	(0.01)	(0.01)	(0.01)	(0.01)
Incumbent	0.98**	1.03**	1.19***	0.96**	1.06	1.23
	(0.38)	(0.44)	(0.40)	(0.47)	(0.54)	(0.47)
Experience as MP	0.60**	0.82***	0.37	0.35	0.42	0.30
	(0.26)	(0.31)	(0.27)	(0.29)	(0.33)	(0.29)
Party (Social Democrats are ref. category)						
Center Party	0.40	0.24	0.25	1.39***	1.52**	0.99*
	(0.36)	(0.43)	(0.36)	(0.45)	(0.51)	(0.47)
Christian Democrats	0.08	−0.17	0.12	0.64	0.74	0.32
	(0.35)	(0.39)	(0.35)	(0.45)	(0.51)	(0.45)
Conservative Party	0.25	0.08	0.34	−0.05	−0.21	−0.02
	(0.36)	(0.42)	(0.36)	(0.44)	(0.50)	(0.45)
Feminist Party	0.97*	0.65	0.11	−0.71	−0.77	−0.86
	(0.55)	(0.59)	(0.55)	(0.68)	(0.78)	(0.68)
Green Party	0.49	0.47	0.50	0.35	0.52	0.21
	(0.33)	(0.39)	(0.34)	(0.43)	(0.48)	(0.43)
Left Party	0.59	0.47	0.49	1.06**	1.25*	0.81*
	(0.37)	(0.44)	(0.38)	(0.47)	(0.53)	(0.47)
Liberal Party	0.21	0.17	0.27	0.86*	1.22**	0.58
	(0.34)	(0.39)	(0.35)	(0.44)	(0.50)	(0.44)
Pirate Party	0.77*	0.55	0.81**	0.83	1.12*	0.64
	(0.41)	(0.47)	(0.41)	(0.51)	(0.57)	(0.52)
Sweden Democrats	−0.57	−0.20	−0.39	−0.18	0.08	−0.42
	(0.49)	(0.56)	(0.51)	(0.57)	(0.64)	(0.58)
Intercept	5.62***	5.11***	5.25***	5.75***	5.10***	5.25***
	(0.44)	(0.51)	(0.45)	(0.52)	(0.58)	(0.53)
Pseudo R^2	0.01	0,01	0.01	0.02	0.02	0.01
N	196	196	196	195	195	195

Note. Standard error in parentheses.
***$p < 0.01$. **$p < 0.05$. *$p < 0.1$.

year before the election (February 2013) and again after the election (January to March 2015). In order to explore differences in actual use and activity between male and female candidates, we collected the number of tweets and the use of retweets, mentions, hashtags, and links. Both retweeting and mentioning can indicate a more interactive style of use, whereas the use of links and hashtags indicates intention to contribute to a debate on an issue at hand or provide further information on topics such as campaign issues. To separate the different uses of Twitter, we created two variables: Twitter interactions (consisting of retweets and mentions) and Twitter information (consisting of links and hashtags). Future studies into communication practices, however, may benefit by taking a more granular approach to different uses based on disaggregate links, hashtags, retweets, and @ replies. Examining the contents of tweets and a possible gendered communication style would also be of interest. In this article, we restricted our scope to a variable for the total number of tweets that candidates sent out (in addition to forms of use). Because our measurements consist of count data with the existence of overdispersion, we used negative binomial regression in our models.[3]

There were no gender differences for either numbers of tweets or Twitter activity during the election campaign (Table 4). Although there was a tendency for women to be more active, the difference was not significant. There were, however, some significant effects in the model. Older candidates were less active on Twitter, tweeting, interacting, and sharing information to a lesser extent than did younger candidates. The same tendency was evident among candidates who were lower ranked on the party list. We correspondingly observed that incumbents were more active on Twitter in comparison to the other candidates; here, it also appears that seniority matters. Candidates who had been members of the national parliament used Twitter to a higher extent. It is difficult to speculate why, but one explanation could be related to party loyalty, as when the election was over and a year had passed, the more senior candidates were no longer more active on Twitter.

The effects of election campaigning were further evident for other candidates' activities a year later. Female candidates were more active on Twitter and also had more interactions with their followers. The difference between male and female candidates who shared Twitter information was nearly significant, as well. It appears that gender is relevant, but not when it is election time. The competition between the candidates makes gender less important during the election campaign than it is before or after the campaign. When the competition is over, however, women candidates are more interested than men in communicating with their followers. This result was not driven by the intensity during the election campaign. In the 2014 election campaign, the candidates tweeted nearly 38,500 times, and in the three first months of 2015, they sent more than 40,500 tweets. To further validate the results, we looked at the candidates' activities a year before the election (February 2013). Here, we found the same pattern: women candidates were more active than men on Twitter (see Appendix 2). These results underscore the relevance of studying what politicians are doing between elections, not only what they are doing during campaigns (Esaiasson & Narud, 2013).

Among the other variables, we observed that higher ranked candidates used Twitter more often even when the election was over. Similarly, younger candidates tweeted more and had more interactions than did their older colleagues. Incumbents were also more active. There were no larger discrepancies between the parties, however, other than candidates from the Center party being more active than the other party candidates after the election.

Conclusions

In this study, we examined the importance of gender in how political candidates use social media for campaigning purposes. Using survey data on Swedish candidates and behavioral data from Twitter during the 2014 European election, we found gender-related patterns in the level of value candidates placed on social media as a campaign tool. Women candidates tended to evaluate social media as more important and more useful than did male candidates, particularly in terms of party-centered campaign approaches. During the election campaign, however, women candidates did not use Twitter more or differently than men. The logic of election campaigning makes candidates act in more predictable ways. The highest-ranked candidates and the incumbents were generally the most active; however, we observed that more senior candidates became more active during the election campaign, but lost their interest after the election was over. Between the elections, we could also see gender patterns for how men and women interacted using Twitter. These patterns have implications for the interpretation of so-called permanent campaigning (see Farrell, 1996) and the logic of online campaigning. During the intense campaign period, the level of activity rose as can be expected, but from these theoretical perspectives, the rationale for social media usage appeared to yield unexpected differences between elections. A distinct normalized or equalized pattern in online campaigning appears difficult to argue for and as this study shows, this especially holds true when considering the period between elections. It would appear that the more experienced and routine candidates value social media to a greater extent, judging by their activity and interactivity during the intense campaign period. This indicates a normalized pattern emerging on social media; however, the pattern was not consistent between elections, where we additionally found that female candidates were more prominent in their use.

The normalization/equalization dichotomy provides a limited understanding of the patterns of social media use in this case. Indicators of equalization, such as gender, offer inadequate explanatory power in a relatively equal setting. In a context of equal representation in parliament but with existing gender differences in de facto political power, it is not unambiguous how a pattern of more extensive social media use by women politicians should best be understood. It could be argued that social media in this case provides more equal conditions but the results from this use can still resemble a normalized pattern. It would be valuable if future references to this rather dated theory provided more elaborate attempts to explain why social media represents a breaking point or continuation of previous conditions. This could be done by, for example, considering different electoral settings, and campaign vs. non-campaign periods. As this article shows, the concept of normalization appears to hold true when looking at a period of intense campaigning, whereas the regular day-to-day basis of political communication on social media platforms indicates a break from this pattern.

Research has shown that women and men are similar in their general campaign styles (Bystrom & Kaid, 2002), as well as in their overall online activity in the recent European elections. Our results suggest that gender does play a role in social media campaigns, which calls for further comparative research in different electoral contexts and with varying degrees of descriptive representation. This study provides insight into the evolution of campaign practices in a context with a relatively gender-equal representation, where candidates adopt and adapt to new media environments. In this regard, social media is seen as an important platform for individual candidates, and its importance can be expected to increase over time. According to Lilleker, Tenscher, and Štětka (2015), indications of development toward a "hypermedia" campaign style can be found in the integration and involvement of several platforms as professional campaigning strategies in Europe. As the European campaign structure has developed toward campaign professionalism, this pattern can help to explain the emphasis put on social media campaigning. Separating these practices as strategic choices in processes of professionalization is necessary (Tenscher, 2013). In line with this reasoning, our results could also indicate that a more strategic use of social media entails a less active presence outside the campaign period. To better understand election campaigns online, we should therefore also study what the candidates are doing between elections. This is perhaps especially true for social media, and such research is necessary to further assess whether social media is used as a professional tool for a more permanent online presence or merely as a temporary additional platform during electoral campaigns.

It has been suggested that, in their effort to sidestep traditional media, female candidates aim to project an image of a more open, personal, and interactive politician (Carlson et al., 2014). The extent to which this could be linked to a typical female conversational style online may be relevant to study, given that some previous research indicates dissimilar gendered behavior on social media and that women in general tend to use technology differently than men (e.g., more sociably; Cunha, Magno, Goncalves, Cambraia, & Almeida, 2014; Lasorsa, 2012; Tufekci, 2008; Walton & Rice, 2013). Given the results presented in this article, gender should be studied in greater detail in relation to the political use of social media platforms. Sweden has one of the highest voter turnouts in European elections and the gender distribution of candidates is one of the most equal; nevertheless, we can detect gendered campaigning. These findings should therefore be expected to be even more prominent in other contexts. In contrast to American and British majority election and candidate-centered systems, Sweden's pluralistic, party-centered parliamentary system can provide different implications for individual online campaigning practices. Research has for example suggested that being online has a significant effect on intra-party competition (Hansen & Kosiara-Pedersen, 2014). In contrast, the relationship between gender and social media practices in this case may not be as strong in the context of national elections, because the European election possibly presents other opportunities for less established candidates, such as younger female contenders.

Political candidates use of social media can possibly yield additional preferential votes (Spierings & Jacobs, 2014). A relevant issue to address in future research could therefore be the extent to which a candidate's individual characteristics, such as gender, make that candidate more or less likely to benefit from using social media as a campaign strategy. If women candidates succeed in establishing themselves online and using social media to connect to voters—

especially female voters, who are more likely to assess female politicians positively (Kosiara-Pedersen & Hansen, 2015)—this could in time strengthen the status of younger women candidates in the electoral system.

Notes

1. All the means in the article were calculated with the margins command in Stata 14.1, while holding other factors constant at their average values.
2. In the party's ethical guidelines from 2011, there are instructions for social media use that state that it is important to be honest and sincere, and treat people the same way on the Internet as in real life. Among other things, the guidelines state that candidates should: not use social media when in an upset state of mind, always think about the political consequences when publishing, avoid internal discussions (the guidelines say this is best handled within the party), and respect the law (pp. 5–6). These statements give a clue as to some of the trouble the party has had with their representatives on social media platforms.
3. Because alpha was significantly different from zero, we preferred negative binomial regression over Poisson regression.

Acknowledgments

We are in great debt to Hampus Brynolf who helped us collect all the Twitter data and made the study possible. In addition we would like to thank Jonathan Polk at the Political Science Department, University of Gothenburg, for invaluable comments and advice, as well as the seminar participants from the Institute for Social Research, Oslo, who gave helpful feedback on the paper draft.

References

Bäck, H., Debus, M., & Müller, J. (2014). Who takes the parliamentary floor? The role of gender in speech-making in the Swedish Riksdag. *Political Research Quarterly*, *67*, 504–518. doi:10.1177/1065912914525861

Barber, B. (2001). The uncertainty of digital politics. *Harvard International Review*, *23*(1), 42–47.

Barber, B. (2003). *Strong democracy: Participatory politics for a new age*. Berkeley: University of California Press.

Berg, L., & Oscarsson, H. (Eds). (2015). *20 år med personval [20 years of preferential voting]. Valforskningsprogrammets rapportserie*. Statsvetenskapliga institutionen, Göteborgs universitet. Göteborg.

Bimber, B., & Davis, R. (2003). *Campaigning online: The Internet in U.S. Elections*. 387–397. New York, NY: Oxford University Press.

Blombäck, S., & De Fine Licht, J. (2015). Feministiskt initiativs sympatisörer [The sympathizers of Feminist initiative]. In A. Bergström, B. Johansson, H. Oscarsson, & M. Oskarson (Eds.), *Fragment*. Göteborgs universitet: SOM-institutet. Göteborg.

Brewer, P. R., Habegger, M., Harrington, R., Hoffman, L. H., Jones, P. E., & Lambe, J. L. (2015). Interactivity between candidates and citizens on a social networking site: Effects on perceptions and vote intentions. *Journal of Experimental Political Science*. doi:10.1017/XPS.2014.29

Bystrom, D., & Kaid, L. (2002). Are women candidates transforming campaign communication: A comparison of advertising videostyles in the 1990s. In C. S. Rosenthal (Ed.), *Women transforming congress*. Norman, OK: University of Oklahoma Press.

Carlson, T. (2007). It's a man's world? *Journal of Political Marketing*, *6*(1), 41–67. doi:10.1300/J199v06n01_03

Carlson, T., Djupsund, G., & Strandberg, K. (2014). Taking risks in social media campaigning: The early adoption of blogging by candidates. *Scandinavian Political Studies*, *37*, 21–40. doi:10.1111/scps.2014.37.issue-1

Cook, J. M. (2016). Gender, party, and presentation of family in the social media profiles of 10 state legislatures. *Social Media + Society*, *2*(2), 1–11. doi:10.1177/2056305116646394

Cunha, E., Magno, G., Goncalves, M. A., Cambraia, C., & Almeida, V. (2014). He votes or she votes? Female and male discursive strategies in Twitter political hashtags. *Plos One*, *9*(1). doi:10.1371/journal.pone.0087041

Dabelko, K. L. C., & Herrnson, P. S. (1997). Women's and men's campaigns for the U.S. house of representatives. *Political Research Quarterly*, *50*(1), 121–135.

Darcy, R., Welch, S., & Clark, J. (1994). *Women, elections, and representation* (2nd ed.). Lincoln: University of Nebraska Press.

Dolan, K. (2005). Do women candidates play to gender stereotypes? Do men candidates play to women? Candidate sex and issues priorities on campaign websites. *Political Research Quarterly, 58*(1), 31–44. doi:10.1177/106591290505800103

Dolan, K. (2010). The impact of gender stereotyped evaluations on support for women candidates. *Political Behavior, 32*, 1. doi:10.1007/s11109-009-9090-4

Dolan, K., & Lynch, T. (2016). The impact of gender stereotypes on voting for women candidates by level and type of office. *Politics & Gender, 12*(3), 573–595. doi:10.1017/S1743923X16000246

Druckman, J., Kifer, M., & Parkin, M. (2007). The technological development of congressional candidate web sites: How and why candidates use web innovations. *Social Science Computer Review, 25*(4), 425–442. doi:10.1177/0894439307305623

Ehin, P., & Solvak, M. (2012). Party voters gone astray: Explaining independent candidate success in the 2009 European elections in Estonia. *Journal of Elections, Public Opinion & Parties, 22*(3), 269–291. doi:10.1080/17457289.2012.682579

Enli, G., & Skogerbø, E. (2013). Personalized campaigns in party-centred politics. *Information, Communication and Society, 16*(5), 757–774. doi:10.1080/1369118X.2013.782330

Esaiasson, P., & Narud, H. (2013). Between-election democracy: An introductory note. In P. Esaiasson & H. M. Narud (Eds.), *Between-election Democracy: The representative relationship after Election Day* (pp. 1–14). Colchester, England: ECPR Press.

European Parliament. (2013). *Women in decision-making: The role of the new media for increased political participation.* Directorate General for Internal Policies, Policy Department C: Citizens' Rights and Constitutional Affairs. Brussels.

Evans, H. K., Cordova, V., & Sipole, S. (2014). Twitter style: An analysis of how House candidates used Twitter in their 2012 campaigns. *PS: Political Science and Politics, 47*, 454–462.

Farrell, D. (1996). Campaign strategies and tactics. In L. Leduc, R. G. Niemi, & P. Norris (Eds.), *Comparing Democracies* (pp. 160–183). London, England: Sage.

Folke, O., & Rickne, J. (2016). The glass ceiling in politics: Formalization and empirical tests. *Comparative Political Studies, 49*(5), 567–599. doi:10.1177/0010414015621073

Fox, R. L., & Lawless, J. L. (2011). Gendered perceptions and political candidacies: A central barrier to women's equality in electoral politics. *American Journal of Political Science, 55*, 59–73. doi:10.1111/ajps.2011.55.issue-1

Freedman, J. (2002). Women in the European parliament. *Parliamentary Affairs, 55*(1), 179–188. doi:10.1093/parlij/55.1.179

Fulton, S. A. (2012). Running backwards and in high heels: The gendered quality gap and incumbent electoral success. *Political Research Quarterly, 65*(2), 303–314. doi:10.1177/1065912911401419

Gainous, J., & Wagner, K. (2013). *Tweeting to power: The social media revolution in American Politics.* New York, NY: Oxford University Press.

Gervais, B. T. (2015). Incivility online: Affective and behavioral reactions to uncivil political posts in a web-based experiment. *Journal of Information Technology & Politics, 12*(2). doi:10.1080/19331681.2014.997416

Gibson, R., Lusoli, W., & Ward, S. (2008). The Australian public and politics on-line: Reinforcing or reinventing representation? *Australasian Political Studies Association, 43*(1), 111–131.

Gibson, R., & McAllister, I. (2015). Normalising or equalising party competition? Assessing the impact of the web on election campaigning. *Political Studies, 63*(3). doi:10.1111/1467-9248.12107

Gilljam, M., Karlsson, D., & Sundell, A. (2010). *Politik på hemmaplan. Tiotusen fullmäktigeledamöter tycker om demokrati [Politics on the Home Turf: Ten-thousand Councilors Thinking About Politics and Democracy].* Stockholm, Sweden: SKL Kommentus.

Grant, W. J., Moon, B., & Grant, J. B. (2010). Digital dialogue? Australian politicians' use of the social network tool Twitter. *Australian Journal of Political Science, 45*(4), 579–604. doi:10.1080/10361146.2010.517176

Gulati, G. J., & Williams, C. B. (2013). Social media and campaign 2012: Developments and trends for Facebook adoption. *Social Science Computer Review, 31*(5), 577–588. doi:10.1177/0894439313489258

Hagen, M., & Mayer, W. (2000). The modern politics of presidential selection: How changing the rules really did change the game. In W. G. Mayer (Ed.), *In pursuit of the White House 2000: How we choose our presidential nominees* (pp. 1–55). New York, NY: Chatham House Publishers.

Hansen, K. M., & Kosiara-Pedersen, K. (2014). Cyber-campaigning in Denmark: Application and effects of candidate campaigning. *Journal of Information Technology & Politics, 11*(2), 206–219. doi:10.1080/19331681.2014.895476

Harrison, L. (2005). Electoral systems and party strategies in Britain: Women candidates in the 1999 and 2004 European parliamentary elections. *Representation, 41*(2), 85–95. doi:10.1080/00344890508523293

Heith, D. (2003). The lipstick watch: Media coverage, gender, and presidential campaigns. In R. P. Watson & A. Gordon (Eds.), *Anticipating Madam President* (pp. 123–130). Boulder, CO: Lynne Rienner.

Hermans, L., & Vergeer, M. (2012). Personalization in E-campaigning: A cross-national comparison of personalization strategies used on candidate websites of 17 countries in EP Elections 2009. *New Media and Society, 15*, 72–92. doi:10.1177/1461444812457333

Hindman, M. (2008). *The myth of digital democracy.* Princeton, NJ: Princeton University Press.

Hogan, R. E. (2007). The effects of candidate gender on campaign spending in state legislative elections. *Social Science Quarterly, 88*, 1092–1105. doi:10.1111/ssqu.2007.88.issue-5

Jackson, N. A., & Lilleker, D. G. (2009). Building an architecture of participation? Political parties and web 2.0 in Britain. *Journal of Information Technology & Politics, 6*(3), 232–250. doi:10.1080/19331680903028438

Jackson, N. A., & Lilleker, D. G. (2011). Microblogging, constituency service and impression management: UK MPs and the use of Twitter. *The Journal of Legislative Studies*, *17*(1), 86–105. doi:10.1080/13572334.2011.545181

Jacobs, K., & Spierings, N. (2016). *Social media, parties, and political inequalities*. New York, NY: Palgrave MacMillan.

Jalalzai, F. (2006). Women candidates and the media: 1992–2000 elections. *Politics and Policy*, *34*(3). doi:10.1111/j.1747-1346.2006.00030.x

Jungherr, A. (2014). *Twitter in politics: A comprehensive literature review*. Retrieved from http://ssrn.com/abstract=2402443, 10.2139/ssrn.2402443.

Just, M., & Crigler, A. (2014). *Gender and self-presentation in social media: An analysis of the 10 most competitive 2012 U.S. Senate races* (APSA 2014 Annual Meeting Paper). Retrieved from http://ssrn.com/abstract=2453741.

Kahn, K. (1996). *The political consequences of being a woman: How stereotypes influence the conduct and consequences of political campaigns*. New York, NY: Columbia University Press.

Karlsen, R. (2011). A platform for individualized campaigning? Social media and parliamentary candidates in the 2009 Norwegian election campaign. *Policy and the Internet*, *3*. doi:10.2202/1944-2866.1137

Karlsen, R., & Enjolras, B. (2016). Styles of social media campaigning and influence in a hybrid political communication system: Linking candidate survey data with Twitter data. *The International Journal of Press/Politics*, *21*(3), 338–357. doi:10.1177/1940161216645335

Kosiara-Pedersen, K., & Hansen, K. M. (2015). Gender differences in assessments of party leaders. *Scandinavian Political Studies*, *38*, 26–48. doi:10.1111/scps.2015.38.issue-1

Krook, M. L. (2006). Reforming representation: The diffusion of candidate gender quotas worldwide. *Politics & Gender*, *2* (3), 303–327. doi:10.1017/S1743923X06060107

Larson, S. G. (2001). Running as women? A comparison of female and male Pennsylvania assembly candidates' campaign brochures. *Women and Politics*, *22*, 107–124. doi:10.1300/J014v22n02_04

Larsson, A. O. (2015a). The EU Parliament on Twitter—Assessing the permanent online practices of parliamentarians. *Journal of Information Technology and Politics*, *12*(2), 149–166. doi:10.1080/19331681.2014.994158

Larsson, A. O. (2015b). Going viral? Comparing parties on social media during the 2014 Swedish election. *Convergence: The International Journal of Research into New Media Technologies*, 23(2), 117–131.

Larsson, A. O., & Kalsnes, B. (2014). "Of course we are on Facebook": Use and non-use of social media among Swedish and Norwegian politicians. *European Journal of Communication*, *29*(6), 653–667. doi:10.1177/0267323114531383

Lasorsa, D. (2012). Transparency and other journalistic norms on Twitter: The role of gender. *Journalism Studies*, *13*(3), 402–417. doi:10.1080/1461670X.2012.657909

Lassen, D., & Brown, A. (2011). Twitter: The electoral connection? *Social Science Computer Review*, *29*(4), 419–436. doi:10.1177/0894439310382749

Lilleker, D. G., & Koc-Michalska, K. (2013). Online political communication strategies: MEPs, E-representation, and self-representation. *Journal of Information Technology & Politics*, *10*(2), 190–207. doi:10.1080/19331681.2012.758071

Lilleker, D. G., Koc-Michalska, K., Schweitzer, E. J., Jacunski, M., Jackson, N., & Vedel, T. (2011). Informing, engaging, mobilizing or interacting: Searching for a European model of web campaigning. *European Journal of Communication*, *26*(3), 195–213. doi:10.1177/0267323111416182

Lilleker, D. G., Tenscher, J., & Štětka, V. (2015). Towards hypermedia campaigning? Perceptions of new media's importance for campaigning by party strategists in comparative perspective. *Information, Communication and Society*, *18*, 747–765. doi:10.1080/1369118X.2014.993679

Lusoli, W. (2005). The Internet and the European parliament elections: Theoretical perspectives, empirical investigations and proposals for research. *Information Polity*, *10*(3), 153–163.

Marcinkowski, F., & Metag, J. (2014). Why do candidates use online media in constituency campaigning? An application of the theory of planned behavior. *Journal of Information Technology and Politics*, *11*, 151–168. doi:10.1080/19331681.2014.895690

Margolis, M., & Resnick, D. (2000). *Politics as usual: The cyberspace revolution*. London, England: Sage.

Meeks, L. (2013). *A woman's place: Gender politics and Twitter in the 2012 elections* (Unpublished doctoral dissertation). University of Washington, Seattle.

Megarry, J. (2014). Online incivility or sexual harassment? Conceptualizing women's experiences in the digital age. *Women's Studies International Forum*, *47*(1), 46–55. doi:10.1016/j.wsif.2014.07.012

Müller, W. C. (2000). Political parties in parliamentary democracies: Making delegation and accountability work. *European Journal of Political Research*, *37*, 309–333. doi:10.1111/1475-6765.00515

Nulty, P., Theocharis, Y., Popa, S. A., Parnet, O., & Benoit, K. (2016). Social media and political communication in the 2014 elections to the European Parliament. *Electoral Studies*, *44*, 429–444. doi:10.1016/j.electstud.2016.04.014

Obholzer, L., & Daniel, W. T. (2016). An online electoral connection? How electoral systems condition representatives' social media use. *European Union Politics*, *17*(3), 387–407. doi:10.1177/1465116516630149

Pearson, K., & McGhee, E. (2013). What it takes to win: Questioning "gender neutral" outcomes in US House elections. *Politics & Gender*, *9*(4), 439. doi:10.1017/S1743923X13000433

Pierre, J. (2015). *The Oxford Handbook of Swedish Politics*. New York, NY: Oxford: Oxford University Press.

Sapiro, V., Walsh, K. C., Strach, P., & Hennings, V. (2011). Gender, context, and television advertising: A comprehensive analysis of 2000 and 2002 House races. *Political Research Quarterly*, *64*(1), 107–119. doi:10.1177/1065912909343583

Schmitt, H. (2009). European parliament elections after eastern enlargement. *Journal of European Integration, 31*(5), 525–535. doi:10.1080/07036330903290629

Scully, R., & Farrell, D. (2003). MEPs as representatives: Individual and institutional roles. *JCMS: Journal of Common Market Studies, 41*(2), 269–288.

Segaard, S. B., & Nielsen, J. A. (2013). Local election blogs: Networking among the political elite. *Information Polity 18, 4*(October), 299–313.

Southern, R. (2015). Is Web 2.0 providing a voice for outsiders? A comparison of personal website and social media use by candidates at the 2010 UK general election. *Journal of Information Technology and Politics, 12*(1). doi:10.1080/19331681.2014.972603

Spierings, N., & Jacobs, K. (2014). Getting personal? The impact of social media on preferential voting. *Political Behavior, 36*(1), 215–234. doi:10.1007/s11109-013-9228-2

Strandberg, K. (2013). A social media revolution or just a case of history repeating itself?—The use of social media in the 2011 Finnish parliamentary elections. *New Media and Society, 15*(85). doi:10.1177/1461444812470612

Strömbäck, J. (2008). Four phases of mediatization: An analysis of the mediatization of politics. *The International Journal of Press/Politics, 13*(3), 228–246. doi:10.1177/1940161208319097

Tenscher, J. (2013). First- and second-order campaigning: Evidence from Germany. *European Journal of Communication, 28*(3), 241–258. doi:10.1177/0267323113477633

Tufekci, Z. (2008). Grooming, gossip, Facebook and Myspace. *Information, Communication and Society, 11*(4), 544–564. doi:10.1080/13691180801999050

Utz, S. (2009). The (potential) benefits of campaigning via social network sites. *Journal of Computer-Mediated Communication, 14*, 221–243. doi:10.1111/jcmc.2009.14.issue-2

Vaccari, C. (2013). A tale of two e-parties: Candidate websites in the 2008 US presidential primaries. *Party Politics, 19*(1), 19–40. doi:10.1177/1354068810391287

Vergeer, M., & Hermans, L. (2013). Campaigning on Twitter: Microblogging and online social networking as campaign tools in the 2010 general elections in the Netherlands. *Journal of Computer-Mediated Communication, 18*(4), 399–419. doi:10.1111/jcc4.2013.18.issue-4

Vergeer, M., Hermans, L., & Cunha, C. (2013). Web campaigning in the 2009 European parliament elections: A cross-national comparative analysis. *New Media and Society, 15*(1), 128–148. doi:10.1177/1461444812457337

Vergeer, M., Hermans, L., & Sams, S. (2011). Is the voter only a tweet away? Micro blogging during the 2009 European parliament election campaign in the Netherlands. *First Monday, 16*(8). doi:10.5210/fm.v16i8.3540

Walton, S., & Rice, R. (2013). Mediated disclosure on Twitter: The roles of gender and identity in boundary impermeability, valence, disclosure, and stage. *Computers in Human Behavior, 29*(4), 1465–1474. doi:10.1016/j.chb.2013.01.033

Wängnerud, L. (2015). *The principles of gender-sensitive parliaments*. New York, NY: Routledge.

Ward, S., Gibson, R., & Lusoli, W. (2003). Online participation and mobilization in Britain: Hype, hope and reality. *Parliamentary Affairs, 56*(4), 652–688. doi:10.1093/pa/gsg108

Werner, B. (1997). Financing the campaigns of women candidates and their opponents: Evidence from three states, 1982–1990. *Women & Politics, 19*, 81–97.

Appendix 1

Table A1. Campaign Activities. Factor Analysis (Principal Component).

	Traditional	Web campaign	Outreach	Personal	Media
Meetings with party group	0.80				
Contact with media	0.72				
Spread the party's campaign material	0.70				
Public speeches	0.59				
Blog		0.83			
Individual Web page		0.81			
Twitter		0.59			
Facebook		0.56			
Calling voters			0.73		
SMS messages			0.72		
Individual e-mail list to inform voters and supporters			0.59		
Visit workplaces and organizations			0.57		
Door knocking				0.75	
Letters to voters				0.72	
Individual election poster				0.70	
Individual commercial in radio, TV, cinema					0.75
Individual ads in newspaper					0.62
Individual election pamphlet or similar print					0.62
Eigenvalue (initial)	4.45	2.34	1.55	1.52	1.11

Appendix 2

Table A2. Gender and Activity on Twitter, February 2013 (NBREG).

	2013 Number of tweets	2013 Twitter interactions	2013 Twitter information
Sex (women)	0.91***	1.02***	0.83***
	(0.31)	(0.36)	(0.31)
Placement on the party list (1–43)	−0.02	−0.01	−0.02
	(0.02)	(0.02)	(0.02)
Age (22–83)	−0.02**	−0.03***	−0.02*
	(0.01)	(0.01)	(0.01)
Incumbent	−0.11	−0.11	−0.12
	(0.62)	(0.75)	(0.62)
Experience as MP	−0.90**	−0.73	−0.98**
	(0.45)	(0.54)	(0.45)
Party (Social Democrats are ref. category)			
Center Party	0.90*	0.93	0.89*
	(0.54)	(0.64)	(0.53)
Christian Democrats	−0.12	−0.39	0.15
	(0.53)	(0.62)	(0.54)
Conservative Party	1.11*	0.67	1.38**
	(0.65)	(0.77)	(0.64)
Feminist Party	−0.42	−0.36	−0.43
	(1.04)	(1.23)	(1.04)
Green Party	0.18	0.15	0.20
	(0.49)	(0.59)	(0.50)
Left Party	0.60	0.43	0.76
	(0.57)	(0.69)	(0.57)
Liberal Party	0.74	0.90	0.64
	(0.56)	(0.67)	(0.56)
Pirate Party	0.74	0.77	0.75
	(0.64)	(0.76)	(0.63)
Sweden Democrats	1.73**	2.20***	1.06
	(0.70)	(0.82)	(0.72)
Intercept	4.34***	3.69***	3.71***
	(0.62)	(0.71)	(0.64)
Pseudo *R*-squared	0.02	0,03	0.02
N	101	101	101

Note. Standard error in parentheses.
***$p < 0.01$. **$p < 0.05$. *$p < 0.1$.

Table A3. Response Rate per Party (%).

Political party	Response rate
Center Party	47
Christian Democrats	47
Conservative Party	30
Feminist Party	44
Green Party	60
Left Party	51
Liberal Party	29
Pirate Party	45
Social Democrats	53
Sweden Democrats	35

Appendix 3. Descriptive Statistics

Table A4. Response Rate per Age Groups (%).

Age groups	Statistics Sweden	The survey
18–29	17	16
30–49	46	41
50–64	30	30
65+	8	13

Note. The statistics are taken from Statistic Sweden's Web page: http://www.scb.se/sv_/Hitta-statistik/Statistik-efter-amne/Demokrati/Allmanna-val/Europaparlamentsval-nominerade-och-valda/#c_undefined

Table A5. Response Rate and Gender (%).

Gender	Statistics Sweden	The survey
Women	47	51

Note. The statistics are taken from Statistic Sweden's Web page: http://www.scb.se/sv_/Hitta-statistik/Statistik-efter-amne/Demokrati/Allmanna-val/Europaparlamentsval-nominerade-och-valda/#c_undefined

Appendix 4 Questionnaire

Importance of Campaign Activities

"Were any of the following activities part of your campaign? And if yes, how important were they?

Items:"

(A) Door-knocking, canvassing
(B) Distributing party campaign material
(C) Calling up voters on the phone
(D) Visiting businesses and social organizations
(E) Meetings with party elites/members and/or party groups
(F) Media activities (interviews, press releases)
(G) Public speeches and rallies
(H) Personal campaign posters
(I) Direct mailing
(J) Personal newspaper ads
(K) Personal spots on radio, TV, movie houses
(L) Personal flyers or other campaign material (give-aways)
(M) Personal Web site
(N) Mailing list to inform supporters and voters about my campaign
(O) Own blog
(P) Facebook
(Q) SMS
(R) Twitter
(S) Other, please specify:

Response options:

(1) little important
(2) somewhat important
(3) very important
(4) most important

Importance of Twitter

"How important was Twitter for you when it comes to:"

(A) Telling people about your daily activities as a politician
(B) Disseminating information of the party's daily activities
(C) Being able to show a more personal side of yourself
(D) Getting into personal contact with voters
(E) Visualizing your personal views
(F) Highlighting the party's positions
(G) Debating with political opponents
(H) Criticizing political opponents
(I) Reaching out to as many voters as possible
(J) Having an impact on traditional media

Response options:

1—To a very low extent, 7—To a very high extent

Evaluations of Twitter

"To what extent have you been successful through Twitter at:

(A) Telling people about your daily activities as a politician
(B) Disseminating information of the party's daily activities
(C) Being able to show a more personal side of yourself
(D) Getting into personal contact with voters
(E) Visualizing your personal views
(F) Highlighting the party's positions
(G) Debating with political opponents
(H) Criticizing political opponents
(I) Reaching out to as many voters as possible
(J) Having an impact on traditional media

1—To a very low extent, 7—To a very high extent

From hybrid media system to hybrid-media politicians: Danish politicians and their cross-media presence in the 2015 national election campaign

Mark Blach-Ørsten, Mads Kæmsgaard Eberholst, and Rasmus Burkal

ABSTRACT
An increasingly complex hybrid system of social and traditional news media surrounds Nordic election campaigns as politically experienced incumbents favor traditional news media and younger, lesser known candidates' social media. Despite little evidence for hybrid-media politicians, politicians' media use is changing rapidly; 15%–16% of Danish candidates used Twitter in 2011 but 68% in 2015. In this large-sample content analysis, party leaders have high traditional news media and low Twitter presence, and younger candidates vice versa, but some politicians have high presence in both. Hybrid-media politicians are younger than the average Danish Parliament member, represent various parties, and likely come from the greater Copenhagen area.

Introduction

Studies on politicians' social media campaigning are becoming as numerous as the politicians with social media profiles. In a recent review of 127 studies focusing on Twitter, Jungherr (2016) finds a number of interesting similarities among the many studies. First, Twitter users are not representative of countries' general population but, rather, make up an elite consisting of politicians, journalists, and the politically interested. Second, members of the opposition are more likely to use Twitter during an election than members of the incumbent government. Third, so far, Twitter appears to have no clear direct effects on electoral success.

Jungherr (2016) also shows that most Twitter studies have focused on the United States and United Kingdom. Considering the Nordic perspective, the review found only two studies that included Denmark, four Sweden, and six Twitter and Norway. Specifically regarding Danish research, a few more studies can be added to the mix, including Skovsgaard and Van Dalen (2013) and Hansen and Kosiara-Pedersen (2014), but this field of research is clearly only emerging in the Nordic countries. The few studies focused on Nordic politicians' use of Twitter in election campaigns indicate that those most active on Twitter are younger and lesser known politicians, whereas the more established and well-known politicians are less active (Enli & Skogerbø, 2013; Skovsgaard & Van Dalen, 2013; Strandberg, 2009). A possible reason is that well-known politicians have high newsworthiness and, consequently, easy, generous access to traditional news media outlets (Blach-Ørsten, 2014; Skovsgaard & Van Dalen, 2013). Thus, well-known politicians have less need to use social media to grab attention for their campaigns, whereas for lesser known politicians, Twitter offers a low-cost way to try to gain both public and media attention.

In a survey study of cyber-campaigning in the 2011 Danish national election, Hansen and Kosiara-Pedersen (2014, p. 216) found no significant effects of any kind from cyber-campaigning when controlling for other campaign activities. Likewise, international and Nordic studies suggest that Twitter should not be singled out as the only social media tool or platform used by politicians in online campaigning. Hansen and Kosiara-Pedersen (2014) argue that Twitter should be analyzed together with other cyber-campaigning platforms, such as Facebook, Web sites, and blogs. Jungherr (2016) contends that Twitter should not

Color versions of one or more of the figures in the article can be found online at http://www.tandfonline.com/WITP.

be seen as a separate communication tool but as part of an increasingly complex media environment in which both traditional news media and (other) social media shape political coverage and thus political communication. Indeed, one future direction of Twitter studies, Jungherr (2016) suggests, is to analyze both social media and traditional news media.

This article adds to this growing body of Twitter studies by examining candidates' presence on Twitter and in traditional news media in Denmark, a country on which so far few studies have focused. Treating Denmark as a case study adds important news aspects to the research on modern-day campaigning. From a media systems perspective, Denmark, which is part of the democratic-corporatist media system, represents a different media system than the liberal media system, seen in, for example, the United States and United Kingdom (Hallin & Mancini, 2004). The Danish media system is characterized by an overall focus on the news media's role in democracy (Blach-Ørsten & Willig, 2016b), and Denmark has a long, strong history of public service television and radio and tradition of providing economic subsidies for newspapers, both traditional and online. Although economic and technological changes have affected the Danish news media, it remains a robust media system (Blach-Ørsten, 2014; Newman, Fletcher, Levy, & Nielson, 2016), in which the traditional news media still dominates, and changes in media use and reach are occurring at different rates than in the UK and United States.

From a political system perspective, the Danish political system is also very different from the UK and U.S. political systems. Denmark's multiparty system featured 10 parties running in the 2015 elections, and while Danish campaigns have become increasingly professionalized and mediatized in the past 10–15 years, campaign budgets remain comparatively low (Hansen & Kosiara-Pedersen, 2014). Finally, in Denmark's proportional election system, candidates from different parties compete against not only each other but also their colleagues within the same party (Esmark & Ørsten, 2008; Skovsgaard & Van Dalen, 2013).

Finally, all the previous Danish studies have been based on surveys of candidates. In this study, a large-sample content analysis investigates the cross-media presence of all 799 candidates for the Folketing (Danish Parliament) in the 2015 general election. Theoretically, the study adopts a hybrid-media perspective focusing on both Twitter and traditional news media. Following the findings of Danish scholars Skovsgaard and Van Dalen (2013) and Hansen and Kosiara-Pedersen (2014), the use of Twitter as a campaign platform is understood in relation to the Twitter users' newsworthiness in the traditional news media. Thus, party leaders and other well-known politicians with high newsworthiness in traditional news media give lower priority to social media (Twitter), whereas lesser known politicians with low newsworthiness in traditional news media give high priority to social media (Twitter), which can offer a low-cost way to gain both public and media attention.

Based on this reasoning, this article is structured as follows. The next section presents the theoretical argument merging media-systems theory (Hallin & Mancini, 2004; Strömbäck, Ørsten, & Aalberg, 2008) and hybrid-media theory (Chadwick, 2013; Moe & Larsson, 2013; Nuernbergk & Conrad, 2016). The discussion then moves to the particulars of the Danish electoral system and the study methodology of large-scale content analysis of both traditional news media outlets and Twitter. Next, the research questions are proposed, and finally, the results are presented and discussed.

Political campaigning in a hybrid-media system

In the media-system theory developed by Hallin and Mancini (2004), Denmark, along with the other Nordic countries, follows the northern European/democratic corporatist model. The countries in this model are all characterized by: (a) the early development of a large newspaper industry; (b) high newspaper circulation; (c) strong professionalization of journalism; and (d) a high level of public intervention in the media sector, in both state subsidies for legacy news media organizations and in a strong public service media, including both radio and television public news services (Hallin & Mancini, 2004, p. 74). A study on political communication in the Nordic countries (Strömbäck et al., 2008) concludes that little if any characteristics of the Nordic countries challenge the fundamentals of Hallin and Mancini's (2004) model.

However, more recent studies (Benson, Blach-Ørsten, Powers, Willig, & Zambrano, 2012; Blach-Ørsten & Willig, 2016b; Hjarvard & Kammer, 2014; Syvertsen, Enli, Mjøs, & Moe, 2015) argue that global trends, such as digitalization and commercialization, are causing profound changes in all media systems, including the democratic-corporatist system. Since the 1990s, print circulation, readership, and advertising revenues have dropped in Denmark (Lund, Willig, & Blach-Ørsten, 2009; Blach-Ørsten & Willig, 2016b; Hjarvard & Kammer, 2014). Traditional public service television and radio still reach large audiences, as do online newspapers, but newspapers have yet to find a business model that makes up for losses in print advertisement (Blach-Ørsten & Willig, 2016b; Hjarvard & Kammer, 2014; Newman et al., 2016). New online news media are also emerging, and online audiences, especially by younger generations, are increasingly using Facebook and Twitter as platforms on which to find and consume news (Newman et al., 2016). These changes within the democratic-corporatist media system resemble Chadwick's (2013) description of a hybrid-media system in which old and new forms of communication and newsmaking coexist and interact in an increasingly complex media ecology (Moe & Larsson, 2013).

Changes are taking place not just within media. As Hallin and Mancini (2004) stress, the relationship between media and politics determines how media systems are shaped and develop over time, and the political side of this equation is also changing (Blach-Ørsten, 2014; Esmark & Ørsten, 2008). During much of the 20th century, the Danish political system could be characterized as a mostly consensual, multiparty parliamentary democracy with a strong corporatist tradition of interest mediation (as implied in the notion of a democratic-corporatist system), making Denmark a strong example of the Nordic welfare state. Since the 1980s, however, the political system has undergone significant changes. Although turnout in national elections remains high (85.9% in 2015) (Statistics Denmark, 2015), fewer voters retain a strong sense of party identification, class-based voting has given way to issue voting, and most parties have seen declining membership (Esmark & Ørsten, 2008), along with, more recently, trust in politicians. During the same time, a broad majority in the Folketing has passed legislation to substantially increase public funding of political parties' professional secretariats (Blach-Ørsten, 2016). This money has largely been invested in professionalizing communication by both party organizations and individual politicians, as well campaign efforts during and between elections (Blach-Ørsten, 2016; Esmark & Ørsten, 2008).

Amid these changes, social media has attracted increased focus from both party organizations and individual politicians. Denmark has high Internet penetration, at 96% in 2016 (Newman et al., 2016), and high adoption of social media in general. Facebook, in particular, is popular among Danes (Nielsen & Schrøder, 2014), with 62% of the Danish population active on Facebook on a daily basis in 2016. In contrast, only 4% of the Danish population is active daily on Twitter (Danielsen, 2016). A survey of Danish politicians in the 2011 election finds that 78% of members of Parliament (MPs) were on Facebook but only 16% were on Twitter (Skovsgaard & Van Dalen, 2013). A more recent survey during the 2015 election reports that 68% of candidates had Twitter profiles, an immense jump up from 2011 (Jensen, Hoff, & Klastrup, 2016). A survey investigating Danish politicians' reasons for using Facebook and Twitter finds that they used social media to attract (a) the attention of journalists and news media organizations and (b) sometimes to aim a specific message at their constituents while avoiding the critical filter of the press (Blach-Ørsten, 2016).

Thus, the Danish democratic-corporatist political system has changed at least as much as the democratic-corporatist media system has in recent decades (Blach-Ørsten, 2014). Despite these structural changes in both news media and politics in Denmark, studies on political communication in Denmark suggest that the traditional news media continues to play the most important role in the emerging hybrid news-media system. Studies on media use from quantitative (Nielsen & Schrøder, 2014) and qualitative (Schrøder, 2014) perspectives find that most Danes use several news platforms on a daily basis (Newman et al., 2016). Thus, public-service television and radio, online newspapers, and social media all play roles in daily use, with younger generations preferring social media, and older generations still favoring television news (Newman et al., 2016; Schrøder, 2015). Studies on agenda setting in Denmark show that the front-page stories of the daily print versions of traditional newspapers are quoted by public service radio and television and online by other major news outlets (Blach-Ørsten & Willig, 2016a; Blach-Ørsten, Willig, & Burkal, 2013; Lund, Willig, & Blach-Ørsten, 2009;). Studies on journalism quality indicate that politicians and journalists themselves consider the three Danish morning newspapers to have the highest journalistic quality, while the Danish public perceives the most quality in public service television news (Willig, Ørsten, Hartley, & Flensburg, 2015). Finally, according to studies on news use and social media, most Danes do not follow breaking news on social media (Nielsen & Schrøder, 2014), and while many do find news on social media, only 12% of the population names social media as their preferred news source (Newman et al., 2016).

From the perspective of political campaigning, these changes in the news media and political system have made Danish politics increasingly mediatized in recent decades (Blach-Ørsten, 2016; Esmark & Ørsten, 2011; Hjarvard, 2008; Ørsten, 2005; Skovsgaard & Van Dalen, 2013). Mediatized politics are largely driven by the media logic of the news media (Ørsten, 2005; Strömbäck, 2008) and its adoption by politicians (Esmark & Ørsten, 2011; Nuernbergk & Conrad, 2016; Strömbäck & Van Alest, 2013). In the Danish context, news values such as conflict, identification, and power figure prominently in the media logic (Blach-Ørsten, 2016; Skovsgaard & Van Dalen, 2013). This logic, however, often skews the news media's attention toward well-known politicians with powerful positions and/or good communications skills and resources, making it harder for the lesser known politicians with fewer resources to gain media attention (Skovsgaard & Van Dalen, 2013).

In a recent report Jensen et al. (2016) track the role of the Internet, online news media, and social media in Danish election campaigns from the late 1990s to the election in 2015. Jensen et al. (2016) trace the first attempts to use new technology in a general election campaign place to 1998, which saw the first significant number of politicians use Web pages as part of their campaign activities. In the 2005 election, candidates added blogs to their campaign toolbox, and in the 2007 general election, Facebook first became a reference point for candidates' campaigns. In the 2011 and 2015 elections, Facebook emerged as the dominant social media used by candidates, as the importance of the blogs and Web pages of individual candidates declined, and YouTube remained a marginal media in Denmark. Twitter entered the campaign toolbox in 2011, with Instagram making its first appearance in the 2015 election.

Despite the focus on social media, Jensen et al. (2016) conclude, based on surveys, that traditional news media remain the most important media for voters, with television being especially important, and newspapers and radio still playing crucial roles. Data from the most recent elections, however, indicate that use of traditional news media is declining in favor of social media. Jensen et al. (2016) also finds that the respondents (voters) believe that social media could influence election outcomes, but the authors argue that other factors, such as party performance, have greater value in changing votes. This argument is in line with Hansen and Kosiara-Perdersen's (2014, pp. 115–116) study of the 2011 election. Hansen and Kosiara-Pedersen (2014) find that, when controlling for other variables (e.g., campaign resources, incumbency, appearance on national television, advertisements in nationwide newspapers, participation in election meetings, and number of volunteers), cyber-camping has an effect only on interparty competition for personal votes, and this effect is not significant when controlling for the other mentioned variables.

In conclusion, the hybridization and increasing complexities of the Danish media system have resulted in increasingly mediatized political campaigning, with the media logic guiding most forms of political communication. Still more communication platforms are coming into play, sometimes interacting with each other, sometimes in competition with each other. Thus, politicians may turn to social media to attract the attention of both journalists and voters, and journalists, in turn, may use social networks to look for both scoops and new sources. However, agenda setting and reaching voters in the Danish media system still largely entail getting a story in traditional news media, such as public service television and radio and morning newspapers.

The Danish electoral system and 2015 national election

Elections to the Danish Parliament are based on proportional representation (Norregaard, 2014). The Parliament has 179 members, including four elected from Greenland and the Faeroe Islands, which belong to the Commonwealth. Denmark is divided into three electoral regions (Metropolitan Copenhagen, Sealand-Southern Denmark and Northern and Central Jutland) and 10 multi-member constituencies subdivided into 92 nomination districts. The distribution of seats takes place at two levels, a multi-member constituency level and a national level. The first 135 seats of the Parliament are allocated among the 10 multi-member constituencies, while the 40 remaining seats are distributed in a compensatory fashion at the higher tier of the national level (Esmark & Ørsten, 2008).

The distribution of mandates among the candidates on the different party lists can follow three principles: (a) distribution of candidates in local constituencies within a regional constituency, with both party votes and preferential (personal) votes determining the outcome; (b) hierarchical running order within a regional constituency, which requires an exceedingly high number of preferential votes for a particular candidate to cause deviations from the running order determined by party; and (c) an equal chance for all candidates on a particular party list within a regional constituency, making the number of preferential votes the most important (Esmark & Ørsten, 2008).

Denmark practices what is known as "negative parliamentarianism," in which the government need not have a majority in the Parliament, but it must not have a majority against it. If there is a majority against the government, it must resign. The system of negative parliamentarianism allows Denmark to be run by a minority government. Indeed, many Danish governments have been minority governments holding less than 90 of the 179 seats in Parliament.

In the 2015 national election, 10 parties making up two blocks (the red and blue blocks) (Kosiara-Pedersen, 2012) fought for votes. On the left, the red block included the Social Democrats (A), Social Liberals (B), Socialist People's Party (F), Red/Green Alliance (Ø) and newly formed Alternative Party (Å). On the right, the blue block included the Liberals (V), Conservatives (C), Danish People's Party (O), Liberal Alliance (I), and Christian Democrats (K), which have no parliamentary representation today. At the time of the election, the incumbent government consisted of the Social Democrats (A) and Social Liberals (B), but the Socialist People's Party (F) had been part of the government until 2014. The prime minister was Helle Thorning-Schmidt from the Social Democrats (S), and the opposition was led by the Liberals (V), headed by former Prime Minister Lars Løkke Rasmussen and the leader of the Danish People's Party (O), Kristian Thulesen Dahl.

Method and data

The guiding principle of data collection in this study is to focus on the news and social media with the most activity, readers, and users. For the legacy media, this means focusing on the national news media with the most readers. The newspapers (and their Web sites) included are *Politiken, Berlingske, Jyllands-Posten* (morning newspapers), *BT, Ekstra Bladet* (tabloids), *Information, Kristeligt Dagblad* (niche newspapers) and *MetroXpress* (free newspaper). The radio news studied are the 8 a.m. broadcasts on public service broadcaster DR's P1, P3, and P4 stations and the corresponding newscast on a second public service broadcaster 'Radio 24syv.' The television news broadcasts included are the most-watched TV news on the two major national television channels, DR1 and TV 2. Thus, candidates might have been quoted in less read, listened to, or watched news media, such as local news media, without being captured in the sample. This is especially likely to have had an effect on the media presence of younger, lesser known politicians outside the capital city in our study.

The content analysis covers news for each day of the entire campaign from May 27, 2015, through

June 18, 2015. The content analysis was conducted in collaboration with the research agency Info-media, which collects all the material published by the Danish news media. The analysis includes all the articles and features in the mentioned news media considered to deal with the general election (n = 9,338) as determined through a manual review of articles and features. All the items are then coded for either quotes from or mentions of the 799 candidates. The preliminary results show very little differences as the leaders of the two biggest parties, the Social Democrats and Liberal Party, had both the most quotes and the most mentions. According to the results, most of the other candidates were quoted more than they were mentioned. This article focuses only on quotes from candidates, understood as the opinion or written statement of a named candidate put in quotation marks or similar punctuation. These statements are counted and coded (n = 7,378 quotes). Quotes are selected for analysis as they are more comparable to the Twitter sample, which can also be seen as a type of "quotes" from the candidates.

In the study of Twitter, the sample is collected by harvesting hashtags, similar to earlier research (Moe, 2012; Moe & Larsson, 2013) explaining that "the presence of relevant hashtags in tweets can be regarded as a suitable delimitory rationale for data collection" (Moe & Larsson, 2013, p. 76). This delimited scope is further supported in the Danish context by the findings of Jungherr (2016) describing Twitter as an elite community of politicians and the politically interested. In Denmark, the general Danish Twittersphere is composed mostly of journalists, politicians, and politically interested citizens. Although the top 25 most-followed Twitter users are celebrities and athletes, by far the most-used hashtag is #dkpol, which refers to Danish politics. A 2014 analysis by a Danish media agency, Overskrift.dk, finds that the #dkpol hashtag has been used a total of 370,000 times in 2014. The closest competitor is #sldk, a hashtag referring to Danish soccer which trails #dkpol by a mere 81,000 tweets. Expanding on these figures, communication agency Bysted maps the content of Danish tweets and argues that 25% of the Danish content on Twitter falls into the category of politics, media, and journalism. Based on these numbers, it is safe to say that Danish political debate is highly popular on Twitter and, by a large margin, accounts for many of the tweets in the Danish Twittersphere. Politicians generally are very aware of this and are keen to position their tweets with the correct hashtags, such as #dkpol.

For the Twitter analysis, all the tweets relevant to the national election were harvested using the open-source tool "Your Twapper Keeper," which was modified to harvest all relevant electoral hashtags from the announcement of the election until the election itself. This method captured 262,000 tweets, their senders, the time and date of posting and other meta-information related to the tweet or tweeter. YourTwapperKeeper is freely available at https://github.com/540co/yourTwapperKeeper. The program has been known to sometimes miss large portions of tweets (Moe, 2012), so to avoid this issue during data collection, tweets were harvested from the mentioned hashtags but only after performing a UNION command in SQL. This command ensured the final data contained no duplicate tweets, although a tweet could have been placed in several of the harvested hashtags. Still, candidates could have been active on Twitter without being captured in the data collection, but if so, they used social media in a way that did not reach large audiences through the use of hashtags.

A user-based harvest was also an option for this research. Given the characteristics of the Danish Twittersphere described earlier, though, this was not done because, in the Danish context, this method would not necessarily have produced more accurate data but simply more data. It is very possible that politicians made tweets without using a hashtag, but these tweets might not pertain to politics. Jungherr (2016) suggests that using hashtags finds results only from Twitter-savvy users, which might create a bias in the data set. However, Jungherr (2016, p. 83) also states that different sampling methods, such as keywords, in no way ensure better or more valid results: "As of now there [are] no systematic comparisons between the results provided by these two modes of data selection (hashtag selecting or keyword-based selecting). This makes it difficult to assess whether the different criteria lead to significantly different data sets." Jungherr (2016) adds that, for the hashtag-based selection method to work best, the researchers must find the best hashtags on which to focus. As mentioned, the political discussion in the Danish Twittersphere is to a large extent hashtag-based, so a hashtag-based sample is a good technique to ensure a consistent data pool of tweets pertaining to politics in general or the particular election investigated.

Research questions

As the abovementioned studies on election campaign and media use in Nordic countries suggests, candidates' media use can be divided into clear groups based on the candidate's newsworthiness and thus their access to traditional news media. However, these studies are based on analysis of surveys inquiring about candidates' election campaign and media preferences. In addition, far more candidates had a Twitter profile (68%) in 2015 than in 2011 (15%–16%). In the present study, a large-sample media content analysis of both Twitter and the traditional news media is conducted. The candidates are divided into three groups, and each group's presence on Twitter and in traditional news media is analyzed. Presence refers to the number of quotes from a candidate in the traditional news media and the number of hashtagged election tweets by the candidate. The candidates are divided into three groups: (a) party leaders, who have high news value and are the natural focus of parties' election campaigns; (b) well-known politicians, or experienced politicians with incumbency status, including top-five-ranking candidates from each party and politicians with otherwise prominent positions or status within their party; and (c) lesser known politicians, who typically are younger and less experienced candidates; candidates not in the top five on their party lists; or first-time candidates with little or no access to traditional news media.

Based on this analysis, the following research questions are proposed:

RQ1: On which media platforms do party leaders, well-known politicians, and lesser known politicians have the highest level of presence?

RQ2: What is the relationship between candidates' communications activities and their election results?

Regarding RQ2, previous studies on both Danish and international election campaigns so far have shown no clear, positive relationship between Twitter use and electoral success. Hansen and Kosiara-Pedersen (2014, p. 213) write: "It is difficult, if not impossible, to link all campaigning activities with individual voters and their voting choices and thus accurately estimate the effects of campaigning due to the plethora of actual campaigning conducted by candidates, parties, media and other political actors." This research question, therefore, is only explorative. The aim here is simply to illustrate through visualization of data the relationship of election results with candidates' media presence in legacy news media and on Twitter.

Results

Turning first to the analysis of legacy news media, the data show that, of the 799 candidates running for parliament in the 2015 election, only 301 had quotes captured in the content analysis. These 301 candidates were quoted 7,378 times in legacy news media during the election campaign. In Table 1, it is clear that the legacy news media still favor party leaders. The top-five most-quoted politicians from both the red and blue blocks were all party leaders, with the incumbent Prime Minister Thorning-Schmidt (A) and the leader of the opposition (and former Prime Minister) Rasmussen (V) by far the most quoted. The two party leaders were the top candidates of the election and also the politicians getting the most quotes in legacy media.

The news media's intense focus on the former prime minister and the opposition leader may be seen to flow from the media logic favoring the most well-known, powerful politicians. This tendency led to a presidentialization (Webb, 2007) of the election in the media coverage, although 10 parties were in the running. Thus, the center-right morning newspaper *Berlingske* launched its election coverage (6. June, 2015) with a front page featuring large pictures of the incumbent prime minister and the opposition leader beneath a headline declaring: "The Duel." Along with signs of presidentialization, the analysis also shows that, of the top-five most-quoted politicians, four were

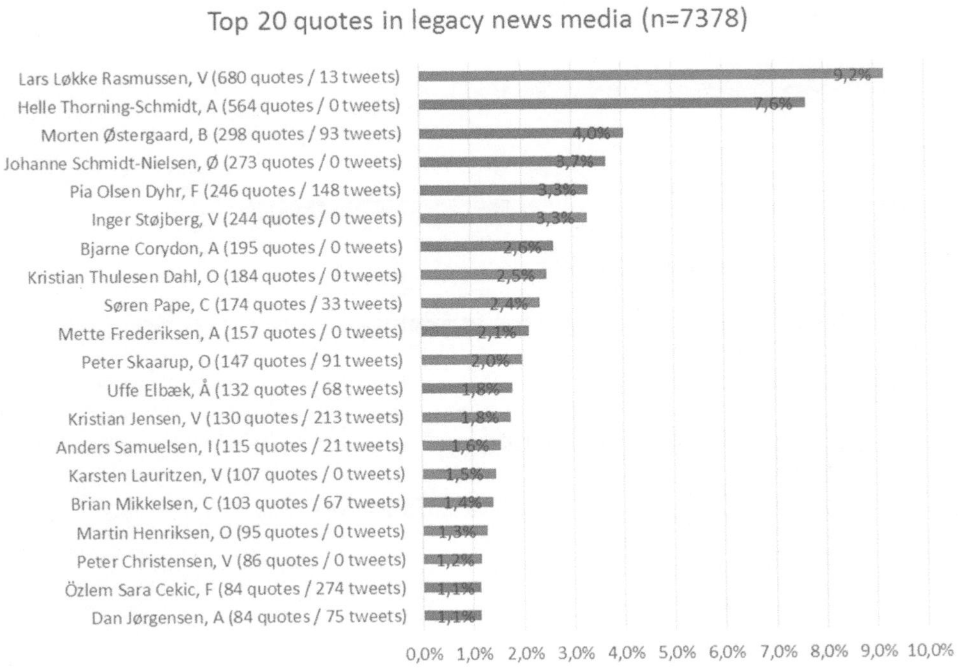

Table 1. Quotes in legacy news media.

party leaders from the red block, demonstrating the incumbency bonus (Hopmann, De Vreese, & Albæk, 2011) found in most election studies regarding which parties gain the most media visibility. Thus, Morten Østergaard (B), who was part of the coalition government at the time of the election, ranked as the third most-quoted politician in the legacy news media. In fourth place was Johanne Schmidt Nielsen (Ø), leader of a party that frequently supported the incumbent coalition government during its four-year term, and in fifth place was Pia Olsen Dyhr, leader of the Socialist People's Party, which was part of the incumbent coalition government until 2014. The rest of the top 20 consisted of party leaders and well-known politicians, supporting previous findings that the news media and media logic favor well-known, powerful politicians in election coverage.

Keeping the focus on party leaders but turning attention to Twitter, Table 2 shows a very different picture.

Incumbent Prime Minister Thorning-Schmidt and opposition leader Rasmussen dominated the legacy news media, but neither candidate was very active on Twitter, with Rasmussen tweeting only 13 times and Schmidt not even once during the election campaign. The highest number of tweets was 148 from Dyhr (F), followed by 93 by Østergaard, party leader for Social Liberals (B). A study of tweets by party leaders during the 2013 national election campaign in Norway (Larsson & Ihlen, 2015) finds that seven party leaders sent higher numbers of tweets. In that study, the leaders of two smaller parties tweeted 669 and 453 times, whereas the incumbent prime minister tweeted 114 tweets. This sizeable deviation may be partly due to differences in data gathering and in election systems. Explaining the results, however, Larsson and Ihlen (2015, p. 8) argue that the leaders of smaller parties lack access to mainstream news outlets and employ social media as a remedy for this predicament. Looking at the Danish election, both Dyhr (F) and Østergaard (B) are leaders of smaller parties, whereas both Thorning-Schmidt (A) and Rasmussen (V) are leaders of larger parties. Although Dyhr and Østergaard are both also quoted in the legacy news media, they are at a far lower rate than both Rasmussen and Thorning-Schmidt. The rest of the party leaders generate only small amounts of tweets, or no tweets at all in the cases of Schmidt and Dahl (O). These generally low levels of activity by party leaders clearly indicate that, despite the massive increase in politicians with Twitter profiles from 2011 to 2015, Twitter, as a campaign tool, remains far from the top of any party leader's

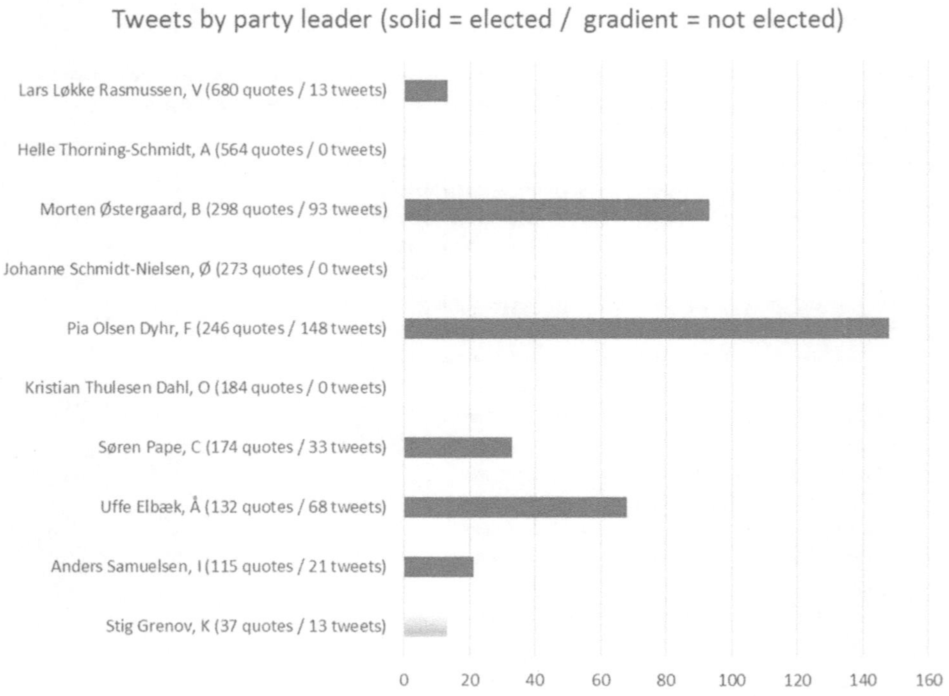

Table 2. Party leaders on Twitter.

list of communication tools. However, it is important to remember that this study only counts the number of tweets made by party leaders and not, for instance, the number of retweets each tweet receives. It is likely that party leaders' tweets may be retweeted more often than those of other politicians, so tweets by party leaders, despite their low frequency, might have more effect and larger reach than tweets by other politicians.

Turning to the candidates most active on Twitter, Table 3 shows the top-30 most-active candidates on Twitter. The candidates are divided into three categories: party leaders, well-known politicians, and a new category tentatively termed hybrid-media politicians. The first two categories are similar to the divisions in media use found in previous studies. The third category is a new division introduced based on the present empirical analysis showing that a small number of politicians have a presence both on Twitter and in traditional news media. Thus, the category of hybrid-media politicians consists of politicians who have an above-average (when excluding the highest scores) presence on Twitter and in traditional news media. For Twitter, this refers to politicians with more than 167 tweets, and for traditional news media, politicians with more than 25 quotes. In relation to the initial three categories of politicians presented in RQ1, the category of hybrid-media politician can best be described as well-known politicians who also have an above-average presence on Twitter. Table 3 also includes the election results, showing whether candidates in any of the three categories were elected in the final vote tally.

By far the most active candidate on Twitter, with 700 tweets, is a young, lesser known female politician from the Social Liberal Party (B). The rest of the top five tweeters sent relatively the same amount of tweets (274–244). The entire top-30 list has 16 female candidates and 14 male candidates. The average age of the top-30 tweeters is 36.8 years, much younger than the average ages of MPs, which in 2015 was 45 years (the average age of MPs since 1953 is 50.1 years). Also, 50% of the top 30 tweeters were running in the greater area of the capital Copenhagen, indicating that Twitter was a tool of lesser known, young, and more urban politicians.

Looking at Table 3 and the three categories of politicians shows that, as found in previous studies, lesser known politicians can be very active on Twitter. The present study, however, also finds a small number of politicians (seven) who have an above-average presence on both Twitter and in

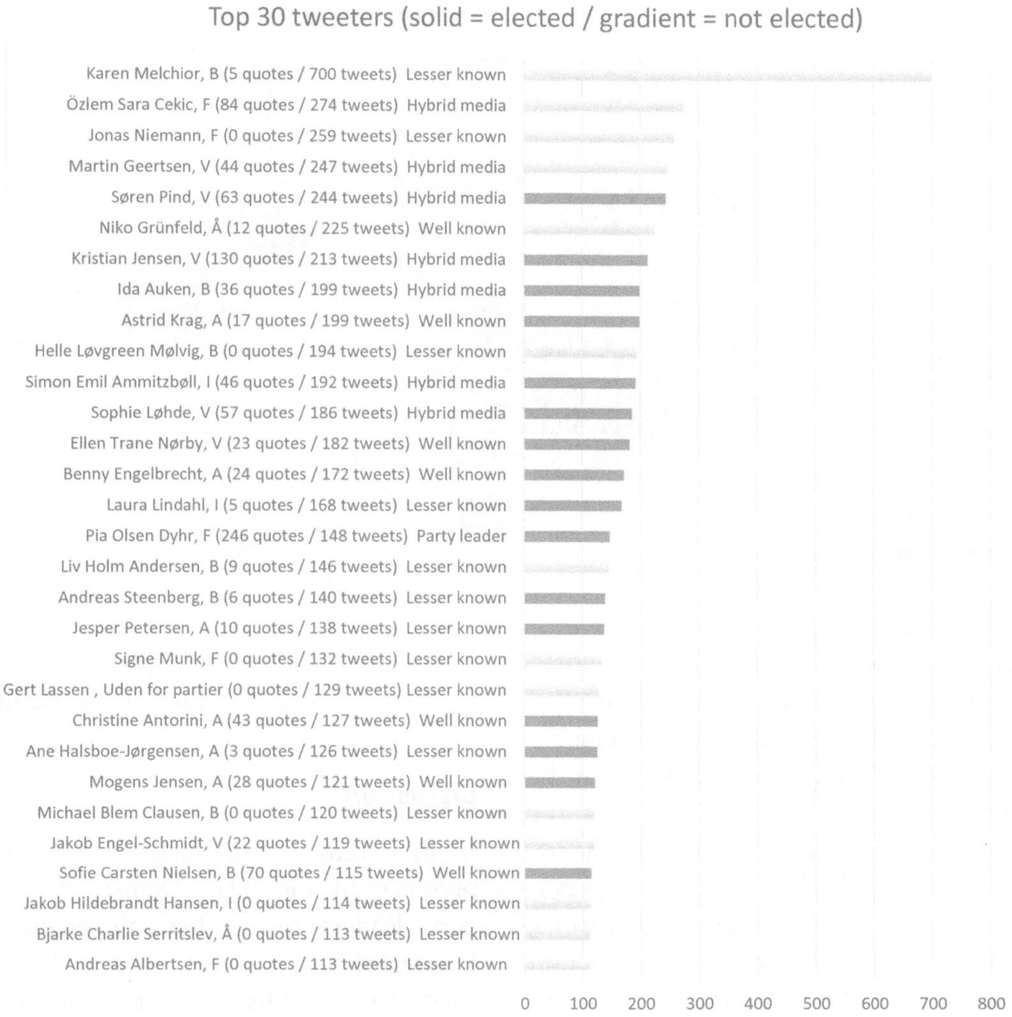

Table 3. Most active candidates on Twitter.

traditional news media. These seven hybrid-media politicians come from four different parties, but four come from the Liberals (V), the major opposition party, and the three other come from smaller parties on the left (F), right (I) and center (B). Regarding gender, three are female, and four are male. Their average age is 39.7 years, slightly older than the average top-30 tweeter. All the hybrid-media politicians are also incumbent politicians with, in most cases, several years of political experience, and most, if not all, had high-ranking positions within their party at the time of the election. Geographically, all but one of the hybrid-media politicians was based in the greater Copenhagen area.

Turning attention to the relationship between communication activities and election results, Figure 1 presents a data visualization of the results. It depicts amount of tweets sent (Y axis), quotes recorded (X axis), personal votes (size), and election results (color). The chart is based on data excluding the highest scores (>300 quotes and >274 tweets) to make the chart easier to read.

Previous research has found no clear relation between Twitter activity and electoral success (Hansen & Kosiara-Pedersen, 2014; Jungherr, 2016). Thus, this study is not intended to investigate the correlation of tweets and quotes and electoral success in the form of votes. However, Figure 1 does indicate (in blue) that tweeting as an activity in itself does not equal to votes. However, this result might have as much to do with the Danish electoral system, the media logic of traditional news media, the candidates' place on the party list, or parties' popularity (or lack of) at the time of the election as anything else. Looking at one clear winner in the election, Dahl (O), the leader of the Danish People's Party, was not active

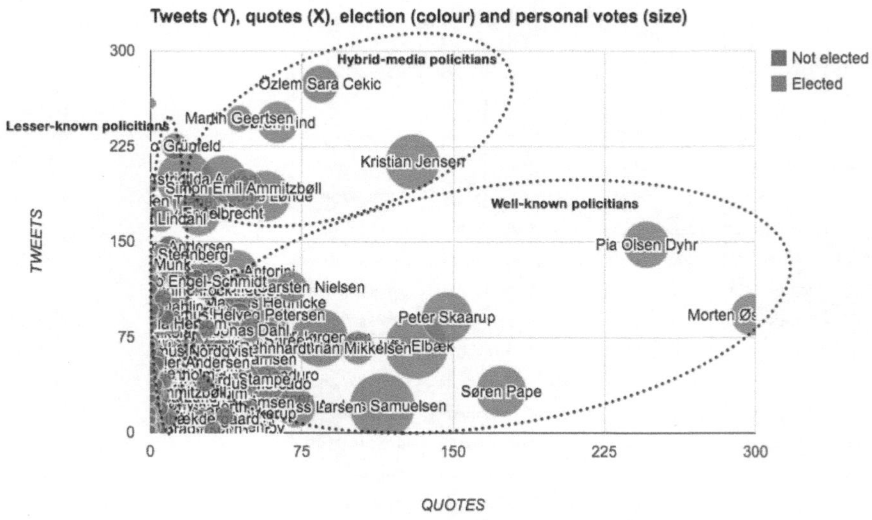

Figure 1. Who tweets, who is quoted, and who is elected.

on Twitter at all and only the eighth-most-quoted politicians in the traditional news media. However, he also received the highest amount of personal votes, close to 60,000. Rasmussen, the leader of the opposition who won the election and was the most-quoted politician in traditional news media, received only the fourth-highest number of personal votes, a little more than 30,000. These results, of course, only indicate that elections and election campaigns are the result of a great number of variables, with communication, even across platforms, only one.

Figure 1 does improve understanding of how candidates' media presence in election campaigns can be divided into groups. Previous studies mostly make such classifications using cluster analysis based on survey data; in this study, the division is done using a large-sample content analysis. The present analysis also shows a clear division in the media presence of party leaders, well-known politicians, and younger politicians. This study also unsurprisingly indicates that most winning election candidates are party leaders and well-known candidates. The study, though, also points to a small group of politicians not identified in previous studies, who have an above-average presence on both Twitter and in traditional news media. Five of seven politicians in this new group were reelected. However, for the moment, the number of hybrid-media politicians is so small that it is impossible to say whether a hybrid-media presence is a new, important stepping-stone on the way to electoral success in Denmark.

Discussion

In this study of candidates and their cross-media presence in the 2015 Danish election campaign, party leaders, by far, have the highest presence in traditional news media, with a low presence on Twitter. On Twitter, this study finds a high presence among candidates who are younger and lesser known to the public and have a very low presence in traditional news media. Thus, this study supports previous research showing that candidates' media use in election campaigns can be divided into clear categories, especially between incumbent, experienced politicians and younger, lesser known politicians. The strong presence of the top two candidates representing the two blocks found in traditional news media may result from the media logic guiding political coverage in traditional news media and does support other studies on political communication in Denmark and other countries indicating the presidentialization of election campaigns, at least in traditional news media coverage. Turning to Twitter, neither of the top-two candidates has a strong presence on this platform; the incumbent prime minister had a Twitter profile but never actively used it in the campaign. Although studies indicate that the opposition may be more inclined to use Twitter in election campaigns, this was not the case in this election, with the leader of the opposition tweeting only 13 times. Other candidates, however, had a higher presence on Twitter, especially lesser known, younger, urban candidates running in the greater Copenhagen area. Leaders of smaller parties also had a Twitter presence. Considering the election results, the data visualization shows that many of the most active tweeters were not elected, and many were quoted in the legacy news media rarely, if at all.

A small number of politicians, though, do have an above-average presence on both Twitter and in traditional news media. The seven hybrid-media politicians come from four different parties, three are female, four are male, and their average age is 39.7 years, slightly older than the average top-30 tweeter. All the hybrid-media politicians are also incumbent politicians with, in most cases, several years of political experience, and most, if not all, had high-ranking party positions at the time of the election. Geographically, all but one of the hybrid-media politicians is based in the greater Copenhagen area. In research on future election campaigns in Denmark and other countries, it would be interesting to further focus on this emerging category of hybrid-media politician. Will the number of hybrid-media politicians increase in the coming years, and in the future, will a high presence in both traditional news media and social media become more decisive in electoral success in Denmark?

In sum, the present study shows that, despite candidates' increased Twitter use between the 2011 and 2015 elections, few candidates had a high presence on Twitter. A possible reason is the hybrid-media context in which modern-day political campaigning takes place. In this complex media system, social media and traditional news media coexist and interact with one another, and the governing media logic gives the most well-known candidates easy access to television, radio, and newspapers, leaving Twitter open to the segment of lesser known, younger, and more urban-based politicians. However, the present study also indicates that this clear division in the media presence of well-known and lesser known politicians might be changing—at least on Twitter.

Considering the election results, being active on Twitter is not enough to secure election. Then again, the candidate with the highest number of personal votes, the leader of the Danish People's Party (O), did not have a Twitter account and was only the eighth-most-quoted politician in traditional news media. The present study, therefore, emphasizes how important is to remember that election outcomes are influenced by much more than campaign communication—whether on social media or in traditional news media.

References

Benson, R., Blach-Ørsten, M., Powers, M., Willig, I., & Zambrano, S. V. (2012). Media systems online and off: Comparing the form of news in the United States, Denmark, and France. *Journal of Communication*, *62*(1), 21–38. doi:10.1111/jcom.2012.62.issue-1

Blach-Ørsten, M. (2014). The emergence of an increasingly competitive news regime in Denmark. In R. Kuhn & R. K. Nielsen (Eds.), *Political journalism in transition: Western Europe in a comparative perspective* (pp. 93–110). London, England: I. B. Tauris.

Blach-Ørsten, M. (2016). Politikkens medialisering: Et ny-institutionelt perspektiv [The mediatization of politics: a new institutional perspective]. In I. S. Hjarvard (Ed.), *Medialisering: Mediernes rolle i social og kulturel forandring* (pp. 185–216). [Mediatization: The role of the media in social and cultural change]. Copenhagen, Denmark: Hans Reitzel.

Blach-Ørsten, M., & Willig, I. (2016a). *Den fælles dagsorden—Og alle de andre* [The common agenda - and all the others]. Frederiksberg, Denmark: Samfundslitteratur.

Blach-Ørsten, M., & Willig, I. (2016b). Det danske mediesystem [The Danish Media System]. In T. Oleson (Ed.), *Medier, politik & samfund* [Media, politics and society] (pp. 13–33). København, Denmark: Hans Reitzel.

Blach-Ørsten, M., Willig, I., & Burkal, R. (2013). *Undersøgelse af citatpraksis ift. Kreditering af mediekilder i nyheder på danske netsteder* [An examination of quoting practices and source crediting in Danish online news media]. Copenhagen, Denmark: Kulturministeriet.

Chadwick, A. (2013). *The hybrid media system: Politics and power*. England: Oxford University Press.

Danielsen, M. (2016, April 29). *Sociale medier statisik 2016 i Danmark* [Social Media Statistics in Denmark]. Retrieved from https://www.socialemedier.dk/sociale-medier-2016-i-danmark

Enli, G. S., & Skogerbø, E. (2013). Personalized campaigns in party-centred politics: Twitter and Facebook as arenas for political communication. *Information, Communication & Society, 16*(5), 757–774. doi:10.1080/1369118X.2013.782330

Esmark, A., & Ørsten, M. (2008). Media and politics in Denmark. In J. Strömbäck, M. Ørsten, & T. Aalberg (Eds.), *Communicating politics: Political communication in the Nordic countries* (pp. 25–45). Gothenburg, Sweden: Nordicom.

Esmark, A., & Ørsten, M. (2011). Et komparativt blik på den politiske kommunikationskultur i Danmark [A comparative look at the culture of political communication in Denmark]. *Økonomi & Politik, 84*(1), 3–18.

Hallin, D. C., & Mancini, P. (2004). *Comparing media systems: Three models of media and politics*. England: Cambridge University Press.

Hansen, K. M., & Kosiara-Pedersen, K. (2014). Cyber-campaigning in Denmark: Application and effects of candidate campaigning. *Journal of Information Technology & Politics, 11*(2), 206–219. doi:10.1080/19331681.2014.895476

Hjarvard, S. (2008). En verden af medier - medialisering af politik, religion og leg (A world of media - the mediatization of politics, religion, language and play). Frederiksberg: Samfundslitteratu

Hjarvard, S., & Kammer, A. (2014). Online news: Between private enterprise and public subsidy. *Media, Culture & Society, 37*(1), 115–123. doi:10.1177/0163443714553562

Hopmann, D., De Vreese, C., & Albæk, E. (2011). Incumbency bonus in election news coverage explained: The logics of political power and the media market. *Journal of Communication, 61*(2), 264–282. doi:10.1111/jcom.2011.61.issue-2

Jensen, J. L., Hoff, J., & Klastrup, L. (2016). *Internettet og folketingsvalget 2015* [Election to Parliament in 2015 and the Internet]. Copenhagen, Denmark: Report, Danske Medier.

Jungherr, A. (2016). Twitter use in election campaigns: A systematic literature review. *Journal of Information Technology & Politics, 13*(1), 72–91. doi:10.1080/19331681.2015.1132401

Kosiara-Pedersen, K. (2012). The 2011 Danish parliamentary election: A very new government. *West European Politics, 35*(2), 415–424. doi:10.1080/01402382.2011.648015

Larsson, A. O., & Ihlen, Ø. (2015). Birds of a feather flock together? Party leaders on Twitter during the 2013 Norwegian elections. *European Journal of Communication, 30*(6), 666–681. doi:10.1177/0267323115595525

Lund, A.B., Willig,I & Blach-Ørsten, M. (ed.) (2009). Hvor kommer nyhederne fra? (Where does news come from). Århus: Forlaget Ajour

Moe, H., & Larsson, A. O. (2012). Methodological and ethical challenges associated with large-scale analyses of online political communication. Nordicom Review, 33(1),117–124.

Moe, H., & Larsson, A. O. (2013). Untangling a complex media system: A comparative study of Twitter-linking practices during three Scandinavian election campaigns. *Information, Communication & Society, 16*(5), 775–794. doi:10.1080/1369118X.2013.783607

Newman, N., Fletcher, R., Levy, D. A. L., Nielson, R. K. (2016). *Reuters Institute Digital News Report 2016.* Retrieved from https://papers.ssrn.com/sol3/papers.cfm?abstract_id=2796534.

Nielsen, R. K., & Schrøder, K. C. (2014). *Danskernes brug af digitale medier og nyheder 2014* [The Danes' use of digital media and news in 2014]. Roskilde, Denmark: Roskilde University.

Norregaard, K. S. (Ed.). (2014, January 27). *Hvem bestemmer* [Who is in charge]. Retrieved from http://www.ft.dk/Demokrati/Hvem_bestemmer.aspx

Nuernbergk, C., & Conrad, J. (2016). Conversations and campaign dynamics in a hybrid media environment: Use of Twitter by members of the German Bundestag. *Social Media+ Society, 2*(1). Ann Arbor

Ørsten, M. (2005). Nyhedsinstitutionen: Et ny-institutionelt perspektiv på den medierede politiske kommunikation [The institution of news: A new institutional perspective on the mediatizied political communication]. *Økonomi & Politik, 78*(3), 13–28.

Poguntke, T. and Webb, P. eds., (2007). The presidentialization of politics: A comparative study of modern democracies. New York: Oxford University press

Schrøder, K. C. (2014). News media old and new: Fluctuating audiences, news repertoires, and locations of consumption. *Journalism Studies, 16*(1), 60–78. doi:10.1080/1461670X.2014.890332

Schrøder, K. C. (2015). *Danskernes brug af nyhedsmedier 2015: Brugsmønstre og nyhedsrepertoirer* [The Danes' use of news media in 2015: Usage patterns and news repetoirs]. Roskilde, Denmark: Roskilde University.

Skovsgaard, M., & Van Dalen, A. (2013). Dodging the gatekeepers? Social media in the campaign mix during the 2011 Danish elections. *Information, Communication & Society, 16* (5), 737–756. doi:10.1080/1369118X.2013.783876

Statistics Denmark. (2015). *Table 44, Election for parliament 18 June 2015.* Retrieved from http://www.dst.dk/pukora/epub/upload/22258/headword/dk/44.pdf

Strandberg, K. (2009). Online campaigning: An opening for the outsiders? An analysis of Finnish parliamentary candidates' websites in the 2003 election campaign. *New Media & Society, 11*(5), 835–854. doi:10.1177/1461444809105355

Strömbäck, J. (2008). Four phases of mediatization: An analysis of the mediatization of politics. The International Journal of Press/ Politics, 13(3),228–246.

Strömbäck, J., & Van Aelst, P. (2013). Why political parties adapt to the media: Exploring the fourth dimension of mediatization. International Communication Gazette, 75 (4),341–358.

Strömbäck, J., Ørsten, M., & Aalberg, T. (Eds.). (2008). *Communicating politics. Political communication in the Nordic countries*. Gothenburg, Sweden: Nordicom.

Syvertsen, T., Enli, G., Mjøs, O. J., & Moe, H. (2014). *The media welfare state: Nordic media in the digital era*. University of Michigan Press.

Webb, P. D. (2007). *The presidentialization of politics: A comparative study of modern democracies*. Oxford University Press on Demand.

Willig, I., Ørsten, M., Hartley, J. M., & Flensburg, S. (2015). *Journalistiske kvaliteter 1999–2014: Specialrapport* [Journalistic qualities 1999–2014: Special report]. København, Denmark: Kulturstyrelsen.

Brute force effects of mass media presence and social media activity on electoral outcome

Marko Kovic, Adrian Rauchfleisch, Julia Metag, Christian Caspar, and Julian Szenogrady

ABSTRACT
In this study, we analyze whether the mere volume of presence in mass media and the mere volume of activity on social media convey advantages to candidates in parliamentary elections. Based on the theoretical model of bounded rationality, we call these potential effects brute force effects. During the last month of the election campaign of the Swiss federal election of 2015, we tracked the presence of all 873 candidates in the canton of Zurich, the most populous canton, in a broad sample of mass media. Additionally, we tracked those candidates' activity on Facebook and Twitter. The results of our multilevel Bayesian estimates show that mass media presence has a consistent nontrivial impact on different aspects of electoral outcome. Furthermore, social media activity also has a nontrivial impact, but only in terms of resonance (reactions to candidates' social media activity). Overall, our results suggest that brute force effects of of mass media presence and social media activity can have substantial impact on voting behavior.

Introduction: Mass media presence and social media activity as brute force effects

To note that, during election times, public communication about the election campaign matters is a truism that verges on the trivial. From the point of view of the political actors who are seeking office, being present in the public discourse is quite obviously a goal—after all, political actors have to mobilize their supporters as well as persuade other potential voters in the hopes of turning them into supporters (Nimmo, 2001; Rohrschneider, 2002). From the voters' point of view, public communication about the campaign is welcome, because it provides them with information that is necessary in order for them to decide which candidates and parties are best aligned with their own preferences (Gelman & King, 1993; Hansen & Pedersen, 2014; Nadeau, Nevitte, Gidengil, & Blais, 2008). From a systemic, democratic point of view, public discourse about electoral campaigns is welcome as well, because, ideally, some rational discourse about the quality of different policy proposals will take place (Habermas, 2006).

Possibly for as long as modern representative democracy has existed, the most important venue of public communication during election campaigns has been professional mass media news outlets. Mass media do not, of course, exhaust the whole conceptual space of public communication, but functionally, they serve as a master forum (Ferree, 2002, p. 10) where communication flows about relevant issues aggregate. In electoral campaigns, the master forum of the mass media plays a crucial role, not least because a large and relevant proportion of the electorate—essentially, what is sometimes referred to as the median voter (Black, 1948; Downs, 1957)—can be addressed via mass media. Research on the role of news media during elections is plentiful, and a number of effects of news media coverage have been observed, mostly hovering around the questions of what and how the media report during electoral campaigns, and how that reporting impacts voter attitudes. Some prominent venues of research include research on the dynamics of agenda-setting and framing (Scheufele & Tewksbury, 2007), research on the reputational consequences of news media reporting in the form of issue ownership (Petrocik, 1996), and research on the nature of the journalistic output in campaign times (Iyengar, Norpoth, & Hahn, 2004). One potentially important aspect of the news media during elections, however, receives relatively little attention, as Hopmann, Vliegenthart, Vreese, and Albæk (2010) note: the question of whether the mere volume of candidate visibility, or presence, in the news media has an impact on electoral outcomes. To some degree, it is understandable that this question receives little scientific attention. Although research on phenomena such as, for example, the aforementioned framing and issue ownership effects focuses on effects that are contingent on the properties of mass media output, possible effects of the sheer volume of mass media content seem less of a sophisticated effect.

The traditional news media are not the only venue of public communication in election times. Campaigning events, billboards (Seidman, 2008), cold calling (Nickerson, 2006, 2007) and direct mail (Green & Gerber, 2015) have long been, and still are, staple methods of campaigning. These venues of public campaign communication have been supplemented by social media. Social media, understood as Internet-based applications that allow for the creation and exchange of user-generated content (Kaplan & Haenlein, 2010), provide candidates with the opportunity to reach significant parts of the public without there being gatekeepers, such as journalists, who wield veto power over the information flows and contents.

The goal of this study is to further explore whether the volume of candidate presence in traditional mass media and the volume of candidate activity on social media have an impact on candidates' electoral fortunes. We call the impact of mass media presence and of social media activity *brute force effects*. We analyze the brute force effects with the following two research questions:

RQ1: Does candidates' presence in the mass media have an effect on their electoral success?

RQ2: Does candidates' activity on social media have an effect on their electoral success?

We analyze these questions in the context of the 2015 Swiss federal election, which took place on October 18, 2015. Our study adds to the existing literature in three ways. First, we include not only social media in our study, but a rather large sample of traditional mass media as well, since mass media most certainly still matter. Second, we aim to embed our study in a broader theory of voter behavior. Third, the peculiarities of the Swiss electoral system are a very fertile ground for conducting this study, because the expected effects can be measured in great detail.

Voter preferences and electoral campaigns

Our overarching theoretical model of voters is one of rational voters. We believe that, generally, voters have preferences, and they act in accordance with their preferences so as to achieve what they want to achieve. This is, in a nutshell, the rational choice model of voting behavior (Shepsle, 2010). But we don't believe that voters are perfectly rational in their behavior, and thus, we don't believe a model of perfect rational choice to be appropriate in the context of voting. Of course, the idea that a pure model of rational choice does not fit reality all that well is not new (Simon, 1955). In contemporary research on rational choice, there is broad and uncontested consensus that the insights of behavioral economics (Mullainathan & Thaler, 2000) about erroneous inference and decision-making do not represent a deviation from regular human cognition, but rather, they demonstrate that regular human cognition is fundamentally error prone.

Given such a behavioral economics view of human cognition, our understanding of voter behavior is one of *bounded rationality* (Jones, 1999). Generally, voters are rational in that they have preferences and act in line with their preferences in the act of voting. But voters' cognitive apparatus makes use of cognitive heuristics to process information, to make inferences about the world, and to partly base decisions—specifically, the act of voting—on those heuristics.

There are many cognitive heuristics that affect inference and decision. In the context of the present study, one particular heuristic is of interest: the so-called mere exposure effect (Hansen & Wänke, 2009; Harmon-Jones & Allen, 2001; Zajonc, 1968, 2001). The mere exposure effect describes the tendency for humans to develop a positive attitude toward information, objects, or people merely by being exposed to that information, those objects, or those people. Mere exposure effects can manifest in many different contexts, not least in the context of elections (Verhulst, Lodge, & Lavine, 2010). The concept of brute force effects of candidates' mass media presence and social media activity is simply a theoretical extension of the mere exposure effect in the context elections. If mere exposure increases familiarity, and with familiarity comes positive attitude, then, in the setting of elections, mere exposure should translate into positive electoral effects. This means that, with the concept of brute force effects, we are describing the expected empirical consequence of the mere exposure effect in the context of elections.

Our model of voting behavior can be summarized as a combination of rational and nonrational voting, whereby brute force effects form a subset of nonrational voting. We argue that nonrational voting, by which we mean voting that is not only a pure function of individual fixed preferences, is a large part of overall voting behavior. Brute force effects as the consequences of the mere exposure heuristic are a subset of nonrational voting. However, we believe that brute force effects form only a minor part of nonrational voting. This rationale is depicted visually in Figure 1.

There are two main sets in Figure 1, the set of rational voting and the set of nonrational voting. There is an area of overlap among those sets (light gray area). This overlap symbolizes the fact that there is not only purely rational and purely nonrational voting, but also voting that is rational in principle, but affected by nonrational mechanisms, such as heuristics. Brute force effects are a subset of nonrational voting—all voting affected by brute force effects is nonrational. However, not all voting affected by brute force effects is necessarily purely nonrational. It is also possible that voting that is rational in principle is affected by brute force effects (dark gray area). The visualization in Figure 1 does not empirically quantify the size of brute force effects, but it contains information that expresses our assumption about the magnitude of brute force effects. Brute force effects, we believe, are only a minor part of all nonrational voting. Furthermore, we believe that brute force effects do not have to be total and exclusive effects: Voters can very well be rational for the most part and be affected by brute force effects in addition to their rational, preferential voting.

Overall, then, we posit that brute force effects of candidates' mass media presence and social media activity are only a minor part of overall voting behavior. We do so for two reasons. First, as we argue above, brute force effects are only a subset of nonrational behavior. Furthermore, there is broad consensus that media effects do exist, but that they are generally small effects, if not minimal ones (Bennett & Iyengar, 2008). Our assumption about the magnitude of brute force effects, then, is both conceptually and empirically motivated.

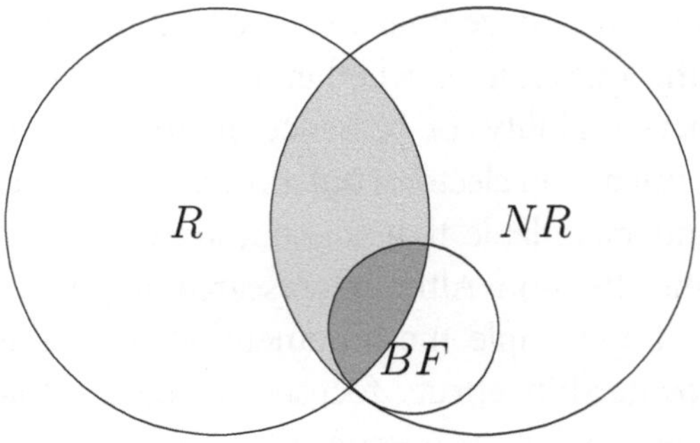

Figure 1. Visual depiction of brute force effects within the sets of rational and nonrational voting. Note: R stands for the set of rational voting, NR for the set of non-rational voting, and BF for the subset of brute force effects.

Existing research

There is a growing body of research that is interested in finding out how social media is used in electoral campaigns, and what results from it (Hansen & Kosiara-Pedersen, 2014; Kreiss, 2015). Social media tends to have a vox populi signaling effect, in that what is visible on social media is presumed to represent public opinion. For example, journalists are prone to this kind of heuristic (Anstead & O'Loughlin, 2015), whereby anecdotal evidence is generalized as indicative of public opinion.

However, more systematic analyses of the connection between social media and elections have yielded more robust and relevant results. One prominent question that has been explored in recent years is whether data from social media has any form of potential predictive power for electoral outcomes (Gayo-Avello, 2012; Gayo-Avello 2013; Metaxas, Mustafaraj, & Gayo-Avello, 2011). Even though the present evidence for the predictive power of social media is far from conclusive, the general idea is not without merit. Samples of social media users can be thought of as an extreme form of nonprobability sampling (Baker et al., 2013). This will become ever more the case as social media penetration rates continue to climb and encompass most population segments and strata.

The literature on the predictive power of social media is certainly relevant in and of itself, but it is only tangentially related to the concept of brute force effects. However, there actually is a small, less prominent body of literature that has explored potential brute force effects of social media activity on electoral outcomes. These studies did not operate with the concept of brute force effects, but what they analyzed are possible brute force effects as we define them in this study. The results of those studies are generally mixed, as Jungherr (2016) summarizes. Some studies find no effect at all (Jungherr, 2013; Marcinkowski & Metag, 2013). Other studies do find an effect, but a rather modest one, in that the relevant question is not so much how active candidates are on social media, but rather whether they are present on social media at all (Gibson & McAllister, 2011; Kruikemeier, 2014). A number of studies report that the degree of activity on social media, either directly by candidates themselves or indirectly through other users reacting to candidates, matters (DiGrazia, McKelvey, Bollen, & Rojas, 2013; Jacobs & Spierings, 2016; Spierings & Jacobs, 2014).

These studies, however, have two shortcomings. First, they analyze only the social media platform Twitter. Twitter matters, of course, but using Twitter as a pars pro toto for social media in general is, at the very least, not something that is self-explanatorily plausible. Second, those studies either completely disregard traditional mass media, or, if they don't, they work yet again with a pars pro toto strategy by generalizing a single media outlet as representative of all media outlets in the given polity. With the present study, we aim to continue the valuable research trajectory outlined by these studies, and we take steps to address the two shortcomings in the literature.

The Swiss electoral system: A precise seismograph of voter preferences

The election of the Swiss federal lower house is carried out both on a party and individual-candidate level. The starting point for voters to vote is individual voting lists that, by and large, correspond to different political parties. Every voter has the right to vote for one voting list. In principle, the amount of voting lists per voting district, that is, per canton, is not limited. In 20 of the 26 Swiss cantons, any political party, loose group, or even singular candidate can register as a voting list if they manage to gather enough signatures in a petition prior to the election.[1] In the remaining six small cantons that only have one seat in the lower house, no signatures have to be collected for candidacy eligibility.[2] The majority of the seats of the lower house, 194 out of 200, are allocated in voting districts where proportional voting actually takes place.[3] The Swiss proportional electoral system, however, is not limiting to choosing only among the voting lists (i.e., among the parties). The voting lists actually only contain the pool of registered candidates, and voters are free to choose among those candidates whatever way they wish. This means that voters are allowed to remove candidates from a list, add candidates from other lists, or even give individual candidates two votes. The latter procedure is referred to as "cumulation," and adding candidates from other lists is known as "panachage." Cumulation and panachage give voters great flexibility, but those procedures are limited. First, only candidates who are within the overall pool of preregistered candidates are eligible for cumulation and panachage. Second, a single voter is only allowed to cumulate two votes per candidate. That means that on a voter's voting list, the same candidate name can only appear twice. Furthermore, the maximum number of candidates per voting list as well as the total amount of votes a voter allocates is fixed because the number of slots on voting lists is fixed. For example, in the canton of Zurich, the 2015 voting lists contained 35 slots, because the canton of Zurich occupies 35 seats in the lower house of parliament. Therefore, a voter in the 2015 election could vote for at most 35 candidates. It was not possible to add more than 35 candidates through panachage, and it was not possible to cumulate a vote for a candidate more than once. By cumulating a vote for a candidate, two of the 35 slots on the voting list were allocated to that candidate.

The Swiss electoral system for proportional allocation of seats to the lower house thus allows voters to express their preferences in a very precise manner. Accordingly, the outcome of the election reflects this, metaphorically speaking, seismographic quality of the electoral system. Not only is it known which candidates are elected to the lower house and how many votes the candidates receive, but there is also data on the amount of panachage as well as the amount of cumulation votes each candidate receives. From the point of view of candidates, then, there are four natural outcome variables of the lower house elections: being elected into office or not, the total amount of votes received, the amount of panachage votes, and, finally, the amount of cumulation votes.

Hypotheses

In the preceding sections, we have first explained our voting behavior model of bounded rationality with relation to brute force effects of candidates' mass media presence and social media activity. Second, we have briefly described the nature of the Swiss electoral system of the lower house elections. If we apply the model of brute force effects to aggregate electoral behavior with regard to the lower house elections, there are four outcome variables where brute force effects might, in principle, materialize: the probability for a candidate to win a seat, the total amount of votes a candidate receives, the amount of panachage votes a candidate receives, and the amount of cumulation votes a candidate receives.

We assume that brute force effects are, generally, weak effects. This means that the rational components of voting behavior, as well as nonrational components other than brute force effects, will probably outweigh brute force effects themselves. We do not expect brute force effects to be decisive factors either for the probability of a candidate receiving a seat in the lower house or for the total amount of votes a candidate receives. We express these two expectations with the hypotheses H1 and H2:

Hypothesis H1: Brute force effects have no substantial impact on a candidate's probability of being elected into the lower house.

Hypothesis H2: Brute force effects have no substantial impact on the total amount of votes a candidate receives.

In hypotheses H1 and H2, we are deliberately referring to substantial impact instead of something such as "no impact." Assuming no effect means expressing a belief in a null model, and we don't think that null models are plausible under any reasonable set of assumptions for the purpose of this study. What is interesting and epistemically more plausible is analyzing what effects actually exist, and how meaningful they are for the given research questions.

We consider brute force effects to have no substantial impact on election chances as well as on the total amount of votes. However, we do think that brute force effects can have nontrivial impact on the other two outcome measures of electoral success: the amount of panachage and cumulation votes. In the model of bounded voter rationality, we expect voter preferences to be, for the most part, fixed. But we do

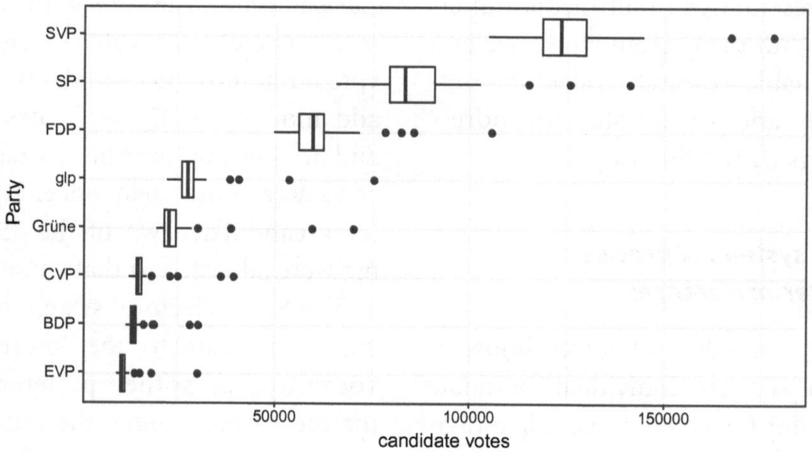

Figure 6. Box plots for all parties with at least one elected candidate. Note: We created box plots for all parties that have at least one elected candidate. The boxplots summarize the distribution of votes that individual candidates received in each party.

believe that brute force effects play a role nonetheless: they have a mobilizing effect on voters' preferences on individual candidates. This means that voters have, in principle, preferences about who they want to vote for, and the brute force of candidate mass media presence and social media activity can "nudge" voters into expressing those preferences. Functionally, this nudging function is the same as nudging in the sense of choice architecture (Sunstein, 2014; Thaler & Sunstein, 2009), but conceptually, of course, it only partly is (brute force effects are "side effects," not the primary intention, of mass media presence and social media activity).

We express the expectation of brute force effects as mobilizing nudges in hypotheses H3 and H4.

Hypothesis H3: Brute force effects have a substantial impact on a candidate's panachage votes.

Hypothesis H4: Brute force effects have a substantial impact on a candidate's cumulation votes.

In hypotheses H1 to H4, we have expressed our expectations regarding the impact of the brute force effect of candidates' mass media presence in conjunction with the brute force effect of candidates' social media activity. We don't believe that those two effects only occur together, but rather that they are separate effects. Even though social media are used ever more widely, mass media are still, as we argue in the introduction, a public master forum. Mass media reach many parts of the public, and thus, candidates' mass media presence does as well. In contrast, the candidates' audience on social media is much more fragmented and self-selected (Prior, 2007). This means, in effect, that voters are more likely to notice candidates in mass media serendipitously, while they notice them on social media because they have already expressed interest in some candidates by following their social media profiles. From the candidates' point of view, mass media presence will simply reach more people than social media activity. In hypothesis H5, we express our expectation that, overall, one effect is stronger than the other:

Hypothesis H5: The brute force effect of mass media presence is stronger than the brute force effect of social media activity.

Voter preferences and electoral campaigns

Data collection

We analyze the final campaigning phase of the 2015 Swiss federal election in this study. The elections took place on October 18, 2015, and we are analyzing the period from September 19 up to and including October 17. For this time period of the final four weeks, we collected data on candidates' mass media presence as well as their social media activity. The data for the dependent variables in this study—whether a candidate was elected; total number of votes per candidate; panachage votes per candidate, and cumulation votes per candidate—is provided by the cantonal statistical office of Zurich Table 1.

The research units for this study are the candidates for the lower house of the Swiss parliament in the canton of Zurich. Zurich is the largest voting district in Switzerland, because it is the largest canton in terms of population size. In the canton of Zurich, there were 35 different voting lists[4] with a total of 873 candidates. We tracked the mass media presence as well as the social media activity of all 873 candidates in the canton of Zurich.

The main predictors in the present study are candidates' presence in mass media and candidates' activity on social media. The mass media presence of the candidates is a fairly straightforward variable: we count how often any one candidate has been present in newspaper articles, in segments of television news shows, or in segments of radio shows between September 16 and October 17, 2015. The media sample that we analyzed is summarized in section A in the appendix. We have performed an automated content analysis within the statistical environment R on a sample of 11 newspapers, three television news shows, and two radio news shows. Additionally, we have manually counted the occurrence of candidates in three television news shows on a regional television channel. We did not calculate an intercoder reliability for these three shows because counting occurrences was very simple: Two of the shows in question[5] are political talk shows where two to four guests appear and stay for the whole show. It was therefore very simple to identify candidates. The third show is a short news show[6] of around 15 minutes in length for which we had segment-by-segment video data available. This also made counting occurrences manually very simple.

When a candidate was mentioned, quoted, or had a direct appearance (in the case of newspaper interviews and studio appearances on television news shows) once or several times in an article or a broadcasting show segment, we counted that as one occurrence. However, if a candidate was mentioned in, for example, several separate newspaper articles in the same newspaper on the same day, we counted that as multiple occurrences. For the radio and television news shows, an explicit appearance of a candidate combined with an explicit mention of that candidate's name was a necessary condition for counting an occurrence.[7] The media sample for this study consists of titles that have a general, broad focus for the whole German-speaking part of Switzerland as well as titles that are of very regional character and mostly have a cantonal audience. In total, our media sample resulted in 125 occurrences of candidates in broadcasting media, and 1,460 occurrences of candidates in newspapers.

We measure candidates' social media activity in a fairly comprehensive manner. First, contrary to many studies interested in social media and politics, we are not analyzing only Twitter as a pars pro toto for social media, but we are analyzing candidates' activity on Facebook as well. Second, we are interested in two conceptual dimensions of candidate activity on each of those two platforms: Direct activity by candidates and candidate resonance. Direct activity is that kind of activity in which candidates directly take some action themselves. On Facebook, direct activity is either posting some content on one's wall, or sharing some other content on one's wall. Direct activity on Twitter is very similar: candidates can either directly "tweet" themselves, or "retweet" some other tweets. The dimension of resonance is social media activity that is not initiated by candidates themselves, but which can make candidates more visible. On Facebook, resonance consists of other users liking, commenting on, and sharing posts by candidates. Similarly, resonance on Twitter consists of other users liking, retweeting, or replying to candidates' tweets. To measure the resonance on Twitter, we tracked the user handles of all politicians to capture the number of replies a politician received. The number of received retweets and likes (favorites) could be accessed over the candidates' wall. The different components of social media activity are summarized in Table 2.

In total, 282 candidates had a Twitter account, and 138 candidates had a Facebook page (see section B in the appendix for more information). We downloaded candidates' tweets from their user walls in an automated fashion within the computational environment R. Furthermore, we regularly searched for all Twitter handles through the Twitter Search API in order to capture all replies to candidates' tweets. Using this approach, we were able to avoid issues that arise when using the Twitter Stream API (Bessi & Ferrara, 2016). With the help of regex functions, we extracted only the replies to tweets by candidates, and we filtered out mere mentions of candidates that are not replies to candidates' tweets. With this approach, it was possible to compare the Twitter data to the Facebook data, since the data from the Facebook pages downloaded via the Facebook API does not contain information about mentions elsewhere of Facebook.

Overall, we are using six variables as independent variables of mass media presence and of social media activity. Two of those independent variables are related to mass media presence: the number of candidate occurrences in newspapers, and the number of candidate occurrences in broadcast news shows. For social media predictors, we end up with four variables: one variable of direct activity and one of resonance for Facebook and Twitter each. The two variables of direct activity on social media are simply the counts of candidates' Facebook posts (including shares) and Twitter tweets (including retweets). The two variables of social media resonance are composite variables. For Facebook, they are the sum of the counts of likes, comments, and shares by other Facebook users. For Twitter, they are the sum of the counts of likes, retweets, and replies by other Twitter users. In the time period covered by this study, the candidates have created 1,595 posts on Facebook and received 49,869 resonance actions on their posts, and they have tweeted 7,036 times and received 15,887 resonance actions on their tweets.

In addition to two variables for mass media presence and the four variables for social media activity, we have collected additional data about the individual candidates. These additional independent variables are summarized in Table 3, together with the variables for social media activity.

Candidates' gender (Dolan, 2008; McDermott, 1998) and age (Piliavin, 1987; Sigelman & Sigelman, 1982) are variables that have been found to possibly play a role in elections as a type of nonrational heuristic. The electoral advantage of incumbents has been observed for some time and in different contexts (Alford & Hibbing, 1981; Ansolabehere & Snyder, 2002; Erikson, 1971; Hogan, 2004; Smith, 2013). The voting list rank is a variable that captures the name order on the voting lists. Name order has been found to have a nontrivial effect on voting outcomes (Ho & Imai, 2008; Koppell & Steen, 2004; Miller & Krosnick, 1998). Name order effects are a very clear type of nonrational, heuristic-driven voting behavior. The voting list variable is included in order to denote the group-level variable for the multilevel modeling strategy.

Data analysis

Our data is of a particular structure. We have collected data on 873 candidates, and those candidates are members of 35 different voting lists. Our data, therefore, has a natural multilevel structure to it. Of course, the data analysis strategy should not be determined only by "accidental" properties of the data at hand, but it should be informed by epistemically reasonable assumptions. We believe our assumptions meet this requirement. The 35 different voting lists represent a wide range of parties, from relatively large ones that have been present in the Swiss federal lower house for decades, to very minor parties and groups that are not very well known. If we pooled all candidates together, we would be committing a rather grave base-rate fallacy (Bar-Hillel, 1980): Given our prior knowledge on, for example, how well different political parties did in the last elections of 2011, it would be fairly irrational to assume that in this election, candidates of all parties would have an equal base-rate probability of being elected. For this reason, we are modeling our estimates as *multilevel models with varying intercepts*: We want to estimate effects of the predictors summarized in Table 3 given our strong expectation that not all parties, that is, not all voting lists, would do equally well absent all predictors. In other words, we believe that voters have preferences, and those preferences, in the sense of rational voting, mostly determine the electoral outcome, and not our set of independent variables. All of this is simply a consequence of our theoretical understanding of voting behavior as explicated in section 1.

We conduct the data analysis as Bayesian multilevel models using Stan (Carpenter et al., 2017) called via the package brms (Bürkner, 2017) from within the computational environment R. We are using a Bayesian procedure for practical as well as philosophical reasons. Practically, Bayesian regression models perform better than frequentist regression models when the data in question has a multilevel structure (Browne & Draper, 2006; Bryan & Jenkins, 2016; Gelman & Hill, 2006; Stegmueller, 2013). Philosophically, the beliefs that are expressed via Bayesian models and the results that Bayesian models produce are more closely aligned to our actual beliefs and our interpretation of parameter estimates than is the case with frequentist models (Morey, Hoekstra, Rouder, Lee, & Wagenmakers, 2016).

We estimate four models, corresponding to the four dependent variables of interest: being elected, the total amount of votes, the amount of cumulation votes, and the amount of panachage votes. In the first of those models, the dependent variable is dichotomous. The model we estimate is the following one:

$$yi,j \sim Bernoulli(\mu)$$

$$\mu = logit(\alpha i,j + \beta i x i)\alpha i,j {\sim} N(\alpha i,\tau)$$

$$\alpha i {\sim} N(0,5)$$

$$\tau {\sim} Cauchy(0,2.5)$$

$$\beta i {\sim} N(0,5)$$

In this model, i stands for the level of the individual candidate, and j denotes the group-level variable, the voting list. We estimate the other three models in the following manner:

$$yi,j \sim t(\mu, \sigma, v)$$

$$\mu = \alpha i,j + \beta ixi \ \alpha i,j \sim N(\alpha i, \tau) \ \alpha i \sim N(0, 10000)$$

$$\tau \sim Cauchy(0, 2.5)$$

$$\beta i \sim N(0, 10000)$$

$$o \sim Cauchy(0, 2.5)$$

$$v \sim Gamma(2, 0.1)$$

For the parameter estimates in all models, we apply only vaguely informative priors. Even though we have suspicions about the model parameters—hence our hypotheses—we do not think that those suspicions rise to the level of information that should be included in the model as prior information.

In our latter three linear models, we do not model the noise distribution as a normal distribution, but rather as a student's *t* distribution (Lange, Little, & Taylor, 1989; Zhang, Lai, Lu, & Tong, 2013). Although the normal distribution is computationally simpler and generally more often used in regression modeling than the *t* distribution, the *t* distribution has the advantage of being more robust against outliers (Kruschke 2013). When using the *t* distribution, it is necessary to specify its scale parameter v (read "nu"). We do not give that parameter a fixed value, but, again, vague priors, as suggested by Juárez and Steel (2010).

Before estimating the models, we have standardized all independent variables that are not nominal by rescaling it relative to their mean and standard deviation. Doing so has two advantages. First, rescaling the data makes the MCMC sampling more efficient. Second, the results become a little more meaningful: the parameter estimates indicate the effect that an independent variable in the model has when it changes by one standard deviation.

Table 1. Dependent variables for the present study.

Variable	Mean	*SD*
Elected (yes/no)	—	—
Total votes	16,588.1	30,973.0
Panachage votes	8,456.3	16,795.2
Cumulation votes	7,399.9	15,175.3

Note. Each variable is used as the dependent variable in one of the four models that are estimated.

Table 2. Components of social media activity.

Platform	Variable	Component	Type
Facebook	Direct activity	Posts (incl. shares)	Count
	Resonance	Likes	Count
		comments	Count
		Shares	Count
Twitter	Direct activity	Tweets (incl. retweets)	Count
	Resonance	Likes	Count
		Retweets	Count
		Replies	Count

An important component of Bayesian estimation is deciding when to stop drawing samples and assume that the stationary distribution of the samples drawn approximates the posterior distribution. Our sampling strategy is twofold. First, we report the potential scale reduction factors (Gelman & Rubin, 1992) for all estimates, with the goal that *R*-hat be close to 1. Second, we present the posterior distribution in visual form in section C of the appendix. A visual inspection can give additional insight into how well the different sampling chains converged.

For all models, we have drawn samples from four sampling chains. For each chain, we drew 2,000 warmup iterations and 2,000 sampling iterations. This modest amount of samples proved good enough for all models except one: for the model of hypothesis 4 where the number of cumulation votes is the dependent variable, we drew 3,000 warmup iterations and 3,000 sampling iterations. This increase in iterations yielded an acceptable level of convergence.

Results

In the following subsection, we present the estimation results for the four models of interest. For the hypotheses one to four, one model per hypothesis was estimated. We present the results in tabular form. Graphical summaries of the posterior distributions of the model estimates are presented in section C of the appendix.

Table 3. List of independent variables.

Variable	Type	Level	Mean	*SD*
Gender	Nominal	Individual	—	
Age	Metric	Individual	44.6	15.2
Incumbency	Nominal	Individual	—	
Voting list rank	Ordinal	Individual	17.2	10.1
Voting list	Nominal	Group	—	
Presence—newspapers	Count	Individual	1.7	5.3
Presence—broadcasting	Count	Individual	0.1	0.9
Facebook—direct activity	Count	Individual	1.8	7.9
Twitter—direct activity	Count	Individual	8.1	44.0
Facebook—resonance	Count	Individual	57.1	555.1
Twitter—resonance	Count	Individual	18.2	109.0

Hypothesis H1: Being elected into office

For the first hypothesis, the dependent variable is dichotomous: Either a candidate is elected into office or not. The estimation results for the first model are summarized in Table 4.

The interpretation of the results is not directly intuitive, because the reported values are log odds. Nonetheless, it is immediately visible that there seem to be only a few estimates that are of practical relevance. The strongest effect on display is incumbency: if a candidate is an incumbent, that translates into a log odds of 4.08. Or, converted into an odds ratio by means of exponentiation: if a candidate is an incumbent, his or her odds of being elected are around 59 times higher than if he or she weren't an incumbent. Of the 873 candidates, 29 were incumbents. Of those 29, 24 got reelected—and only 11 of the 844 other nonincumbent candidates got elected. The second effect of practical importance is sex: Female candidates are more likely to be elected than male ones, with log odds of 2.02, which translates to an odds ratio of about 7.5. Finally, presence in newspapers has an effect of 1.19, which translates into an odds ratio of 3.3. This means that a change of one standard deviation of newspaper presence has a nonnegligible impact on being elected.

Overall, the first hypothesis is only partly supported. Contrary to the hypothesis, one aspect of brute force effects, the presence in newspapers, does have a positive nonnegligible impact. Even though the effect is rather small, it cannot be ignored.

Overall, hypothesis H1 is only partly supported by the evidence. The effects of presence in broadcasting media, social media activity, and social media resonance are all either small, inconsistent, or both. Presence in newspapers, however, is not: Being present in a newspaper article increases a candidate's odds of being elected to around 1.27; this effects posterior distribution lies almost completely in the positive range.

Hypothesis H2: Total amount of votes

For the second hypothesis, the dependent variable is the total amount of votes. The summary of the model estimates that tests hypothesis H2 is reported in Table 5.

One estimate is immediately striking: If a candidate is an incumbent, he or she will receive, on average, an additional 17,012 votes. This finding goes hand in hand with the one reported for the odds of being elected—there seems to be a strong incumbency bonus in the Swiss lower house elections. A second noticeable effect is Facebook resonance. An increase in one standard deviation of resonance, 555.1, translates into an average of some additional 1,213 votes. Presence in broadcasting and in newspapers both have positive effects. An increase in one standard deviation of broadcasting presence, 0.9, translates into an average of around 345 additional votes. However, the 95% credible interval does not lie wholly in the positive region; the posterior distribution's lower end dips slightly into the negative range. An increase in one standard deviation of newspaper presence, 5.3, translates into some 715 additional votes on average. The effect of the voting list rank is slightly negative; the lower the candidates are on the voting list, the fewer votes they receive.

Overall, hypothesis 2 is only partly supported. The average amount of votes a candidate received is around 16,500, with a standard deviation of about 30,900. In light of these magnitudes, the brute force effects are, contrary to our expectation, partly substantial. An increase in one standard deviation in newspaper presence results in an average of about 750 additional votes, and an increase in one standard deviation of Facebook resonance results in around 1,213 additional votes; both of these effects are nontrivial.

Hypothesis H3: Amount of panachage votes

In hypothesis H3, we posit that mass media presence and social media activity will increase the amount of panachage votes a candidate receives.

The results of the estimation for this hypothesis are summarized in Table 6.

Once again, the strongest effect by far is a candidate's incumbency status: On average, incumbents receive around 6,500 more panachage votes than nonincumbents. The second most notable effect is presence in newspapers. An increase in one standard deviation of newspaper presence on average leads to some 440 additional panachage votes. Presence in broadcasting also has an average positive effect for an increase in one standard deviation, 0.9, but the lower end of the distribution dips into the negative, meaning that the effect is less consistent. Out of the social media variables, resonance on Facebook is, once again, the only notable effect. An increase in one standard deviation, 555.1, leads to around 178 additional panachage votes on average. Voting list rank is, once again, displaying a small negative effect: the lower the candidates are on the voting list, the fewer panachage votes they receive.

The results only partly support hypothesis 3. Even though some of the brute force variables do have a nonnegligible effect, only presence in newspapers has an effect that can be regarded as substantial. The average amount of panachage votes per candidate is around 8,400, and the standard deviation is around 16,800. Within such a context, about 440 votes gained from an increase in one standard deviation of newspaper articles can be relevant. Similarly, resonance on Facebook can also have a smaller, but still substantial impact, with an average of about 178 votes per an increase in one standard deviation of resonance.

Hypothesis H4: Amount of cumulation votes

In hypothesis H4, we posit that the brute force effects of mass media presence and social media activity will increase a candidate's cumulation votes. Before delving into the results, it is necessary to briefly explain why and how the amount of cumulation votes candidates receive can be, and almost certainly is, biased. In principle, every voter is allowed to cumulate votes for candidates, meaning that a voter is allowed to place one candidate on a voting list twice. Most parties have as many different candidates as they are allowed to have. In the Swiss federal election of 2015, each voting list in the canton of Zurich could contain up to 35 candidates, because Zurich occupies 35 seats in the lower house. Most parties had 35 different candidates on their voting lists. Some smaller ones, however, did not have 35 candidates, and some of those smaller parties put one or several candidates on their list twice.

Cumulating the potential votes in this manner by putting a candidate's name twice on a voting list a priori is completely legal, since, in the end, if a voter decides not to change such a list, the voter has expressed his or her will to cumulate votes for the candidates in question. In principle, then, this type of cumulation is simply cumulation, nothing more. But in reality, this is a prototypical scenario where a prominent cognitive heuristic, the status quo bias (Fernandez & Rodrik, 1991; Samuelson & Zeckhauser, 1988), comes into play. The status quo bias is the observation that people tend to disproportionately favor not changing things over changing them. In the context of cumulation votes, it is highly probable that voters will also favor the status quo, which means that those candidates whose names are cumulated a priori are more likely to receive cumulation votes than candidates whose names are not cumulated a priori. The nature of this kind of a priori cumulation is, in the end, a case of nonrational voting through nudging. Nonetheless, it is worth having a look at the estimation results, even if there is some bias present with the dependent variable. The results are summarized in Table 7.

Once again, incumbency has the strongest effect. On average, incumbents receive around 5,812 additional cumulation votes. Furthermore, the presence both in broadcasting as well as in newspapers has a positive effect. On average, an increase in one standard distribution of broadcasting presence, 0.9, leads to around 113 additional cumulation votes, and an increase in one standard deviation of newspaper presence, 5.3, leads to around 165 additional cumulation votes. Among the social media variable, only resonance on Facebook has a notable effect. An increase of one standard deviation of Facebook resonance, 555.1, leads to around 150 additional cumulation votes. Also, as with the previous models, voting list rank has a small negative effect.

Table 4. Estimates of the first model. The dependent variable is the dichotomous election outcome of being elected or not.

Parameter (log odds)	Mean	2.5% Quantile	97.5% Quantile	Odds ratio
Presence—newspapers	1.19	0.54	1.98	3.29
Presence—broadcasting	−0.10	−0.68	0.56	0.90
Activity—Facebook	−0.24	−0.88	0.38	0.79
Resonance—Facebook	0.58	−0.28	1.61	1.78
Activity—Twitter	−0.72	−2.54	0.29	0.49
Resonance—Twitter	0.68	0.09	1.59	1.97
Voting list rank	−1.10	−2.49	0.00	0.33
Incumbency	4.08	2.11	6.18	59.14
Age	0.15	−0.72	1.09	1.16
Gender (female)	2.02	0.47	3.81	7.54

Notes. The range between the 2.5% and 97.5% quantiles is the so-called 95% credible interval (CI). Given the data, there is a 95% probability that the parameter of interest lies in this range. Credible intervals are not the same as frequentist confidence intervals; the latter are oftentimes, incorrectly, interpreted as the former Hoekstra et al. (2014). All ^R are 1.00. Odds ratios are the exponentiated log odds.

The results do not support hypothesis 4. The average amount of cumulation votes each candidate received is around 7,400, with a standard deviation of around 15,100. The brute force effects of mass media presence and social media activity are all too small to be considered substantial. The strongest effect, an additional 165 votes, on average, by an increase in one standard deviation in newspaper presence (5.3 articles), is fairly small.

Hypothesis H5: The force is stronger with mass media presence

In our final hypothesis H5, we posit that the brute force effects of mass media presence are stronger than the brute force effects of social media activity. Given the results of the models described above, this seems to be the case. From the two variables of mass media presence, the presence in newspaper articles displays a consistent effect: Newspaper presence slightly increases candidates' odds of getting elected, and it increases the amount of total votes, the amount of panachage votes, and the amount of cumulation votes. There are also signs that presence in broadcasting has a positive effect, but the effect is overall somewhat weaker and less consistent than newspaper presence. Among the social media variables, only resonance on Facebook has produced relevant effects. But those effects are consistent and for one model—the total amount of votes—Facebook resonance is even the strongest brute force effect.

Discussion: Brute and forceful, but not quite as expected

The results of our analysis of the 2015 Swiss federal election naturally only paint a partial picture of brute force effects of candidates' mass media presence and social media activity. But that picture, we believe, is mostly plausible, and at least to some degree generalizable beyond the context of Swiss elections.

We started out with the general expectation that brute force effects are minor effects. Our results are very much compatible with that assumption: even in scenarios where brute force effects are potentially maximized, they are unlikely to completely make or break an election. But at the same time, they are also nontrivial. Within a given voting list, candidates sometimes receive very similar amounts of votes, and several hundred to a few thousand potential additional—or missing—votes can make a difference in terms of electoral prospects if several candidates are competing closely.

However, the impact of brute force effects did not play out exactly as we expected in our hypotheses. In the context of the first hypothesis, we actually observed an effect, namely, that of presence in newspapers, that does constitute a nontrivial impact. The results for the second hypothesis are surprising: contrary to our expectation, the effects of mass media presence and social media activity were substantial. Specifically, the effects of newspaper presence and of Facebook resonance are strong. The results for the third

Table 5. Estimates of the second model. The dependent variable is the total amount of votes.

Parameter	Mean	2.5% Quantile	97.5% Quantile
Presence—newspapers	714.69	492.91	936.33
Presence—broadcasting	345.04	−30.04	604.57
Activity—Facebook	−63.73	−132.59	18.09
Resonance—Facebook	1,213.55	1,084.55	1,458.07
Activity—Twitter	38.35	−129.70	246.29
Resonance—Twitter	−9.48	−187.67	206.69
Voting list rank	−210.21	−244.47	−176.26
Incumbency	17,012.03	15,969.69	18,029.76
Age	−9.21	−43.03	25.07
Gender (female)	16.88	−42.00	78.15

Note. All ^R are 1.00. Only Resonance—Facebook has 1.02.

hypothesis were consistent with our expectation. Specifically, the effects of newspaper presence and Facebook resonance have a relatively strong impact. The results for the fourth hypothesis, however, only partly support the hypothesis. Mass media presence and social media activity does have a number of consistent effects, but they have, at best, a modest impact. The final hypothesis was supported by the results. Overall, the effects of mass media presence are stronger and more consistent than the effects of social media activity.

Overall, and contrary to our expectations, possible brute force effects are not only present for the amount of panachage and cumulation votes, but also for the total amount of votes as well as the odds of getting elected. Those effects are only present for mass media presence, not for social media activity and resonance. This forms an important general insight of the present study: In the context of brute force effects, traditional media still matter, and they matter a lot. That is not to say that social media is not important, both for candidates and for voters. But professional journalistic mass media still exert a centripetal force whereby large parts of society become informed. Consequently, it is unlikely that professional mass media will become obsolete for political campaigning anytime soon. It is important, we believe, to try and keep such a "global" perspective in mind when conducting research in the context of politics and social media. It is tantalizing to conduct research exclusively within the context of social media, not least because it is often easier to collect social media data than mass media data. However, social media should not be analyzed in total isolation, and, furthermore, electoral behavior should not be reduced to media effects, be they induced by mass or by social media. That is precisely the rationale of our concept of brute force effects, because they are only a minor, but relevant, part of voter behavior.

Table 6. Estimates of the third model. The dependent variable is the amount of panachage votes.

Parameter	Mean	2.5% Quantile	97.5% Quantile
Presence—newspapers	441.39	328.58	541.59
Presence—broadcasting	69.28	−14.45	139.56
Activity—Facebook	−10.50	−40.82	23.26
Resonance—Facebook	178.21	8.89	302.81
Activity—Twitter	8.81	−22.45	71.55
Resonance—Twitter	−1.30	−36.29	29.27
Voting list rank	−80.82	−97.89	−64.35
Incumbency	6,499.10	4,852.06	8,096.97
Age	−7.43	−24.39	9.46
Gender (female)	25.15	−4.79	56.47

Note. All $\hat{R}$ are 1.00. Only Resonance—Facebook has 1.01 and Incumbency 1.02.

Social media: Resonance, not direct activity, matters

One of the most intriguing aspects of the results of this study is the unequal impact of different social media variables. Facebook activity, Twitter activity, and Twitter resonance are, essentially, meaningless and inconsistent. However, Facebook resonance has a consistent and substantial effect. There are two possible conclusions that can be drawn from this result. First, in the Swiss context, Facebook might matter more than Twitter as a platform for political candidates. Facebook has far more monthly active users than Twitter in Switzerland (about 3.5 million compared to 0.7 million; Statista GmbH, 2017). Second, and more important, resonance on social media might matter more than activity in general. This is, of course, rather plausible. A candidate might be very active on social media, but if she or he has no audience, then that activity will not, obviously, translate into votes. It is even possible that candidates who are "desperate" will be more active on social media, to no avail, since nobody is listening.

The electoral Matthew effect

In our models, the strongest predictor of electoral success was incumbency: Candidates who are sitting members of the lower house do much better, on average, than challengers. This electoral Matthew effect in the sense of $Pr(e|i) > Pr(e|c)$, where e stands for being elected, i for incumbent, and c for challenger, is no big surprise. After all, we specifically included incumbency as an independent variable because it has been shown time and again that incumbency matters. How important, then, could incumbency be in the context of brute force effects? Specifically, could incumbency be a driver of mass media presence and social media activity? Indeed, there is ample evidence that the incumbency bonus extends to mass media presence (Green-Pedersen, Mortensen, &

Thesen, 2015; Hopmann, De Vreese, & Albæk, 2011). The potential impact of the incumbency effect in the context of brute force effects can thus be described as a two-step Matthew effect. First, incumbents receive more air time and more presence in newspapers on account of their prominence. Second, being more visible in the mass media, in turn, has an effect on voters, part of which consists of brute force effects.

The incumbency effect as a two-step Matthew effect is, to some degree, a double status quo bias. Incumbents enjoy a disproportionate amount of media coverage because they are incumbents, and in turn, incumbents' higher visibility as a brute force effect strengthens voters' general status quo bias as the preference for incumbents. Given the data of this study, such a two-step mechanism is conceivable: incumbents commanded 55% of total candidate TV and radio presence, and 38% of total candidate newspaper presence, while being only a small minority of 3.3% within the total candidate pool.

Limitations and future research

Our study has a number of limitations. First, we have conducted our analysis only in the context of one election, and it is therefore impossible to say whether the results are generalizable in a temporal (future elections in the same political context) and geographical (elections in different contexts) manner. A second major limitation is the question of how important the potential brute force effects are for different parts of the public. Not all people have the same mass media and social media repertoires and habits. It is therefore conceivable that a much clearer picture of brute force effects would emerge if they were studied directly by analyzing individual voting behavior instead of aggregated population-level votes. For example, the effects of social media activity might be much stronger for voters who are heavy users of social media and who rarely consume mass media. Another limitation of this study is that we have condensed the analyzed time period into a cross-sectional data set. Looking at brute force effects with a time series design would allow us to extend the analysis to effects of intermedia agenda setting: it is possible that candidate mass media presence has a relevant impact on their social media activity and resonance, and vice versa.

Table 7. Estimates of the fourth model, with the amount of cumulation votes as the dependent variable.

Parameter	Mean	2.5% Quantile	97.5% Quantile
Presence—newspapers	164.88	88.19	244.05
Presence—broadcasting	113.40	2.23	211.94
Activity—Facebook	−9.49	−32.84	16.67
Resonance—Facebook	149.69	−8.19	272.69
Activity—Twitter	17.97	−32.29	85.84
Resonance—Twitter	−14.80	−73.23	38.04
Voting list rank	−58.42	−69.78	−47.44
Incumbency	5,811.99	4,222.20	7,854.54
Age	−6.92	−18.85	5.00
Gender (female)	18.64	−3.13	40.01

Note. All $\hat{R}$ are 1.00. Only Activity—Twitter has 1.01, Presence—newspapers and Resonance—Facebook have 1.02, Incumbency 1.03, and Presence—broadcasting 1.10.

We encourage further research on the concept of brute force effects; with the present study, brute force effects have been explored only tentatively in the context of one single election. The general theoretical strategy we adopt in this study should be pursued further. That is not to say that all future research has to rely on exactly the same notions of bounded rationality, but we do think it necessary to embed features of biase-prone human cognition, such as brute force effects, within a more generalizable model of voter behavior. That being said, we think there are two general ways future research could further explore brute force effects. The first prospect for future research is quasi-replication in different political contexts. By this we simply mean studying potential brute force effects in a similar manner as we do presently, but for different political contexts. After all, not all political campaigns, not all voting systems, and not all mass media systems are the same. The second prospect for future research is research with different research designs. As explained above, one major limitation of our study is the fact that we did not have access to the micro-level of individual voting behavior; that is precisely what should be in future research, be it in the form of experimental or in the form of survey-type designs. Only then can the exact share of nonrational voting influenced by brute force effects be estimated (see Figure 1).

Normative implications

The primary motivation for the present study is to put expectations that arise from theory to the empirical test. Given our model of bounded voter rationality and brute force effects as a form of nonrational voting behavior, we set out to analyze whether the effects we expected are present. From our results, however, some normative implications arise. Political decision-making by citizens should be as rational as possible, and nonrational voting behavior as the result of cognitive heuristics is therefore a normative problem. Consequently, brute force effects are also a problem. How much of a problem? Not a great one, for at least two reasons.

First, we imagine brute force effects, conceptually, as only a minor part of nonrational voting. Nonrational voting in general might be a problem (quantifying the overall amount of irrational behavior in voting is far beyond the scope of the present paper), but brute force effects of mass media presence and social media activity are only a minor slice of that problem. Furthermore, our empirical results support our theoretical assumption that brute force effects are, at most, moderate effects. Second, brute force effects are likely to be universal effects, since they are a consequence of cognitive heuristics. Cognitive heuristics are a universal property of human cognition, and therefore, the magnitude of brute force effects should be more or less equally distributed among the population. That might hardly sound like something to take solace in. But if brute force effects exist, then it is normatively preferable that they be present and weak in the general population rather than disproportionately concentrated within some population segments or strata.

Notes

1. The number of signatures required for a candidacy varies according to the cantonal population sizes, but does not exceed the relatively low amount of 400.
2. In four of these small cantons, any one Swiss citizen from the respective canton is eligible to be elected into the lower house, even without prior official registration of the candidacy.
3. In the six small cantons with only one seat per canton, the election, naturally, defaults to a majority vote.
4. Most of those voting lists correspond to a political party. However, a few voting lists did not directly represent political parties, but different types of political groups, some of them only semi-serious, such as the "Anti PowerPoint Party." Any one individual can form a voting list and become a candidate in the canton of Zurich if they manage to collect 400 signatures from Swiss citizens living in the canton of Zurich.
5. *TalkTäglich* and *SonnTalk*.
6. *Züri-News*.
7. We had access to the official database of the Swiss Broadcasting Corporation. For each segment in the news, the mentioned and quoted politicians are listed in the database. For newspapers, we automatically extracted all politicians. For common names and all politicians with more than ten mentions, we checked manually for false positives and subtracted them. The newspaper articles were downloaded from the comprehensive Swiss Media Database (Schweizerische Mediendatenbank).

References

Alford, J. R., & Hibbing, J. R. (1981). Increased incumbency advantage in the house. *The Journal of Politics*, *43*(4), 1042–1061. doi:10.2307/2130188

Ansolabehere, S., & Snyder, J. M. (2002). The incumbency advantage in U.S. elections: An analysis of state and federal offices, 1942–2000. *Election Law Journal: Rules, Politics, and Policy*, *1*(3), 315–338. doi:10.1089/153312902760137578

Anstead, N., & O'Loughlin, B. (2015). Social media analysis and public opinion: The 2010 UK general election. *Journal of Computer-Mediated Communication, 20*(2), 204–220. doi:10.1111/jcc4.12102

Baker, R., Brick, J. M., Bates, N. A., Battaglia, M., Couper, M. P., Dever, J. A., ... Tourangeau, R. (2013). Summary report of the AAPOR task force on non-probability sampling. *Journal of Survey Statistics and Methodology, 1*(2), 90–143. doi:10.1093/jssam/smt008

Bar-Hillel, M. (1980). The base-rate fallacy in probability judgments. *Acta Psychologica, 44*(3), 211–233. doi:10.1016/0001-6918(80)90046-3

Bennett, W. L., & Iyengar, S. (2008). A new era of minimal effects? The changing foundations of political communication. *Journal of Communication, 58*(4), 707–731. doi:10.1111/j.1460-2466.2008.00410.x

Bessi, A., & Ferrara, E. (2016). Social bots distort the 2016 U. S. presidential election online discussion. *First Monday, 21* (11). Retrieved from http://journals.uic.edu/ojs/index.php/fm/article/view/7090

Black, D. (1948). On the rationale of group decision-making. *Journal of Political Economy, 56*(1), 23–34. Retrieved from http://www.jstor.org/stable/1825026 doi:10.1086/256633

Browne, W. J., & Draper, D. (2006). A comparison of Bayesian and likelihood-based methods for fitting multilevel models. *Bayesian Analysis, 1*(3), 473–514. doi:10.1214/06-BA117

Bryan, M. L., & Jenkins, S. P. (2016). Multilevel modelling of country effects: A cautionary tale. *European Sociological Review, 32*(1), 3–22. doi:10.1093/esr/jcv059

Bürkner, P.-C. (2017). *brms: Bayesian regression models using stan*. Retrieved from https://cran.r-project.org/web/packages/brms/index.html

Carpenter, B., Gelman, A., Hoffman, M., Lee, D., Goodrich, B., Betancourt, M., ... Riddell, A. (2017). Stan: A probabilistic programming language. *Journal of Statistical Software, 76*(1), 1–32. doi:10.18637/jss.v076.i01

DiGrazia, J., McKelvey, K., Bollen, J., & Rojas, F. (2013). More tweets, more votes: Social media as a quantitative indicator of political behavior. *Plos One, 8*(11), e79449. doi:10.1371/journal.pone.0079449

Dolan, K. (2008). Is there a "gender affinity effect" in American politics? Information, affect, and candidate sex in U.S. House elections. *Political Research Quarterly, 61*(1), 79–89. doi:10.1177/1065912907307518

Downs, A. (1957). An economic theory of political action in a democracy. *Journal of Political Economy, 65*(2), 135–150. Retrieved from http://www.jstor.org/stable/1827369 doi:10.1086/257897

Erikson, R. S. (1971). The advantage of incumbency in congressional elections. *Polity, 3*(3), 395–405. doi:10.2307/3234117

Fernandez, R., & Rodrik, D. (1991). Resistance to reform: Status quo bias in the presence of individual-specific uncertainty. *The American Economic Review, 81*(5), 1146–1155.

Ferree, M. M. (2002). *Shaping abortion discourse: Democracy and the public sphere in Germany and the United States. Communication, society and politics*. Cambridge, England: Cambridge University Press.

fög-Forschungsbereich Öffentlichkeit und Gesellschaft. (2015). *Jahrbuch 2015 Qualität der Medien*. Basel, Switzerland: Schwabe Basel.

Gayo-Avello, D. (2012). "I wanted to predict elections with Twitter and all I got was this lousy paper"—A balanced survey on election prediction using Twitter data. *arXiv:1204.6441 [physics]*

Gayo-Avello, D. (2013). A meta-analysis of state-of-the-art electoral prediction from Twitter data. *Social Science Computer Review, 31*(6), 649–679. doi:10.1177/0894439313493979

Gelman, A., & Hill, J. (2006). *Data analysis using regression and multilevel/hierarchical models*. New York, NY: Cambridge University Press.

Gelman, A., & King, G. (1993). Why are American presidential election campaign polls so variable when votes are so predictable? *British Journal of Political Science, 23*(4), 409–451. doi:10.1017/S0007123400006682

Gelman, A., & Rubin, D. B. (1992). Inference from iterative simulation using multiple sequences. *Statistical Science, 7*(4), 457–472. doi:10.1214/ss/1177011136

Gibson, R. K., & McAllister, I. (2011). Do online election campaigns win votes? The 2007 Australian "YouTube" election. *Political Communication, 28*(2), 227–244. doi:10.1080/10584609.2011.568042

Green, D. P., & Gerber, A. S. (2015). *Get out the vote: How to increase voter turnout* (3rd ed.). Washington, DC: Brookings Institution Press.

Green-Pedersen, C., Mortensen, P. B., & Thesen, G. (2015). The incumbency bonus revisited: Causes and consequences of media dominance. *British Journal of Political Science, FirstView*, 1–18. doi:10.1017/S0007123415000022

Habermas, J. (2006). Political communication in media society: Does democracy still enjoy an epistemic dimension? The impact of normative theory on empirical research. *Communication Theory, 16*(4), 411–426. doi:10.1111/j.1468-2885.2006.00280.x

Hansen, J., & Wänke, M. (2009). Liking what's familiar: The importance of unconscious familiarity in the mere-exposure effect. *Social Cognition, 27*(2), 161–182. doi:10.1521/soco.2009.27.2.161

Hansen, K. M., & Kosiara-Pedersen, K. (2014). Cyber-campaigning in Denmark: Application and effects of candidate campaigning. *Journal of Information Technology & Politics, 11*(2), 206–219. doi:10.1080/19331681.2014.895476

Hansen, K. M., & Pedersen, R. T. (2014). Campaigns matter: How voters become knowledgeable and efficacious during election campaigns. *Political Communication, 31*(2), 303–324. doi:10.1080/10584609.2013.815296

Harmon-Jones, E., & Allen, J. J. B. (2001). The role of affect in the mere exposure effect: Evidence from psychophysiological and individual differences approaches. *Personality and Social Psychology Bulletin, 27*(7), 889–898. doi:10.1177/0146167201277011

Ho, D. E., & Imai, K. (2008). Estimating causal effects of ballot order from a randomized natural experiment: The California alphabet lottery, 1978–2002. *Public Opinion Quarterly, 72*(2), 216–240. doi:10.1093/poq/nfn018

Hoekstra, R., Morey, R. D., Rouder, J. N., & Wagenmakers, E.-J. (2014). Robust misinterpretation of confidence intervals. *Psychonomic Bulletin & Review, 21*(5), 1157–1164. doi:10.3758/s13423-013-0572-3

Hogan, R. E. (2004). Challenger emergence, incumbent success, and electoral accountability in state legislative elections. *The Journal of Politics, 66*(4), 1283–1303. doi:10.1111/j.0022-3816.2004.00300.x

Hopmann, D. N., De Vreese, C. H., & Albæk, E. (2011). Incumbency bonus in election news coverage explained: The logics of political power and the media market. *Journal of Communication, 61*(2), 264–282. doi:10.1111/j.1460-2466.2011.01540.x

Hopmann, D. N., Vliegenthart, R., Vreese, C. D., & Albæk, E. (2010). Effects of election news coverage: How visibility and tone influence party choice. *Political Communication, 27*(4), 389–405. doi:10.1080/10584609.2010.516798

Iyengar, S., Norpoth, H., & Hahn, K. S. (2004). Consumer demand for election news: The horserace sells. *The Journal of Politics, 66*(1), 157–175. doi:10.1046/j.1468-2508.2004.00146.x

Jacobs, K., & Spierings, N. (2016). Saturation or maturation? The diffusion of Twitter and its impact on preference voting in the Dutch general elections of 2010 and 2012. *Journal of Information Technology & Politics, 13*(1), 1–21. doi:10.1080/19331681.2015.1131652

Jones, B. D. (1999). Bounded rationality. *Annual Review of Political Science, 2*(1), 297–321. doi:10.1146/annurev.polisci.2.1.297

Juárez, M. A., & Steel, M. F. J. (2010). Model-based clustering of non-Gaussian panel data based on skew-*t* distributions. *Journal of Business & Economic Statistics, 28*(1), 52–66. doi:10.1198/jbes.2009.07145

Jungherr, A. (2013). Tweets and votes, a special relationship: The 2009 federal election in Germany. In *PLEAD '13, Proceedings of the 2nd Workshop on Politics, Elections and Data* (pp. 5–14). New York, NY: ACM. doi: 10.1145/2508436.2508437

Jungherr, A. (2016). Twitter use in election campaigns: A systematic literature review. *Journal of Information Technology & Politics*, ed. Ingmar Weber, Ana-Maria Popescu, Marco Pennacchiotti, *13*(1), 72–91. doi:10.1080/19331681.2015.1132401

Kaplan, A. M., & Haenlein, M. (2010). Users of the world, unite! The challenges and opportunities of social media. *Business Horizons, 53*(1), 59–68. doi:10.1016/j.bushor.2009.09.003

Koppell, J. G. S., & Steen, J. A. (2004). The effects of ballot position on election outcomes. *The Journal of Politics, 66* (1), 267–281. doi:10.1046/j.1468-2508.2004.00151.x

Kreiss, D. (2015). Digital campaigning. In S. Coleman & D. Freelon (Eds.), *Handbook of digital politics* (pp. 118–135). Cheltenham, England: Edward Elgar.

Kruikemeier, S. (2014). How political candidates use Twitter and the impact on votes. *Computers in Human Behavior, 34*, 131–139. doi:10.1016/j.chb.2014.01.025

Kruschke, J. K. (2013). Bayesian estimation supersedes the t test. *Journal of Experimental Psychology*. General, *142*(2), 573–603. doi:10.1037/a0029146

Lange, K. L., Little, R. J. A., & Taylor, J. M. G. (1989). Robust statistical modeling using the *t* distribution. *Journal of the American Statistical Association, 84*(408), 881–896. doi:10.1080/01621459.1989.10478852

Marcinkowski, F., & Metag, J. (2013). Lassen sich mit dem Internet Wählerstimmen gewinnen? *Publizistik, 58*(1), 23–44. doi:10.1007/s11616-013-0168-y

McDermott, M. L. (1998). Race and gender cues in low-information elections. *Political Research Quarterly, 51*(4), 895–918. doi:10.1177/106591299805100403

Metaxas, P. T., Mustafaraj, E., & Gayo-Avello, D. (2011). How (Not) to Predict Elections. In Institute of Electrical and Electronics Engineers (Ed.), IEEE Third International Conference on Privacy, Security, Risk and Trust (PASSAT), 2011 and 2011 IEEE Third International Conference on Social Computing (SocialCom). 9 – 11 Oct. 2011, Boston, Massachusetts, USA (pp. 165–171). Piscataway, NJ: IEEE.

Miller, J. M., & Krosnick, J. A. (1998). The impact of candidate name order on election outcomes. *The Public Opinion Quarterly, 62*(3), 291–330. Retrieved from http://www.jstor.org/stable/2749662 doi:10.1086/297848

Morey, R. D., Hoekstra, R., Rouder, J. N., Lee, M. D., & Wagenmakers, E.-J. (2016). The fallacy of placing confidence in confidence intervals. *Psychonomic Bulletin & Review, 23*(1), 103–123. doi:10.3758/s13423-015-0947-8

Mullainathan, S., & Thaler, R. H. (2000). *Behavioral Economics* (NBER Working Paper No. 7948). Cambridge, MA: National Bureau of Economic Research.

Nadeau, R., Nevitte, N., Gidengil, E., & Blais, A. (2008). Election campaigns as information campaigns: Who learns what and does it matter? *Political Communication, 25*(3), 229–248. doi:10.1080/10584600802197269

Nickerson, D. W. (2006). Volunteer phone calls can increase turnout evidence from eight field experiments. *American Politics Research, 34*(3), 271–292. doi:10.1177/1532673X05275923

Nickerson, D. W. (2007). Quality is job one: Professional and volunteer voter mobilization calls. *American Journal of Political Science, 51*(2), 269–282. doi:10.1111/j.1540-5907.2007.00250.x

Nimmo, D. D. (2001). *The political persuaders: The techniques of modern election campaigns.* New Brunswick, NJ: Transaction Publishers.

Petrocik, J. R. (1996). Issue ownership in presidential elections, with a 1980 case study. *American Journal of Political Science, 40*(3), 825–850. Retrieved from http://www.jstor.org/stable/2111797 doi:10.2307/2111797

Piliavin, J. A. (1987). Age, race, and sex similarity to candidates and voting preference. *Journal of Applied Social Psychology, 17*(4), 351–368. doi:10.1111/j.1559-1816.1987.tb00318.x

Prior, M. (2007). *Post-broadcast democracy: How media choice increases inequality in political involvement and polarizes elections.* New York, NY: Cambridge University Press.

Rohrschneider, R. (2002). Mobilizing versus chasing: How do parties target voters in election campaigns? *Electoral Studies, 21*(3), 367–382. doi:10.1016/S0261-3794(00)00044-5

Samuelson, W., & Zeckhauser, R. (1988). Status quo bias in decision making. *Journal of Risk and Uncertainty, 1*(1), 7–59. doi:10.1007/BF00055564

Scheufele, D. A., & Tewksbury, D. (2007). Framing, agenda setting, and priming: The evolution of three media effects models. *Journal of Communication, 57*(1), 9–20. Retrieved from. doi:10.1111/j.0021-9916.2007.00326.x

Seidman, S. A. (2008). *Posters, propaganda, and persuasion in election campaigns around the world and through history.* Peter Lang. New York.

Shepsle, K. A. (2010). *Analyzing politics: Rationality, behavior, and instititutions.* W. W. Norton & Company. New York.

Sigelman, L., & Sigelman, C. K. (1982). Sexism, racism, and ageism in voting behavior: An experimental analysis. *Social Psychology Quarterly, 45*(4), 263–269. doi:10.2307/3033922

Simon, H. A. (1955). A behavioral model of rational choice. *The Quarterly Journal of Economics, 69*(1), 99–118. doi:10.2307/1884852

Smith, T. H. (2013). Are you sitting comfortably? Estimating incumbency advantage in the UK: 1983–2010—A research note. *Electoral Studies, 32*(1), 167–173. doi:10.1016/j.electstud.2012.12.002

Spierings, N., & Jacobs, K. (2014). Getting personal? The impact of social media on preferential voting. *Political Behavior, 36*(1), 215–234. doi:10.1007/s11109-013-9228-2

Statista, GmbH (2007). Social Media in der Schweiz - Statista-Dossier. Retrieved from HYPERLINK. https://protect-us.mimecast.com/s/rx4mBRUOvg38fa?domain=marketing.ch"http://www.marketing.ch/Portals/0/social-media-in-der-schweiz-statista-dossier.pdf?ver=2016-08-02-141729-547

Statista GmbH. (2017). Social Media in der Schweiz - Statista-Dossier. Retrieved from HYPERLINK "https://protect-us.mimecast.com/s/rx4mBRUOvg38fa?domain=marketing.ch"http://www.marketing.ch/Portals/0/social-media-in-der-schweiz-statista-dossier.pdf?ver=2016-08-02-141729-547

Stegmueller, D. (2013). How many countries for multilevel modeling? A comparison of frequentist and Bayesian approaches. *American Journal of Political Science, 57*(3), 748–761. doi:10.1111/ajps.12001

Sunstein, C. R. (2014). *Why nudge?: The politics of Libertarian paternalism.* New Haven, CT: Yale University Press.

Thaler, R. H., & Sunstein, C. R. (2009). *Nudge: Improving decisions about health, wealth, and happiness* (Revised and expanded ed.). New York, NY: Penguin Books.

Verhulst, B., Lodge, M., & Lavine, H. (2010). The attractiveness halo: Why some candidates are perceived more favorably than others. *Journal of Nonverbal Behavior, 34*(2), 111–117. doi:10.1007/s10919-009-0084-z

WEMF AG für Werbemedienforschung. (2015). *WEMF Auflgebulletin 2015.* Zurich: WEMF AG.

Zajonc, R. B. (1968). Attitudinal Effects of Mere Exposure. *Journal of Personality and Social Psychology, 9*(2, Pt. 2), 1–27. doi:10.1037/h0025848

Zajonc, R. B. (2001). Mere exposure: A gateway to the subliminal. *Current Directions in Psychological Science, 10*(6), 224–228. doi:10.1111/1467-8721.00154

Zhang, Z., Lai, K., Lu, Z., & Tong, X. (2013). Bayesian inference and application of robust growth curve models using student's *t* distribution. *Structural Equation Modeling: A Multidisciplinary Journal, 20*(1), 47–78. doi:10.1080/10705511.2013.742382

Appendix

A Media Sample

The television and radio shows as well as the newspaper titles analyzed in the present study are summarized in Table 8.

The newspaper titles in the sample account for around 77% of total newspaper circulation in the canton of Zurich, according to a nonprofit corporation that collects and verifies data on newspaper circulation (WEMF, 2015). All newspapers with medium and major circulation (75,000 and more) in the canton of Zurich are contained in the sample, with the exception of the *Tagblatt der Stadt Zürich*, which is not focused on politics. The selection criteria for the television and radio titles are less straightforward. The selection of the television shows was pragmatic: we have selected all regional and national news shows and political talk shows that are available in the canton of Zurich. This resulted in a number of public broadcasting news shows and political talk shows (*Tagesschau, 10vor10, Arena*). There is only one regional television channel with political news content, "Tele Züri," and we have analyzed all news shows and political talk shows on that channel. In the case of radio, we have only selected news shows on public broadcasting, one of which focuses on regional content. Private radio stations in the canton of Zurich are less listened to than public radio stations, and the amount and duration of news shows on private radio stations is kept to or near the regulatory minimum (fög-Forschungsbereich Öffentlichkeit und Gesellschaft, 2015).

B Social Media

In order to collect social media data, we proceeded in two steps: first, we manually identified candidates' Twitter accounts and Facebook pages, and second, we automatically extracted data from those accounts and pages. For Twitter, we manually checked for every one of the 873 candidates whether a Twitter account exists for them. The criteria applied for identifying Twitter accounts are the following:

- A candidate's first and last name had to be present.
- In addition, at least one of the following additional conditions had to be satisfied:

(1) Their political affiliation was mentioned in their Twitter profile.
(2) They tweeted about their political affiliation in the analyzed time period.

The identification of candidates' Facebook pages was similar. We manually searched for public Facebook pages of all 873 candidates. The identification criteria for Facebook pages and profiles are the same as the above ones for Twitter, only applied to Facebook.

Table 8. Media sample.

Medium type	Title	Geographic focus	Description
Television	*TalkTäglich*	Regional	Daily political talk show
	SonnTalk	Regional	Weekly political talk show
	ZüriNews	Regional	Daily news show
	Tagesschau	National	Daily news show
	10 vor 10	National	Daily news show
	Arena	National	Weekly political talk show
Radio	*Echo der Zeit*	National	Daily news show
	Regionaljournal	Regional	Daily news show
	Rendez-vous	National	Daily news show
Newspaper	*Tages-Anzeiger*	National	Daily newspaper
	Neue Zürcher Zeitung	National	Daily newspaper
	Blick	National	Daily newspaper
	Blick am Abend	National & regional	Daily newspaper
	20 Minuten	National & regional	Daily newspaper
	SonntagsZeitung	National	Weekly newspaper
	NZZ am Sonntag	National	Weekly newspaper
	SonntagsBlick	National	Weekly newspaper
	ürcher Oberländer	Regional	Daily newspaper
	Zürcher Unterländer	Regional	Daily newspaper
	Zürichsee-Zeitung	Regional	Daily newspaper
	Der Landbote	Regional	Daily newspaper

Note. The newspapers "Blick am Abend" and "20 Minuten" are distributed nationally, but in regional editions. We analyzed the Zurich editions in our sample.

(1) **C Posterior distributions of the estimates**

(2) **C.1 Posterior distributions of the estimates of the first modelal Media**

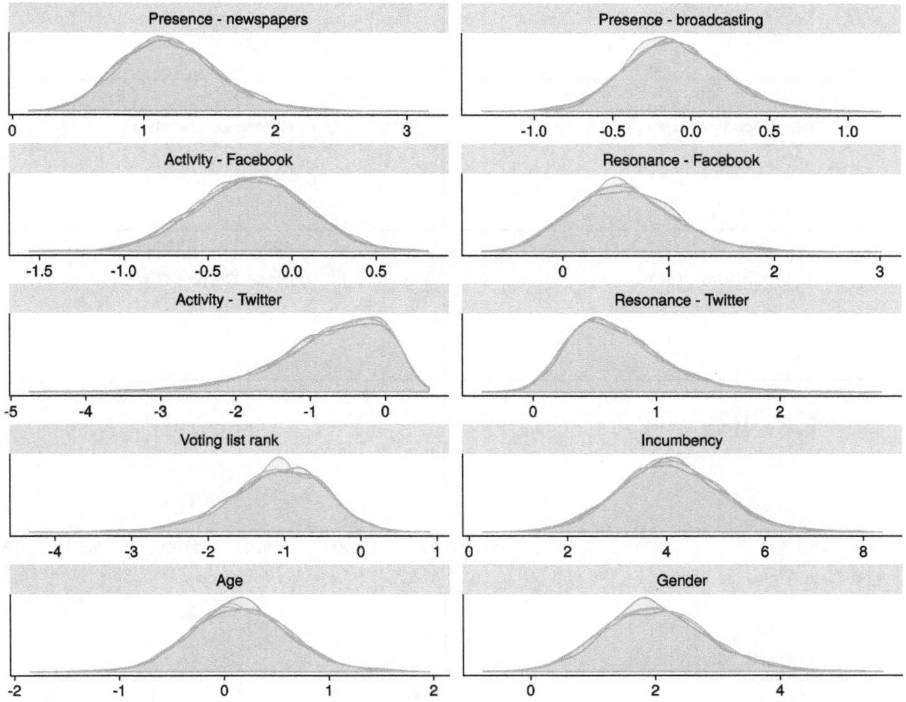

Figure 2. Posterior probability densities of the parameter estimates for the first model. The dependent variable is the dichotomous election outcome of being elected or not. Note: The different colors represent the four sampling chains; the better the overlap of the four chains, the better the model convergence. The distribution shows the relative proportion of samples that estimate the effect at some value, as depicted on the x-axis of the parameter estimates.

(3) **C.2 Posterior distributions of the estimates of the second model**

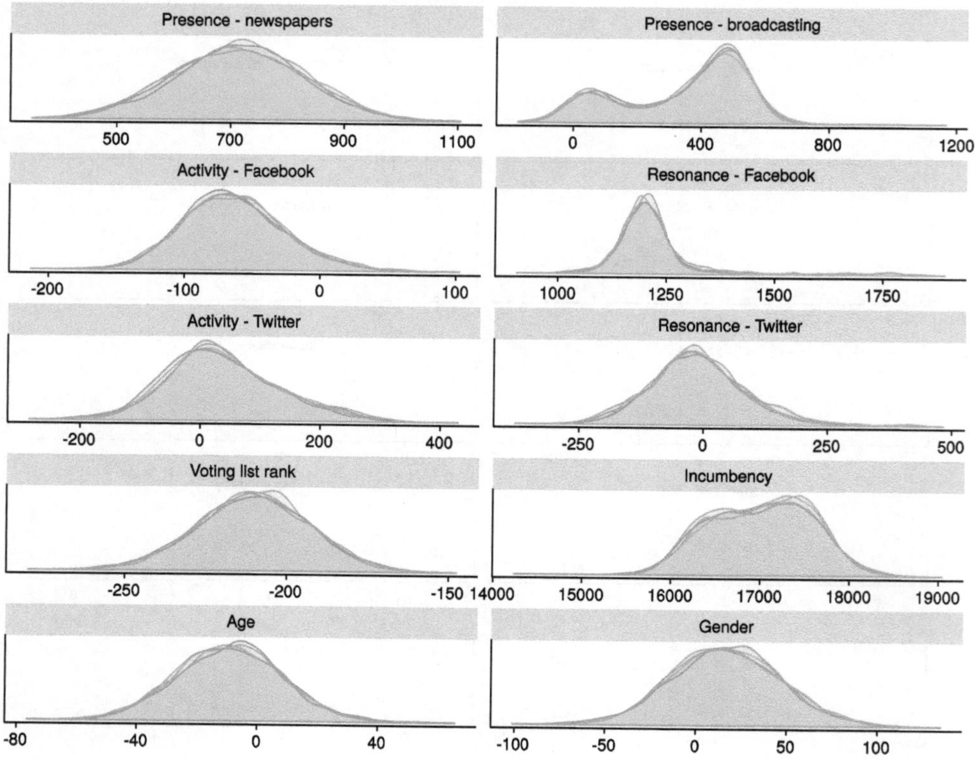

Figure 3. Posterior probability densities of the parameter estimates for the second model. The dependent variable is the total number of votes. Note: The different colors represent the four sampling chains; the better the overlap of the four chains, the better the model convergence. The distribution shows the relative proportion of samples that estimate the effect at some value, as depicted on the x-axis of the parameter estimates.

(4) **C.3 Posterior distributions of the estimates of the third model**

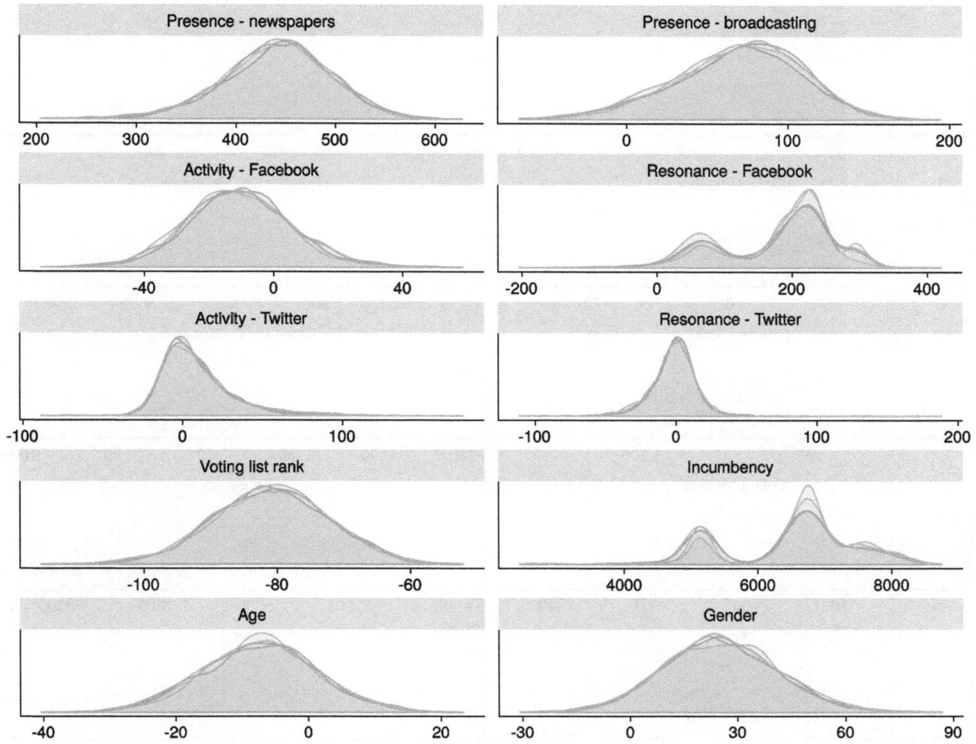

Figure 4. Posterior probability densities of the parameter estimates for the third model. The dependent variable is the number of panachage votes. Note: The different colors represent the four sampling chains; the better the overlap of the four chains, the better the model convergence. The distribution shows the relative proportion of samples that estimate the effect at some value, as depicted on the x-axis of the parameter estimates. The distributions for resonance on Facebook and for incumbency suggest a bimodal effect.

(5) **C.4 Posterior distributions of the estimates of the fourth model**

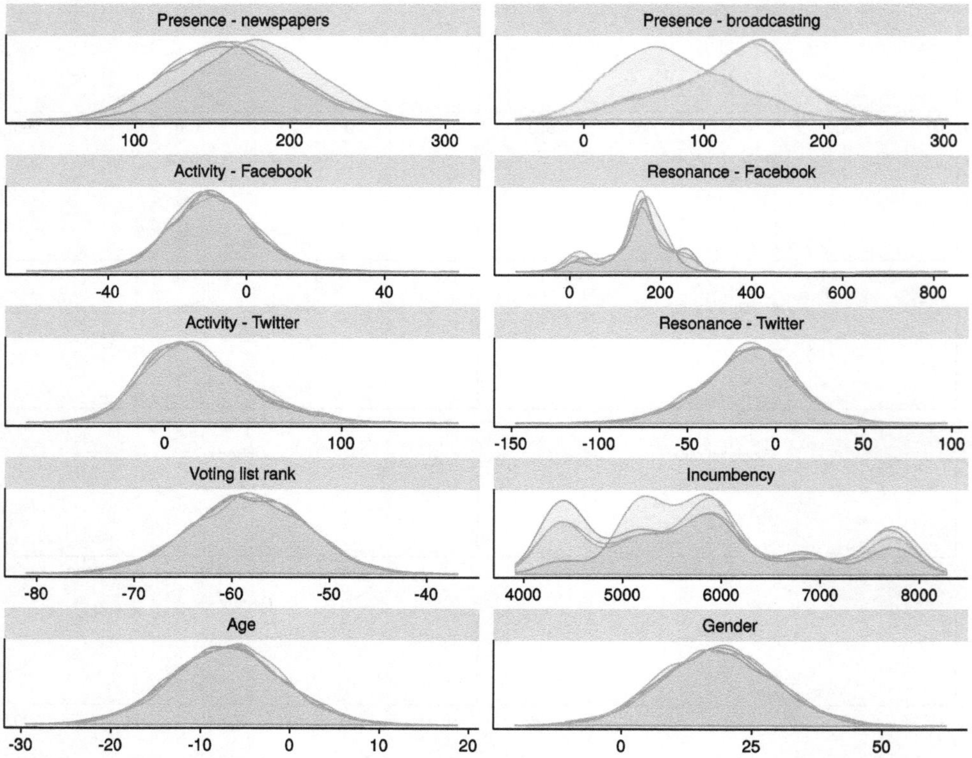

Figure 5. Posterior probability densities of the parameter estimates for the fourth model. The dependent variable is the number of cumulation votes. Note: The different colors represent the four sampling chains; the better the overlap of the four chains, the better the model convergence. The distribution shows the relative proportion of samples that estimate the effect at some value, as depicted on the x-axis of the parameter estimates. Presence in broadcasting has one divergent chain, which potentially suggests a bimodal effect. The distribution for incumbency is multimodal. The general range of the effect, between around 4000 and 8000 votes, is plausible.

(6) D Comparison of frequentist and Bayesian parameter estimates

Table 9. Comparison of frequentist and Bayesian estimates for model one, with being elected into office as the dependent variable.

Parameter	Frequentist	Bayesian (Bernoulli)
Presence—broadcasting	−0.14	−0.10
Presence—newspapers	1.04	1.19
Activity—Facebook	−0.23	−0.24
Resonance—Facebook	0.38	0.58
Activity—Twitter	−0.04	−0.72
Resonance—Twitter	0.31	0.68
Voting list rank	−1.00	−1.10
Incumbency	3.87	4.08
Age	0.16	0.15
Gender (female)	1.99	2.02

Note. The distribution in the brackets is the sampling distribution used in the Bayesian model.

Table 10. Comparison of frequentist and Bayesian estimates for model two, with the total amount of votes as the dependent variable.

Parameter	Frequentist	Bayesian (normal)	Bayesian (student's *t*)
Presence—broadcasting	−269.14	−266.58	345.04
Presence—newspapers	3,839.01	3,842.17	714.69
Activity—Facebook	6.09	6.77	−63.73
Resonance—Facebook	733.75	735.72	1,213.55
Activity—Twitter	−190.47	−189.77	38.35
Resonance—Twitter	126.38	125.53	−9.48
Voting list rank	−757.44	−757.99	−210.21
Incumbency	10,936.72	10,879.96	17,012.03
Age	−6.70	−4.24	−9.21
Gender (female)	429.35	430.84	16.88

Note. The distributions in the brackets are the sampling distribution used in the Bayesian models.

Table 11. Comparison of frequentist and Bayesian estimates for model three, with the amount of panachage votes as the dependent variable.

Parameter	Frequentist	Bayesian (normal)	Bayesian (student's *t*)
Presence—broadcasting	274.86	276.52	69.28
Presence—newspapers	1,630.37	1,629.64	441.39
Activity—Facebook	472.87	473.11	−10.50
Resonance—Facebook	25.15	23.70	178.21
Activity—Twitter	12.78	12.72	8.81
Resonance—Twitter	77.32	77.57	−1.30
Voting list rank	−205.69	−206.10	−80.82
Incumbency	7,105.07	7,091.28	6,499.10
Age	5.60	5.84	−7.43
Gender (female)	263.01	264.24	25.15

Note. The distributions in the brackets are the sampling distribution used in the Bayesian models.

Table 12. Comparison of frequentist and Bayesian estimates for model four, with the amount of cumulation votes as the dependent variable.

Parameter	Frequentist	Bayesian (normal)	Bayesian (student's *t*)
Presence—broadcasting	−536.22	−536.51	113.40
Presence—newspapers	2,189.78	2,191.01	164.88
Activity—Facebook	−456.73	−455.90	−9.49
Resonance—Facebook	700.39	699.74	149.69
Activity—Twitter	−194.24	−193.17	17.97
Resonance—Twitter	34.42	34.39	−14.80
Voting list rank	−564.14	−564.45	−58.42
Incumbency	3,739.42	3,727.27	5,811.99
Age	−1.97	−4.44	−6.92
Gender (female)	190.58	190.94	18.64

Note. The distributions in the brackets are the sampling distribution used in the Bayesian models.

In this section, we compare frequentist and Bayesian parameter estimates. More specifically, we present the frequentist point estimates estimated with the R package lme4 in tabular form with the estimates of the four Bayesian models presented in our study. In addition, for models two to four, we present the mean Bayesian estimates for our models two to four, but with the normal distribution as a sampling distribution instead of student's *t* distribution. The frequentist point estimates and the Bayesian mean estimates using the normal distribution are quite similar to one another, whereas the estimates of the models with student's *t* distribution are slightly different (smaller, for the most part). This demonstrates the advantage of student's *t* distribution for data that contains outliers.

E Election results

Figure 6 is a summary of the party-level election results.

When David and Goliath campaign online: The effects of digital media use during electoral campaigns on vote for small parties

Carol Galais and Ana Sofía Cardenal

ABSTRACT
Challenger parties might have an advantage online compared to mainstream parties, since digital technologies increase their visibility at a low cost and connect them with niche audiences. Previous research has examined this phenomenon focusing on parties' use of the Internet, yet we need to focus on voters' behavior to quantify the effect. To this end, we use data covering 21 national and regional elections from four countries. Our results confirm that digital media use during the campaign boosts uncertainty about one's own vote choice and, ultimately, increases the chances to change one's voting intention from mainstream to small parties.

Introduction

Almost 20 years after concluding that the emergence of the Internet will not have major effects on politics, but just reproduce "politics as usual" (Gibson & Ward, 1998; Margolis & Resnick, 2000; Margolis, Resnick, & Levy, 2003), some authors still claim that digital media can seriously alter the political landscape. A growing strand of the literature examines the effects of digital media on electoral politics, and more particularly, on the fortune of challenger parties (i.e., Gibson & McAllister, 2015; Lusoli, 2005). According to this perspective, challengers might have an advantage online given that digital technologies are creating opportunities for small contenders to increase their visibility (equalization effect). Moreover, an increasing number and plurality of media might prompt political fragmentation, connecting small parties to niche audiences and undermining the appeal of mainstream parties (fragmentation effect).

However, studies examining the impact of digital media on challengers (or "small" parties) generally focus on the supply side of the question; most pay attention to parties' use of digital technologies for campaigning, with some also examining how campaigning online affects the vote (D'Alessio, 1997; Gibson & McAllister, 2006, 2015; Sudulich & Wall, 2010), and few focusing solely on audience behavior, that is, on how using digital technologies for political information affects the vote (Balcells & Cardenal, 2013; Lusoli, 2005). In this paper, we follow the latter less-traveled road to ask whether digital technologies affect the electoral fortunes of challengers from the demand perspective. More particularly, we ask whether digital media contribute to electoral fragmentation by moving citizens' vote from mainstream to third parties thanks to the equalizing effect of the Internet.

Our first contribution is to address the causal mechanisms connecting digital media and vote for challenger parties by relying on some of the ideas and expectations drawn from the equalization hypothesis. To this end, we put to empirical test the role of two potential mediators for the effects of digital media use during the campaign, both connected to the alleged advantage that small parties have online. The first one is the perceived electoral chances of small parties; the second, voters' indecision caused by exposure to online political information.

Besides opening the black box of the causal mechanisms that link digital media use and electoral fragmentation, this study presents a series of methodological innovations. First, most previous research has examined the effect of the Internet on

Color versions of one or more of the figures in the article can be found online at http://www.tandfonline.com/WITP.

the vote focusing on single-case studies. This is one of the first studies we know of that tests the fragmentation potential of the Internet on the vote using a cross-country study that explores digital media impact on a variety of electoral contexts. In this respect, this research uses data from the Making Electoral Democracy Work project to test the effects of Internet use on small parties' chances with regional and national data from 21 elections held in four countries (nine regions).

Our second methodological contribution to the study of digital media effects on electoral competition is the use of individual panel data to measure fragmentation at the individual level. We compare voting intention in pre-electoral surveys with vote reported in post-electoral surveys. We investigate whether vote for small parties or, more precisely, voting intention change from mainstream to small parties are related, ceteris paribus, to digital media use during the campaign. Our results confirm that digital media use benefits small parties and that off-line media use harms small parties while benefitting big ones. We also find that some of the effect of digital media use during electoral campaigns travels through the two causal mechanisms suggested, particularly boosting uncertainty about one's own vote choice.

Digital technologies and vote for third parties

Two decades after the publication of the first studies on the general effects of the Internet on politics, this research field concluded that its impact was more modest than expected initially. Since then, the broad question on the political effects of the Internet has spawned several subfields aimed at better understanding the subtleties of digital media use effect. One of these research fields focuses on electoral competition, and more particularly, on the implications for the fate of small parties in competitive democracies.

Indeed, there is currently a lively debate on the electoral consequences of digital technologies for the performance of mainstream and challenger parties, with some scholars pointing to a potential advantage for small parties or challengers (the equalization hypothesis) and others pointing to a persisting dominance of mainstream parties (the normalization hypothesis).

Scholars pointing to an advantage of small parties online tend to highlight transaction-cost reduction, network effects, and media fragmentation. First, small parties may benefit from the dramatic reduction in transaction costs associated with Web-mediated communications (Benoit & Laver, 2003; Hill & Hughes, 1999; Lupia & Sin, 2003). For a start, once a candidate or a party site is created, large quantities of issue content can be added for little additional cost (Benoit & Laver, 2003; Xenos & Foot, 2005). This makes this environment accessible to a broad range of political actors, including independent candidates and third parties (Xenos & Foot, 2005). Digital technologies thus allow Web presence to all political organizations regardless of monetary investments (Mazzoleni & Schulz, 1999). In addition to lowering the barriers of entry, digital technologies allow campaigns to circumvent the gatekeepers responsible for filtering and agenda-setting in traditional broadcast and print media (Hill & Hughes, 1999; Norris, 2001; Xenos & Foot, 2005).

Second, small parties may also take advantage of the rise of Web 2.0. Unlike Web 1.0, these new technologies would make even more affordable campaigning online for small parties because most infrastructure is already available through interactive platforms (Strandberg, 2013). Also, as large numbers of people share political information with family and friends through social media (Copeland & Römmele, 2013), Web 2.0 technologies allow for network effects to take place, that is, the value of a site increasing as the use by others increases (Hamilton, 2005). This might especially benefit minor parties because their supporters tend to be more active online (i.e., Gibson & McAllister, 2015; Samuel-Azran, Yarchi, & Wolfsfeld, 2015; Xu, 2015; for counter-examples, however, see Larsson & Moe, 2014; Klinger, 2013). Both lower transition costs and network effects may help increase the visibility of third parties relative to mainstream parties online, and lead to expectations of a more equal playing field in online electoral competition—the so-called *equalization hypothesis.*

Finally, small parties may take advantage of the fragmentation of news outlets brought about by digital media. The number of media outlets resulting from the digital revolution has forced media to offer specialized messages and carve new niche markets (Coe et al., 2008; Greyes, 2011; Hamilton, 2005; Mullainathan & Shleifer, 2005). This may pave the way for new cleavages to appear or reinforce, dragging citizens from mainstream politics. As a result, issue-oriented groups and small parties take advantage of this situation to send tailor-made campaign messages, break official narrative, gain momentum, and erode the electoral bases of mainstream parties (Layman, Carsey, & Horowitz 2006; Masket 2009).

In contrast, observers pointing to the dominance of mainstream parties generally highlight unequal resources, the centralized nature of networks, and the dominance of traditional media online. Proponents of the "big-party-dominance" thesis tend to see the disparity in resources between big and small organizations as the main reason for normalization in the online domain (Margolis & Resnick, 2000; Margolis et al., 2003; Margolis, Resnick, & Tu, 1997; Margolis, Resnick, & Wolfe, 1999). Indeed, big organizations have been found to have the best Web sites, and their sites, to concentrate most links (Gonzalez-Bailón, 2009). Some also point to the hierarchical nature of networks; recent research finds that far from promoting horizontal relations as early studies contented (e.g., Castells, 1996), networks are highly centralized structures, where most content is produced and consumed by a minority of users (González-Bailón & Wang, 2016). This centralized and hierarchical nature of networks would tend to benefit organizations with the greatest resources (Gonzalez-Bailón, 2009).

In addition, current research shows that networks do not favor the viral diffusion of messages; although networks have the potential to create informational cascades, studies find that most messages die in the vicinity of the person that initiates them (Borge-Holthoefer, Baños, González-Bailón, & Moreno, 2013), making successful informational cascades something exceptional. Finally, despite increasing fragmentation of digital media, studies find that traditional media continue to play a dominant role in the online news domain (e.g., Brossard & Scheufele, 2013). This would reduce opportunities for small parties to exploit the fragmentation of digital media and grant big parties still considerable visibility online.

Although this debate calls for studies examining digital media effects on electoral outcomes, most studies to date have looked at these effects from a supply-side perspective, focusing on parties' use of digital technologies during the electoral campaign. Yet if one goes back to early discussions about the electoral effects of digital technologies, it seems clear that the real test of these effects is not primarily on whether parties gain prominence online but whether this greater visibility has any real impact on the vote. In the words of Margolis, Resnick, and Wolfe: "the critical question still is: What impact, if any, will a minor party's relatively greater Web presence have on that party's political fortunes over time?" Unfortunately, their own answer to this question is that "Until we collect more data, we can only offer speculative answers to this question" (Margolis et al., 1999, p. 43).

Among studies looking at the effects of digital media on electoral competition, a few match supply and demand by studying the influence of online campaign on parties' vote share (D'Alessio, 1997; Gibson & McAllister, 2006, 2015; Sudulich & Wall, 2010). Others have provided some "demand-side" evidence, showing how the use of these sites by (small) party supporters may be affecting these parties' fortunes in the ballot box (Gibson & McAllister, 2015; Samuel-Azran et al., 2015; Ward, 2011; Xu, 2016). Although these are important contributions, Margolis et al.'s warning still applies, as these studies focus on single cases and the evidence they provide is thus limited and, in some cases, even anecdotal.

In spite of the limitations affecting this strand of research, we follow its previous works to derive expectations concerning the effect of digital technologies on vote for small parties. We expect changes in the structure of costs brought about by digital technologies to increase small parties' relative visibility and this, in turn, to shift some of the vote in their favor. Our first hypothesis is thus a general, optimistic one on the effects of digital media use on party system fragmentation by enhancing the chances of small parties. Hence:

H1: Exposure to webs of political content during the electoral campaign will increase the probability of voting for small parties.

Even if we expect a generally positive effect of digital media use on vote for small parties, it is not really clear how small parties' hypothetical advantage online translates into votes. Previous studies on equalization, by focusing mainly on the supply side of this hypothesis (i.e., parties' campaigning online), do not fully make explicit or test the manner in which this advantage is delivered.

One possibility by which small parties' alleged greater visibility online may affect the vote is suggested by studies looking at the demand side: they find that use of digital media during elections increases uncertainty. For example, Sudulich, Wall, and Baccini (2015) find that using the Internet during the campaign makes voters significantly more likely to consider multiple parties as alternatives. Also, in their study of party Web sites' audience during the 2000 U.S. presidential campaign, Bimber and Davis (2003) found that around half of the people visiting third-party Web sites or candidates had not yet decided their vote. In contrast, among the audience of big-parties' Web sites, the undecided represented a bit more than 20% (p. 111). Because digital media contains detailed information about minor alternatives that are invisible in the traditional media, browsing through digital media during the campaign might put voters with specific, minority preferences in contact with parties that match their inclinations, making them hesitate between their usual mainstream choice and a new, challenging one. In fact, previous works have proven that online media allow voters to learn about other parties that are not visible in the off-line media (Bimber & Davis, 2003; Margolis et al., 1999; Samuel-Azran et al., 2015).

Another possibility by which the alleged greater visibility of small parties online might affect their electoral fortunes is implicit in the equalization hypothesis. According to this rationale, small parties are more present online than off-line. This stronger online presence would make voters perceive them as "bigger" and more viable than they really are, therefore overestimating their electoral chances. Nevertheless, this remains to be tested. We therefore explore the following indirect effects. We argue that the use of digital media during the campaign might cause two effects that are previous to vote choice: first, to get in touch with previously unknown alternatives that may match voters' preferences better than their initial choices, creating doubts about the voting decision; second, to perceive higher chances of success for these minor—but comparatively very visible—parties, believing that they are more viable (and worthy of voting for them) than they really are.

This would lead to our last two hypotheses:

H2. *Indecision about one's vote choice will mediate the effects of digital media. Because of digital media consumption during the campaign, individuals will be more likely to consider multiple alternatives and to become less sure about their initial choice. This indecision will benefit small parties, resulting in higher chances to switch initial vote intention in their favor.*

H3: *Perceived increased chances of small parties will mediate the effects of digital media. As a result of consuming digital media during the campaign, individuals will overestimate the chances of small parties and, ultimately, will vote for them with a higher probability.*

Research design and methods

We have decided to address the effects of digital media use on the fate of small parties by tackling individuals' voting intention change during the electoral campaign. In order to tap this phenomenon we resorted to a series of pre and post-electoral surveys conducted in 21 elections held in nine regions within four countries (Canada, France, Germany, and Spain). These surveys were carried out in the framework of the Making Electoral Democracy Work (MEDW) project (Blais, 2010). The surveys are online quota-based polls that guarantee the representativeness of the regional samples of the population under study regarding age, gender, education, and region. The study gathers elections held at the regional, national, and European level (when available).[1]

Table 1 shows the main characteristics of the case studies in which this research relies. All the surveys were conducted between 2011 and 2015. For some of the countries (i.e. Germany, Spain) we have surveys covering the regional, national, and European levels, while for Canada we lack the European level and for France the regional level.

Table 1. Elections, main parties, and contextual factors considered in this research.

					ENEP	
	Year	Two main parties (highest vote shares in the previous election)	Seat criteria (Norris, 2003) First two parties > 20% seats	Electoral system	Current election	Previous election
GERMANY						
Lower Saxony						
Federal	2013	CDU, SPD	Yes	MMPR	3.43	4.30
State	2013	CDU, SPD	Yes	MMPR	3.79	3.44
European	2014	CDU, SPD	—	SD-Party list—PR	4.53	4.57
Bavaria						
Federal	2013	CSU, SPD	Yes	MMPR	3.38	4.05
State	2013	CSU, SPD	Yes	MMPR	3.48	4.02
European	2014	CSU, SPD	—	SD-Party list—PR	4.65	4.57
CANADA						
Ontario						
Federal	2015	CP, NDP	Yes	FPTP	2.84	3.05
Provincial	2011	OLP, PCP	Yes	FPTP	3.13	3.19
Quebec						
Federal	2015	NPD, BC	No	FPTP	3.88	3.49
Provincial	2011	QLP, PQ	Yes	FPTP	3.61	3.04
British Columbia						
Federal	2015	CP, NDP	Yes	FPTP	3.48	2.97
SPAIN				FPTP		
Catalonia						
National	2011	CiU, PSC/PSOE	No	Party list—PR: Closed lists	4.72	3.52
Regional	2012	CiU, PSC	Yes	Party list—PR: Closed lists	5.96	4.76
European	2014	PP, PSOE	—	SD-Party list—PR	7.10	3.00
Madrid						
National	2011	PP, PSOE	Yes	Party list—PR: Closed lists	2.90	2.48
Regional	2015	PP, PSOE	Yes	Party list—PR: Closed lists	4.43	2.86
European	2014	PP, PSOE	—	SD-Party list—PR	7.10	3.00
FRANCE						
Île-France						
Legislative	2012	UMP, PS	Yes	Two round system	5.37	4.42
European	2014	UMP, PS	—	Party list-PR	6.74	6.68
Provence						
Legilslative	2012	UMP, PS	Yes	Two round system	5.37	4.42
European	2014	UMP, PS	—	Party list—PR	6.74	6.68

Key: CDU: Christian Democratic Union; SPD: Social Democratic Party; CSU: Christian Social Union (Bavaria); CP: Conservative Party; NDP: New Democratic Party; OLP: Ontario Liberal Party; PCP: Progressive Conservative Party; BC: Bloc Québecois; QLP: Quebec Liberal Party; PQ: Party Québecois; PSOE: Partido Socialista Obrero Español; ICV/IU: Iniciativa per Catalunya-Els Verds-Esquerra Unida i Alternativa; CiU: Convergència i Unió; PSC: Partit dels Socialistes de Catalunya; PP: Partido Popular; ENEP: effective number of parties; MMPR: mixed-member proportional representation; FPTP: first past the post; PR: proportional system.

The electoral systems vary across and within countries, including mixed-member proportional representation (e.g., Germany at the federal/national and the state/regional levels), first-past-the-post (Canada), proportional representation (e.g., Spain) and two-round system (French legislative elections). This results in a considerable amount of variation regarding the party system fragmentation, as the last column shows. The effective number of parties (ENEP) is clearly lower in plurality systems (Canada, about 3) than in proportional systems, such as Spain or France, particularly at the European level. This variation suggests that context features must be considered in our analyses, so they do not bias our results.

In each pre-electoral survey respondents were asked to indicate what was their vote intention. In the post-electoral survey they were asked about their actual voting behavior, as well as a series of retrospective questions regarding the electoral campaign. Hence, we will use variation between the pre- and the post-election to operationalize the dependent variable, and the post-electoral survey to operationalize the attention and exposure to political information during the electoral campaign.

As for the dependent variable, our goal was to tap the change between the will to vote for a party and changing one's mind during the campaign. For this, we first identified the two main parties running in each of the 21 elections that we have characterized as "big," as opposed to the rest. The distinction between "big" and "small" parties is consistent with De Vries and Hobolt's (2012) differentiation between mainstream parties, main opposition parties, and challenger parties. Both mainstream and main opposition parties alternate in power, a reason to consider them "big" in a particular context. In our case, we consider a party "big" when it came first or second in the previous election, taking into account its vote share (see column 3 in Table 1). We focus on the share of votes and not on the share of seats (see Norris, 2003) so we can compare between plurality and proportional systems, and between levels of elections.[2]

We used this classification to compare voting intentions in the pre-electoral survey with the reported vote for the individuals who took the second round of each study. This way we got a four-category dependent variable: (a) stick to big parties, (b) stick to small parties, (c) change to big parties, and (d) change to small parties. The last category is obviously the one we are most interested in, as it taps any possible vote fragmentation effect due to online media use during electoral campaigns. In our estimations, the reference category for the dependent variable is "stick to big parties," which includes those who voted for one of the two biggest parties they wanted to vote initially and also those who switched from the first to the second party, and vice versa. All individuals claiming that they were not voting (pre-electoral) or who reported having abstained or casted a blank vote were coded as missing observations. Our final N for the dependent variable (once the data set is weighted; see below) is 11,176 individuals.

Figure 1 depicts the distribution of our dependent variable. The largest category consists of individuals who have stuck to big parties. About 51% of the weighted sample falls into this category. The next one gathers all those who have stuck to a myriad of small parties (36%), followed by those who changed their mind and finally voted for a big (8%) or a small party (5%). As the graph below shows (see Figure 1), the proportion of those who changed in favor of a small party is slightly higher in France (9%); while Germany stands out for a greater fidelity to "big" parties.

The variables tapping attention and exposure to political information during the campaign covered both off-line (traditional) media, and online (digital) media. A battery asked the amount of attention paid "to news about the election" on television, newspapers and on the radio. The

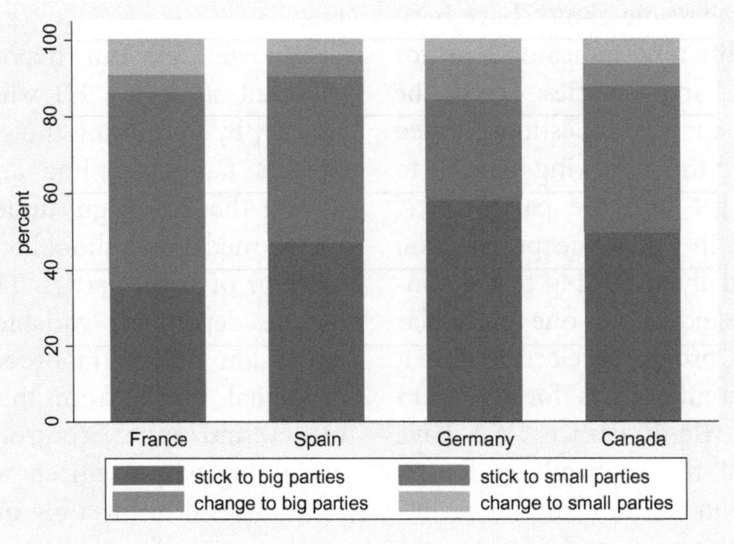

Figure 1. Distribution of the dependent variable, by country.

respondent could select a value between a 0 and 10 scale where the poles were labeled as "No attention at all" and "A lot of attention." These questions have been added and averaged to build a scale of campaign attention using off-line, traditional media. The scale ranges from 0 to 1, the maximum value gauging the maximum level of attention for all of the three traditional media.

Three more questions referred to attention and use of digital media during the campaign. The first is a question on "attention paid to news about the election" on the Internet. It has the same wording and values as the three questions aforementioned referring to off-line media, and it will be used to control for the effects of campaign attention online. For the sake of simplicity in the interpretation of the multivariate estimations, we have rescaled these questions to range between 0 and 1. Two additional dichotomous questions asked about the use of two digital resources "to find out about the election": a party or candidate Web site and "some other Web site with political content." Given the parallel wording of the last two questions, they have been added and recoded to build a scale on digital media use during the campaign, which takes three values: 0 if none of the digital supports have been used during the campaign, 0.5 if only one of them were used, and 1 if both were used. This scale constitutes the main independent variable of our study, tapping on exposure to digital media during the campaign.[3]

Perceptions about the chances of small parties and indecision about one's vote choice have been captured using three different indicators. As for the perceived chances of small parties, one of the MEDW pre-electoral surveys questions asked "How likely is each of the following parties to gain enough votes to get into the parliament?" The question, included in 18 of the pre-election surveys, varied substantially according to the context, in that it only asked about one particular party in Ontario's 2011 provincial election, but it asked about nine different parties for the 2014 European elections in Île-de-France. We have added and averaged all the probabilities for all the parties asked within an election, and the resulting scale has values between 0 and 1, the maximum value pointing to the maximum probability that all the relevant extra-parliamentary parties get into the parliament in that election.

As for indecision, the measure refers to individual's doubts about his/her own choice. Respondents were asked about the difficulties that the individual faced to make up her mind. The question, included in the post-electoral survey, asked "did you consider the possibility of voting for another party/candidate?" Individuals answering affirmatively are considered to be in doubt before casting their vote.

Other relevant variables that will be included in the analyses include basic sociodemographic controls as well as interest in politics in general, interest in the campaign, and strength of party identification. Also, and bearing in mind that the MEDW data gather information for very different types of elections, we include a control for the level of the election, whether it is a regional, a national, or a European one. Indeed, according to the second-order election theory (Reif & Schmitt, 1980), citizens usually take advantage of less important elections to show their true colors, hence voting less strategically. Because they are therefore less prone to vote for big parties than in national (first-order) elections, it seems reasonable to control for the saliency of the election. Similarly, we include dummies for countries to account for contextual variables (e.g., electoral systems, level of fragmentation) that might facilitate or hinder change to small parties and affect other relevant variables, such as the estimated chances of extra-parliamentary parties to obtain seats.

We will test our hypotheses following three different strategies. H1 will be tested straightforwardly, by examining the significance of the coefficients tapping online and off-line media use during the campaign, under the assumption that online media uses should boost change and fidelity in favor of small parties. The nature and measure of the dependent variable require multinomial regression models in order to isolate the effects of digital media from the effects of traditional media and other controls when it comes to explaining why a citizen would vote for a small party instead of for a big one.

The rest of our hypotheses refer to causal mechanisms and conditional effects. Our second hypothesis refers to the possibility that the perceived chances of small parties mediate the effects of online media on the final vote decision. The third hypothesis specifies the same kind of conditional effects for indecision as a mediator. This implies that the perceived chances of small parties and indecision are also allegedly effects of digital media use (see Sudulich et al., 2015), and hence, are also dependent variables affected by digital media use, like the ultimate decision to vote. Although there are several ways to put mediation effects to empirical test, we will use a structural equation model (SEM) to quantify and test the significance of the indirect effects, that is, of the effects of digital media that are actually mediated by the perceived chances of small parties and indecision.[4] The SEM estimation will therefore test a multiple mediation model in which the perceived viability of (very) small parties and indecision mediate exposure to digital media during the campaign.

A final note concerns the nature of the data. Because the survey samples are designed to be representative of each one of the nine regions included, model errors for individuals from the same region may be correlated, which constitutes a violation of regression assumptions that can lead to small standard errors, narrow confidence intervals, and misleading significant coefficients. Hence, our estimations take into account the structure of the data by clustering the standard errors by region. Also, respecting the survey design, we have applied a weight that guarantees that the surveys are indeed representative in terms of sex, age, education, region, mother tongue, and voting behavior.

Table 2. Multinomial logistic estimation for vote change and campaign media use.

	(1)	(2)	(3)
	Stick to small parties	Change to big	Change to small
Female	−0.04	0.13	0.06
	(0.07)	(0.09)	(0.13)
Education	−0.18	−0.01	0.04
	(0.27)	(0.18)	(0.34)
Age	−0.63*	−0.92**	−1.04**
	(0.32)	(0.20)	(0.31)
Strength partyID	−0.75*	−1.02**	−0.84**
	(0.29)	(0.23)	(0.18)
Pol. interest	0.01	−0.06	0.55+
	(0.31)	(0.47)	(0.31)
Interest campaign	−0.08	−0.81**	−0.60*
	(0.34)	(0.18)	(0.27)
Election attention off-line media	−1.00**	0.17	−0.69*
	(0.21)	(0.30)	(0.24)
Election attention: Internet	0.06	−0.16	0.02
	(0.10)	(0.22)	(0.29)
Consultation of digital media	0.64**	0.28	0.63**
	(0.17)	(0.19)	(0.18)
Election level: Regional	0.81*	0.46*	0.08
	(0.29)	(0.19)	(0.25)
Election level: European	1.35**	−0.08	0.25
	(0.18)	(0.24)	(0.20)
France	1.54**	0.54	1.36*
	(0.42)	(0.52)	(0.56)
Spain	0.88+	−0.16	0.16
	(0.46)	(0.50)	(0.58)
Germany	0.05	0.52	0.26
	(0.33)	(0.47)	(0.52)
_cons	−0.60+	−1.18*	−1.79*
	(0.34)	(0.54)	(0.67)
Pseudo R-Squared	.08		
N	9,678		

Notes. Standard errors in parentheses. The reference category for the dependent variable is "stick to big parties." Canada is the reference category for countries. National is the reference category for level of elections.
$+p < .1$. $*p < .05$. $**p < .01$.

Results

Table 2 presents the results of estimating the consistency or change between vote intention (wave 1) and voting behavior (wave 2). Only four control variables show significant effects on the dependent variable: older people are less prone to change their initial choice of party or to stick to small ones than to stick to a big party (the reference category). The stronger the party identification, the greater the loyalty toward big parties. Also, interest in the campaign makes voters less prone to change their initial choice than to stick with a big party. Finally, the effect of the level of election is partially consistent with the second-order election theory. Regional and especially European elections enhance loyalty to small parties significantly more than loyalty to big parties.

As for the main variables of our interest, election attention through off-line media reduces the chances of sticking or switching to small parties, as compared to sticking with big ones. Election attention through the Internet, in turn, does not play any significant role on any voting behavior. Finally, use of political Web sites during the campaign boosts the chances of vote switching and of sticking to small parties as compared to the chances of sticking with big parties—from which we can deduce that online media use is detrimental to "big parties" and enhances party fragmentation. This is in line with our first hypothesis.

Computing the marginal effects of off-line and digital media use during the campaign helps us understand the magnitude of their impact.[5] Going from no election attention at all to maximum election attention through off-line media causes a 17% increase in the probabilities of sticking to big parties, and a 4% increase in the case of change in favor of big parties. On the other hand, it causes a 19% decrease and a 1% decrease in the likelihood of sticking and changing to small parties, respectively.

Conversely, moving from not consulting digital media at all to maximum use during the campaign causes a 13% decrease in the likelihood of sticking to big parties, and has no significant effect on the likelihood of changing vote intention for big parties. In the case of small parties, maximum variation in the use of digital media during the campaign causes a 11% increase in the likelihood of sticking to small parties, and a 2% increase when it comes to changing vote intention for a small party. The magnitude of the effects is remarkable—even in the case of change for a small party, given that only 5% of the sample fits into this category—and confirms our first hypothesis. Not only does digital media use during the campaign benefit small parties, but it also hampers the chances of big parties, and this effect is practically the opposite for off-line media attention.

Our next analysis concerns mediation. The purpose of this analysis is twofold: first, to determine whether some of the effect of digital media use during the electoral campaign on vote for small parties travels through any of these mediators; second, to determine how important these indirect effects are.[6] Figures 2 and 3 present the results of a generalized structural equation model that accounts for the indirect effects of digital media through our indicators of indecision and perceived chances of (very) small parties. This multiple mediation model includes all the controls and specifications already presented (see Table 2), and was estimated using maximum likelihood method and equation wise deletion of missing cases, which explains why the number of observations is higher. For the sake of clarity in the interpretation of the results, each figure only displays a set of indirect effects, but because they spawn from the same estimation, most information—from direct effects to total indirect effects—is redundant[7].

Figure 2 reproduces the section of the model that puts to empirical test the mediator role of having "doubted between two parties."[8] The mediator variable is tapped using a retrospective

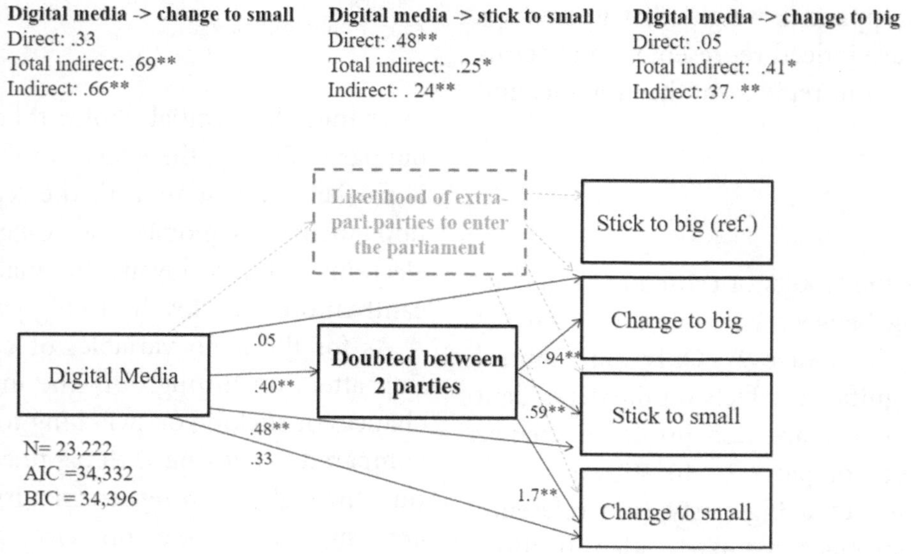

Figure 2. Doubted between two parties as a mediator. Structural equation model.
+$p < .1$. *$p < .05$. **$p < .01$.

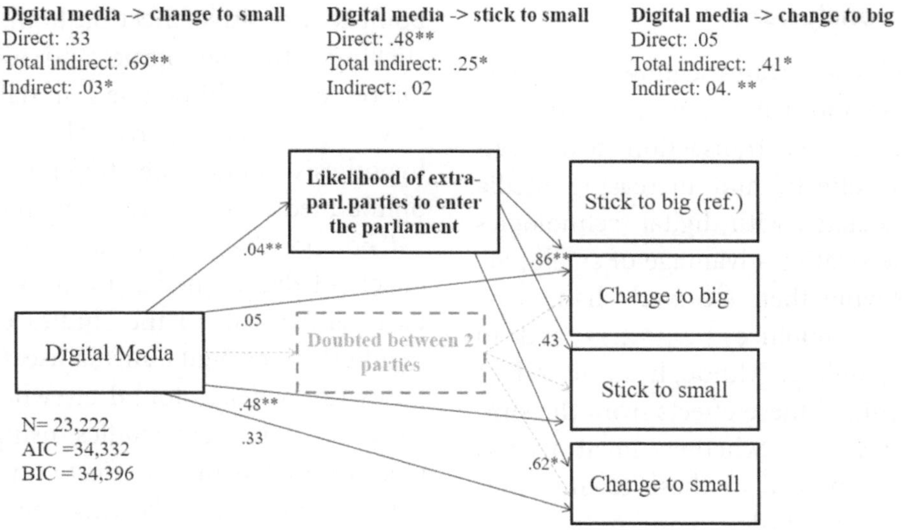

Figure 3. Estimated chances of extra-parliamentary parties as a mediator. Structural equation model. +$p < .1$. *$p < .05$. **$p < .01$.

question asked in the second wave of the survey, hence referring to the time before the voting decision. We assume here that the effects of digital media during the campaign (which had already started in the first wave of the panel) were previous to these doubts.

The total effects of digital media use on voting decision change are greater for "stick to small" than for "change to small" or "change to big." The direct effects of digital media use on voting intention change are positive and significant only for the "stick to small" (as compared to the reference category), which might suggest a reinforcement effect of digital media use among small parties' supporters.

The coefficient for the effect of digital media use on the "doubt" variable is positive and significant (.40), and so are the effects between the alleged mediator and the categories of the independent variable. This implies that the mediated effect for each of these three categories is significantly larger than the one exerted over "stick to big," yet the highest coefficient is found for the category "change to small," implying an indirect effect almost twice as big as the one observed for "change to big."

There are significant total indirect effects for "stick to big," "change to small," and, particularly, for "change to big." When read against the results of our previous estimations (Table 2), these indirect effects are consistent with partial mediation for "stick to small"—as the direct effects of digital media are lesser but still significant—and total mediation for "change to small"—as the direct effects of digital media are not significant anymore.

Figure 3 displays the role of the estimated chances of extra-parliamentary parties to enter the parliament as a mediator. The effect of digital media use during the campaign on the mediator is significant and positive, although modest. The indirect effects are modest and only significant for the "change" categories, somewhat larger for "change to big." Although both seem very similar, different logics might apply. On the one hand, sympathizers of small parties—currently willing to vote for a mainstream party—might feel encouraged to vote for a challenger if the latter seems more visible online and therefore likely to succeed. On the other hand, current voters of challengers might feel tempted to switch their vote in favor of a big party out of fear that very small, extremist parties will enter the parliament.

To sum up the story that this model tells us, digital media use during the campaign strengthens small parties' sympathizer's loyalty, but also drives to an overestimation of the chances of small parties, and, above all, to doubts about vote choice. The indirect effects of digital media use during the campaign—particularly when it boosts doubts about one's vote choice—enhance the chances of vote change, mostly in favor of small parties.

Discussion and conclusions

Digital technologies are transforming the supply side of information and, with it, we contend, electoral competition. Lower transaction costs, network (horizontal) effects, and increasing media fragmentation associated with digital technologies might increase the relative advantage of small parties online, improving their electoral chances by managing them to mobilize supporters and to attract new voters online. Although an abundant literature has examined these effects from the supply-side perspective (i.e., whether small parties make a more efficient use of these technologies for campaigning), very little attention has been paid to the demand side of the electoral equation with regard to digital media and challenger parties. Combining a supply- and demand-side perspective, some studies have analyzed the effect of online campaigning on parties' vote share, but because most focus on single-case studies, their results are limited in scope. Here, we have addressed the question of whether digital technologies affect the electoral fortunes of third parties from a demand-side, individual perspective and we have contended that using digital media during the electoral campaign increases the chances of voting for small parties.

Our study contributes to the studies concerned with digital media effects on political competition in electoral democracies. We have used a non-U.S. large cross-country data set to measure the effects of digital media on the vote for third parties and studied these effects across four different countries with very different electoral and party systems, submitting them to the hard test of contextual variation.

Our data have revealed that individuals changing their voting intention during the campaign are a minority, with only 5% of total voters having changed their initial intention from a big party to a small one (namely, to a party that is none of the two biggest contenders). We have estimated the effect of old and new media exposure during the campaign on the probabilities of sticking to big parties, sticking to small parties, and changing to big and small parties, paying special attention to this last category. Old, traditional media seem to have a concentration effect, benefitting big parties. As for the effects of online media, our analyses point to a positive effect on both the likelihood of sticking with small parties and, especially, the likelihood of switching one's initial vote choice in favor of a smaller party. This confirms our first hypothesis about the fragmentation effects of online media use during campaigns.

The positive, significant, and strong direct effects of digital media use on sticking to a small party also speak to the studies on the reinforcement effects of digital media use. Our results are in line with evidence found elsewhere. For example, in one of the few studies using panel data to measure digital media effects on the vote, Padró-Solanet finds that following the campaign online strengthens the probability of voting for a small party among small party voters (2009), while it increases the probability of abstention among mainstream parties' voters. In the same vein, Bimber and Davis (2003) found that an important part of the audience of third parties' Web sites declared already voting for these parties. Our results confirm a reinforcement effect of digital media use that would be especially acute among small parties' supporters. This effect would be the result of underdog's sympathizers being more likely to consume electoral information online because detailed information regarding third parties is scarce or nonexistent in traditional media (Gibson & McAllister, 2015).

Our next hypotheses posit a series of conditional effects. Although other factors could also enhance or suppress the electoral impacts of digital media use, we contend that the indecision about one's vote and the perceived chances of small parties will increase with digital media use, and that this, in turn, will positively affect the chances to vote (stick with or switch to) a small party. We thus model a multiple mediation model that we tested by means of structural equations. We found evidence of partial mediation for the effect of digital media on the chances to stick with a small party and a greater mediation effect (compatible with total mediation) when it comes to the chances of switching vote intention, mainly through doubts between two parties. The robustness and coherence of our results make us inclined to interpret that these mediation models partially open the black box of the effects of media use on vote choice.

According to our evidence, the more an individual uses the Internet during the electoral campaign, the more dubious he will be about his vote choice, which, ultimately, increases the chances to vote for a small party. This is consistent with previous research pointing to the crucial role of uncertainty as a link between digital media use during the electoral campaign and electoral behavior (Bimber & Davis, 2003; Sudulich et al., 2015). The results could only be more convincing with a more complete panel that would allow us to measure the independent variable at $t - 1$, the mediator at t, and the outcome at $t + 1$. Nevertheless, the time at which the fieldwork was conducted and the retrospective wording of the questions tapping the variables make us inclined to think that we are respecting the time sequence implied in a mediation relationship.

Nevertheless, the mediating role of the perceived chances of extra parliamentary parties is only marginal, and it works better for the chances to switch in favor of a big party. This points to two limitations of our study. First, the perceived chances to get into the parliament of very small parties is an imperfect measure for the perceived viability of not-so-small (e.g., "third," "challenger") parties. Indeed, not all small parties are the same. A third—challenger—party might one day lead the opposition or rule the country, while an extra parliamentary party is not only less likely to play an important role, but probably stands out for its minority and/or extremist views. Also, digital media use might have different effects on them. The relative advantage of small parties online might translate into convincing big party supporters to change their vote in favor of a smaller—but not tiny—party that is as credible a challenger. But it also might deter partisans of small parties from voting for them—casting instead a useful, strategic vote for a mainstream party—if they perceive that extremist extra parliamentary parties can achieve representation.

Our results also raise some intriguing questions about our measures that cannot be answered with the data at hand. For example, why do we not find any effect of election attention to the Internet on the vote? The reason why electoral attention to the Internet does not capture any significant effect is probably because more and more the Internet is used as a multimedia platform that integrates different behaviors, from watching TV to using social media. Because electoral attention to the Internet may encompass such divergent uses, these uses might cancel each other out (we would expect using the Internet to follow the campaign on TV to have the same effect as following the campaign through social media). Also, the myriad sources that a reference to "the Internet" implies (from digital versions of newspapers to social networking sites) suggests that the individual cannot pay too much attention to all of them, even if he or she is consciously or unconsciously getting lots of political stimuli through this medium. In this respect, we acknowledge another limitation. Although we managed to tap some concrete uses of digital media during the campaign, these uses are limited and do not include the use of social media directly, which is expected to have a greater effect for challenger parties. We expect to address these limitations and to study the influence of social media in future research.

Notes

1. Each regional survey has a sample size of around 1,000 respondents, making a total of 2,000–3,000 observations per region, with the exception of Bavaria, where we have about 6,000, and the Canadian provinces of Quebec, Ontario, and British Columbia, where we have only one survey and about 1,000 respondents. Note as well that the study included data for Zurich and Lucerne, but we have excluded these cases for one main reason: Switzerland is the epitome of a consociational democracy, whose main characteristics—according to Lijphart—are grand coalitions and mutual veto between elites; all of which hinders referring to "big" or "small" parties, as a small party can be in fact a ruling one. Finally, note that the national election included for the French case was the one meant to select the 14th National Assembly, held a little over a month after the French presidential election in May.
2. Our criterion is also partially consistent with Norris's conception of major and minor parties (Norris, 2003). According to Norris, major parties have at least 20% of the seats in the lower house of parliament, while minor parties have less than 20%. Our classification fulfills Norris's categorization in all cases except in two—both criteria conflict. These conflicting cases are all federal elections in idiosyncratic regions such as Quebec and Catalonia, where

major electoral parties at the regional level become minor parliamentary parties at the federal level. In these cases, our classification diverges from Norris's categorization because we use vote share and not seat share to classify parties as either big or small. The fact that the level of party nationalization of the Canadian electoral system is very low in comparison with the rest and that seat share cannot be used to determine which parties are big and small in European elections are two additional reasons to choose vote share and not seat share as our main classification criteria.

3. Note that the use of composite measures (scales) for both off-line media attention and digital media exposure during the campaign reduces the amount of measurement error and simplifies our models, reducing the risk of multicollinearity. We still acknowledge that using two dichotomous variables (albeit in a composite index) to tap digital media use is not ideal. Frequency of exposure would have been a better measure of digital media use and more indicators of digital media use—including, for instance, social media use—before and during the electoral campaign would have helped to tap more accurately this phenomenon. Please find the exact question wording behind these variables and their descriptive statistics in appendix I and II, respectively.
4. More precisely, we will test a generalized linear model via maximum likelihood by means of the *gsem* STATA 13 command.
5. See Appendix III.
6. We are not computing the total or indirect effects for the "stick to big parties" category, as this would be beyond the scope of the paper.
7. The AIC (Akaike Information Criterion) and BIC (Bayesian Information Criterion), both maximum likelihood estimates that assess model fit, should be interpreted against a reference model. Should we drop the mediators, both model fit measures would improve, although our goal is not to find the most efficient predictive model of voting behavior, but to test the causal path through perceived viability of small parties and indecision.
8. Each coefficient is represented under its respective arrow.

Disclosure statement

The authors report no conflicts of interest. The authors alone are responsible for the content and writing of the article.

References

Balcells, J., & Cardenal, A. S. (2013). Internet & competición electoral: El caso de Esquerra Republicana de Catalunya. *Revista Española De Investigaciones Sociológicas (REIS), 141*(1), 3–28.

Benoit, K., & Laver, M. (2003). Estimating Irish party policy positions using computer wordscoring: The 2002 election —A research note. *Irish Political Studies, 18*(1), 97–107.

Bimber, B., & Davis, R. (2003). *Campaigning online: The Internet in US elections.* Oxford University Press.

Blais, A. (2010). Making electoral democracy work. *Electoral Studies, 29*(1), 169–170.

Brossard, D., & Scheufele, D. A. (2013). Science, new media, and the public. Science, 339(6115), 40–41.

Borge-Holthoefer, J., Baños, R., González-Bailón, S., & Moreno, Y. (2013). Cascading behaviour in complex socio-technical networks. *Journal of Complex Networks, 1* (1), 3–24.

Castells, M. (1996). *The rise of the network society. Information age: Economy, society and culture* (Vol. I). Malden, MA: Blackwell.

Coe, K., Tewksbury, D., Bond, B. J., Drogos, K. L., Porter, R. W., Yahn, A., & Zhang, Y. (2008). Hostile news: Partisan use and perceptions of cable news programming. *Journal of Communication, 58*(2), 201–219.

D'Alessio, D. (1997). Use of the World Wide Web in the 1996 US election. *Electoral Studies, 16*(4), 489–500.

De Vries, C. E., & Hobolt, S. B. (2012). When dimensions collide: The electoral success of issue entrepreneurs. *European Union Politics, 13*(2), 246–268.

Gibson, R. K., & McAllister, I. (2006). Does cyber-campaigning win votes? Online communication in the 2004 Australian election. *Journal of Elections, Public Opinion and Parties, 16*(3), 243–263.

Gibson, R. K., & McAllister, I. (2015). Normalising or equalising party competition? Assessing the impact of the web on election campaigning. *Political Studies, 63*(3), 529–547.

Gibson, R. K., & Ward, S. J. (1998). UK political parties and the Internet "politics as usual" in the new media? *The Harvard International Journal of Press/Politics, 3*(3), 14–38.

González-Bailón, S. (2009). Traps on the web: The impact of economic resources and traditional news media on online traffic flow. *Information, Communication & Society, 12*(8), 1149–1173.

González-Bailón, S., & Wang, N. (2016). Networked discontent: The anatomy of protest campaigns in social media. *Social Networks*, *44*, 95–104.

Greyes, N. (2011). The untapped potential of social media: A primer for savvy campaigners. *Campaigns and Elections*, *300*, 45–47.

Gueorguieva, V. (2008): Voters, MySpace, and YouTube: The impact of alternative communication channels on the 2006 election cycle and beyond. *Social Science Computer Review*, *26*(3), 288–300.

Hamilton, J. T. (2005). The market and the media. In G. Overholser, & K. H. Jamieson (Eds.), *The press* (pp. 351–370). Oxford University Press on Demand. New York: Oxford: The Annenberg Foundation Trust at Sunnylands.

Klinger, U. (2013). Mastering the art of social media: Swiss parties, the 2011 national election and digital challenges. *Information, Communication & Society*, *16*(5), 7.

Larsson, A. O., & Moe, H. (2014). Triumph of the underdogs? Comparing Twitter use by political actors during two Norwegian election campaigns. *Sage Open*, *4*(4), 2158244014559015.

Layman, G. C., Carsey, T. M., & Horowitz, J. M. (2006). Party polarization in American politics: Characteristics, causes, and consequences. Annu. Rev. Polit. Sci., 9, 83–110.

Lupia, A., & Sin, G. (2003). Which public goods are endangered? How evolving communication technologies affect the logic of collective action. *Public Choice*, *117*(3–4), 315–331.

Lusoli, W. (2005). A second-order medium? The Internet as a source of electoral information in 25 European countries. *Information Polity*, *10*(3, 4), 247–265.

Margolis, M., & Resnick, D. (2000). *Politics as usual: The cyberspace "Revolution"* (Vol. 6). London, England: Sage Publications.

Margolis, M., Resnick, D., & Levy, J. (2003). Major parties dominate, minor parties struggle. In R. K. Gibson, P. Nixon, & S. Ward (Eds.), *Political parties and the Internet: Net gain?* (pp. 53–69). London, England: Routledge.

Margolis, M., Resnick, D., & Tu, C. (1997). Campaigning on the Internet parties and candidates on the World Wide Web in the 1996 primary season. *The Harvard International Journal of Press/Politics*, *2*(1), 59–78.

Margolis, M., Resnick, D., & Wolfe, J. D. (1999). Party competition on the Internet in the United States and Britain. *The Harvard International Journal of Press/Politics*, *4*(4), 24–47.

Masket, S. E. (2009). No middle ground: How informal party organizations control nominations and polarize legislatures. Ann Arbor: University of Michigan Press.

Mazzoleni, G., & Schulz, W. (1999). "Mediatization" of politics: A challenge for democracy? *Political Communication*, *16*(3), 247–261.

Mullainathan, S., & Shleifer, A. (2005). The market for news. *The American Economic Review*, *95*(4), 1031–1053.

Newell, J. L. (2001). Italian political parties on the web. *The Harvard International Journal of Press/Politics*, *6*(4), 60–87.

Norris, P. (2001). *Digital divide: Civic engagement, information poverty, and the Internet worldwide*. UK: Cambridge: Cambridge University Press.

Norris, P. (2003). Preaching to the converted?: Pluralism, participation and party websites. *Party Politics*, *9*(1), 21–45.

Padró-Solanet, A. (2010, September 16–17). *Internet and votes: The impact of new ICTs in the 2008 Spanish parliamentary elections*. Paper presented at the Internet, Politics, and Policy conference, Oxford Internet Institute, Oxford, England.

Reif, K., & Schmitt, H. (1980). Nine second-order national elections–A conceptual framework for the analysis of European election results. *European Journal of Political Research*, *8*(1), 3–44.

Römmele, A., & Copeland, L. (2013). Beyond the Base? Political Parties, Citizen Activists, and Digital Media Use in the 2009 German Federal Election Campaign.

Samuel-Azran, T., Yarchi, M., & Wolfsfeld, G. (2015). Equalization versus normalization: Facebook and the 2013 Israeli elections. *Social Media & Society*, *1*(2), 1–9.

Strandberg, K. (2013). A social media revolution or just a case of history repeating itself? The use of social media in the 2011 Finnish parliamentary elections. *New Media & Society*, *15*(8), 1329–1347.

Sudulich, M. L., & Wall, M. (2010). "Every little helps": Cyber-campaigning in the 2007 Irish general election. *Journal of Information Technology & Politics*, *7*(4), 340–355.

Sudulich, M. L., Wall, M., & Baccini, L. (2015). The effects of Internet use on voters' electoral uncertainty. *British Journal of Political Science*, *45*(4), 853–881.

Ward, I. (2011). Does the Internet encourage small parties? A case study of the minutiae of BC politics, 1996–2009. *Australian Journal of Political Science*, *46*(2), 229–242.

Williams, C. B., & Gulati, G. J. (2007, August). Social networks in political campaigns: Facebook and the 2006 midterm elections. In annual meeting of the American Political Science Association (Vol. 1, No. 11, pp. 49–62). Chicago.

Xenos, M. A., & Foot, K. A. (2005). Politics as usual, or politics unusual? Position taking and dialogue on campaign websites in the 2002 US elections. *Journal of Communication*, *55*(1), 169–185.

Xu, X. (2015). David vs Goliath: Twitter's role in equalising big-party dominance. In T. H. Tan, A. Mahizhnan, & P. H. Ang (Eds.), *Battle for hearts and minds. New media and elections in Singapore* (pp. 163–177). Singapore: World Scientific Publishing.

Appendix I: Question wording. Main independent variables.

- PQ9A. How much attention did you pay to news about the election on television?
- 0: no attention at all—10: A lot of attention
- PQ9B. How much attention did you pay to news about the election: In the newspapers?
- 0: no attention at all—10: A lot of attention
- PQ9C. How much attention did you pay to news about the election: On the radio?
- 0: no attention at all—10: A lot of attention
- PQ9D. How much attention did you pay to news about the election: On the Internet?
- 0: no attention at all—10: A lot of attention
- PQ10A. During the campaign, did you use the following to find out about the election: A party or candidate Web site?
- Yes
- No
- PQ10B. During the campaign, did you use the following to find out about the election: Some other Web site with political content?
- Yes
- No
- PQ6C. When did you decide to vote for [party you voted for]?
- Months before election day
- A few weeks before election day
- A few days before election day
- On election day
- PQ6A. Did you consider the possibility of voting for another party?
- Yes
- No
- Q24: How likely are the following parties to gain enough votes to get into parliament?
- 0: very unlikely—10: very likely

Appendix II. Main variables descriptive statistics.

Variable	Obs (weighted)	Mean	*SD*	Min	Max
Change intention to vote	11,175.9	1.68	.84	1	4
Female	33,839.4	.52	.5	0	1
Education	29,194.3	.49	.23	0	1
Age	27,413.4	.41	0.2	0	1
Strength of party ID	31,037.8	.27	.36	0	1
Pol. interest	28,943.7	.61	.28	0	1
Interest campaign	33,510.1	.62	.31	0	1
Election attention off-line media	26,187.3	.43	.28	0	1
Election attention: Internet	26,259.4	.37	.35	0	1
Use of digital media during the campaign	25,431.4	.17	.31	0	1
Election level	33,839.4	1.78	.79	1	3
Country	33,839.4	3.8	.92	1	4
Doubted between two parties	15,792.3	.39	.49	0	1
Estimated chances of extra-parl. parties	18,522.5	.38	.19	0	1

Appendix III: Alternative table: Predictive margins of media effects

	Stick to big parties	Stick to small parties	Change to big	Change to small
Election attention off-line media at its minimum value	.41 [.36–.47]	.47 [.41–.52]	.06 [.05–.08]	.06 [.05–.07]
Election attention off-line media at its maximum value	.58 [.51–.66]	.28 [.21–.34]	.10 [.08–.12]	.05 [.04–.06]
Consultation of digital media at its minimum value	.53 [.47–.59]	.34 [.29–.40]	.08 [.07–.09]	.05 [.05–.06]
Consultation of digital media at its maximum value	.40 [.34–.45]	.45 [.39–.52]	.08 [.06–.10]	.07 [.06–.08]

Note. Numbers in brackets indicate the 95% confidence intervals.

Sharing Is Caring! Investigating Viral Posts on Politicians' Facebook Pages During the 2014 General Election Campaign in Hungary

Marton Bene

ABSTRACT

The study investigates 25 viral posts during the Hungarian general election campaign in 2014. These are posts whose numbers of shares were much higher than the average shares of their posters' posts. The study addresses the question of what kind of content may go viral and how this happens. First, it investigates the most specific and common features of the content of these posts. Second, the way they are shared and the effects they may evoke within personal networks are examined. Results show the prominence of negativity, undistorted message transmission, and a low reactivity level to the shares.

Over the last few decades, "sharing" has become a "crucial concept in contemporary culture and society" (John, 2013, p. 179). Its popularity stems from the social media where the object of "share" has been increasingly obscured and extended to anything: by now it has become a sort of cultural imperative well beyond the online world. "Share your moment!", "Share your life!", "Share your world!" or even "Share yourself!"—these are calls we are continually flooded with (John, 2013).

In this context, politics is also becoming a "shared experience." Social media, most notably Facebook, plays an increasingly important role in voters' political orientation and information consumption, especially among less politically involved segments of society. Politics can be widely visible and communicable, that is, viral, through Facebook sharing. Sharing operates by citizens' communication within their personal networks. Consequently, politics aiming at virality should target these "conversations" and be injected into them. When it comes to political campaigning on Facebook, achieving virality is especially important. Nielsen & Vaccari (2013) show that, as during the 2010 U.S. congressional election, most candidates were hardly followed; consequently, politicians' messages can reach wider segments of voters only if they are shared. In default of a large immediate audience, getting viral is vitally important.

Nonetheless, we know very little about political virality, and even less about the virality of candidates' campaign communication. In a recent project, I investigated what post elements are conducive to a post being shared, using a database with more than 7,000 Facebook posts of 183 single-member district candidates during the 2014 Hungarian general election campaign (Bene, 2017a). Although these results offered a general picture of how political sharing operates in a campaign context, in order to obtain undistorted results, outliers had to be excluded from the quantitative analysis. However, these outliers are posts shared in extremely large numbers. To understand virality, it is crucial to take most shared posts into account, as virality is mostly about extraordinariness. Although these posts are extreme cases in their numbers of shares, for virality they seem to be the most typical cases.

In this research, the typical cases of virality, 25 highly shared posts during the 2014 Hungarian general election campaign, are investigated through a mixed-method content analysis research design. I look at posts whose numbers of shares are much higher than average numbers of shares of their posters' posts. The study addresses the question of what kind of content gets viral and how it happens. As for content, I explore whether there are any fairly common or particularly specific features of these highly shared posts, and these features are qualitatively analyzed. For this purpose, this content is contrasted with posts from the total sample of 7,294 posts.

If we hardly know anything about the content aspect of virality, we know even less about how users share viral posts. Another novelty of this work is that it investigates how viral content is shared and what happens to the posts after being taken out of their original context, namely the politicians' pages. All publicly available shares of posts (1,822 shares) are analyzed regarding the way they were shared and the reactions they received from users' Facebook friends.

This approach offers a complex and comprehensive picture of virality during political campaigns, supplementing the general results of previous quantitative work. The findings reinforce the dominant role of negativity in political virality and give a fine-grained analysis of how this negativity is used in viral content. Surprisingly, it turns out that shares mostly lack any individual contributions, and even when some short text is added to the shared content, it never contradicts the original message. The reactivity of these shares is extremely low; the friends of the users who share posts seem to ignore this viral political content. Finally, the research demonstrates the important role of highly followed pages and accounts that are able to boost the virality of candidates' content. In the first part of the paper, I draw up the theoretical background followed by presenting data and methods. Next, I discuss the findings and finish the article with some concluding remarks.

Theoretical background

The growing significance of Facebook on political communication

Over the last few years, Facebook has become one of the most important political information resources for voters. In the United States, 44% of the adult population, or 66% of all Facebook users, obtains news from Facebook at least sometimes (Pew Research, 2016b). In Hungary, Facebook penetration is lower (46%) than in the United States (67%), but almost one third of the voting age population are informed about politics from Facebook "at least sometimes" (31%), which is 69% of all Facebook users.[1] However, among Hungarian university students, for example, Facebook has become the top political information resource, with half of them "regularly" and a further third "sometimes" informed about politics from it (Bene, 2017b).

A special feature of Facebook as an information resource is that it can easily reach the politically uninterested segments of voters who otherwise tend to avoid political information in the current high-choice media environment. The dominance of accidental exposure on Facebook is well supported by the Pew Research data, showing that 62% of Facebook users get news by accident when they are doing other things on the site (Pew Research Center, 2016b); moreover, a similarly high degree of accidental exposure has been found in Italy, Great Britain, and Germany (Valeriani & Vaccari, 2015). Furthermore, Valeriani & Vaccari (2015) show that accidental exposure to political information may also influence political behavior; moreover, this effect is stronger on voters with low political interest.

The effectiveness of political information on Facebook is further increased by the fact that it is usually transmitted by personal acquaintances, that is, Facebook friends (see, Pew Research, 2016a). Some research has demonstrated that social cues and the social transmission of messages could induce their pervasive power (Bond et al., 2012; Messing & Westwood, 2014; Turcotte, York, Irving, Scholl, & Pingree, 2015). In addition, political information on Facebook appears in a typically nonpolitical, highly personalized context where political predisposition and reflexes may be less activated. Wojczieszak and Mutz have found that political conversations in nonpolitical contexts are more tolerant of political disagreement (2009). To sum up, political information on Facebook does not only inform a large number of voters, but strong evidence demonstrates its effectiveness because of accidental exposure, peer transmission, and nonpolitical contexts (see Bene, 2017b).

"Viralization" of politics on Facebook

Facebook's reach, effectiveness, and nonpolitical nature have increased its significance in political communication. In the past, the primary way of reaching voters was to fit to media logic(s) (for the mediatization approach in politics, see, e.g., Strömbäck, 2008). Now, voters can also be reached through social media platforms, which operate on different logics.

Facebook is based on sharing. Users create communication networks, including mostly their offline acquaintances (see Boyd, 2014), kept alive by the activity of sharing. Users are perceived by members of their network only if they share, and they see these members' shares and can interact with them. Sharing is the soul of these communication networks and can literally be anything: a moment, an experience, an opinion, public information, others' content, links, etc.

The distribution logic of network media is virality (Klinger & Svensson, 2015). The term is taken from marketing and defined as "network-enhanced word-of-mouth" (Jurvetson & Draper, 1997; see Nahon, Hemsely, Walker, & Hussain, 2011). This definition well captures the original dual meaning of sharing, namely an act of communication as well as an act of distribution, meanings that are collapsed in the context of social media (see John, 2013). Broadly speaking, getting viral on Facebook means being shared in many different communication networks.[2] The more people share a content, that is, use it within their ongoing communication with members of their networks, the more extended reach and influence it can achieve. On social media, there are no stable audiences as in the case of mass media, but there is an abundance of information where content from a wide spectrum of topics and creators competes for attention and for being shared (Klinger & Svensson, 2015). Content has to create its own audience by being viral and injected in many communication networks. However, numbers of shares are generally unevenly distributed (see Klinger & Svensson, 2015). A small amount of content enjoys disproportionately huge attention and is shared within large numbers of personal networks, while most content is shared very little or not at all. The term "virality" captures this extraordinariness and "viral content" refers to content shared to an extreme extent.

In order to be effective, political communication on social media has to be intended to get viral. For gaining visibility, political messages have to break into these share-driven "conversations" between users and their friends. Content is successful if users can use it for these conversations with their personal networks. This means that the direct purpose and way of communication is different from traditional mass media-centric communication. Whereas the direct purpose of the latter type of communication is to affect mass media communication and thereby the reception and cognitive or affective processes of citizens, the former is intended to make citizens communicate about its content, and thereby to target their communicative, social nature. It is easy to see that reaching these goals requires different strategies and content. This is a significant challenge, as the sharing behavior is strongly shaped and constrained by impression management (see Boyd, 2014). This is especially true for political sharing because the conflicting nature of politics restrains many users from interacting with political content (Costera Meier & Groot Kormelink, 2015; Vraga, Thorson, Kligler-Vilenchik, & Gee, 2015). Consequently, the motives to express oneself are crucial in Facebook political communication (see Marichal, 2013), and political actors have to take this fact into account by aiming to affect citizens' communication.

Turning to candidates and their campaign, the above argument suggests that the most important goal of candidates' Facebook campaigns is to get viral. Generally, a campaign may seek two main goals: mobilizing supporters ("Get out of the vote"—GOTV) or persuading nonsupporters (see Holbrook & McClurg, 2005). Candidates on Facebook can directly communicate with their followers who are likely to be their supporters. However, for most candidates, direct followers are only a very narrow circle of all supporters (see Nielsen & Vaccari, 2013), thus no significant gain on the election results can be expected from their mobilization on Facebook. The wider circle of supporters, undecided voters, and especially voters leaning toward opponents can only be reached through getting viral, if the message is injected into as many "conversation networks" as possible.

Political virality

Although political virality is a fairly new phenomenon, politics flowing through social networks was examined before social media. Several effects on the spread and patterns of political and other information have been highlighted by personal influence and information diffusion research. Some approaches have emphasized the key actors in the information diffusion process (e.g., opinion leaders or early adopters) and their characteristics (see Katz & Lazarsfeld, 1955; Rogers, 1962). Others highlight the time of the day when information is released and the role of daily routines (Budd, MacLean, & Barnes, 1966), the community's demographical character (Hill & Bonjean, 1964) or the network composition (Huckfeldt & Sprague, 1995). But for nonpolitical information diffusion, see the seminal study by Coleman, Katz, and Menzel, 1957, or the environment where political discussions take place (Mutz, 2006). Content aspects have received less attention, even though some results suggest they have a crucial role in the diffusion process (see J-curve by Greenberg, 1964). Whereas all of the above discussed factors may be relevant in social media political information diffusion, the present work focuses only on the content aspect of political virality.

Although the question of social media information diffusion has recently received scholarly attention, it has been examined in many different fields (see Zhang & Vos, 2015). Overviewing the field, Zhang and Vos (2015) detect many different aspects of virality: these studies are concerned with diffusion mechanisms, network characteristics, or even the specific features of social network sites (SNS) facilitating information spreading. As for the content dimension of virality considered worthwhile, emotions, entertainment value or positive sentiments, news value, and content people want to be identified with are identified as key characteristics of messages shared on SNS platforms.

Regarding political virality, our knowledge is still rather insufficient. Three thin streams of literature are relevant here. The first is reflected in studies that examine the sharing of news articles. In their seminal paper, Berger and Milkman, examining online articles of *The New York Times*, show that emotionality, especially positivity, significantly affects whether an article will be among the top e-mailed pieces. In addition, they have found that virality is influenced by physiological arousal as well: articles with high-arousal emotions, whether positive or negative, trigger more e-mails (Berger & Milkman, 2012). Heinbach and Hinz replicated this study in a German context examining online articles of *der Spiegel*, but expanded their focus to more SNS platforms where articles could be shared. Regarding Facebook, they found that emotions affecting virality on this platform were anger and awe, but emotionality was not a significant predictor in itself. However, thorough investigation has revealed that positivity could affect sharing on Facebook but in a nonlinear way: slightly positive content is conducive to virality but extremely positive articles are not (Heimbach & Hinz, 2016). Bastos focuses on the topics rather than sentiments of articles on two news sites (*The New York Times* and the *Guardian*) and shows that there are differences between topics shared by SNS users and those highlighted by editors. Editors emphasize economy and sport more strongly than the extent to which these topics are shared on SNS sites, whereas on Facebook, arts, entertainment, and opinion pieces are more frequently shared. Articles from the political section are moderately shared, showing that political news content appears on Facebook mainly in the form of opinion pieces (2015). In a similar study, examining Swedish online newspapers, Larsson has found an identical pattern regarding the infrequent sharing of political news articles on Facebook, and has demonstrated the popularity of health and crime issues in Facebook news sharing (2016).

Another stream of literature examines factors affecting retweets of political tweets on Twitter. Twitter is a widely available SNS platform, and is thereby conducive to automatized data collection and conducting large-*N* content analysis. Stieglitz and Dang-Xuan investigated political tweets during regional elections in two German states in 2011 and found that the more emotion-filled a tweet, the more likely it is retweeted. In addition, both positivity and negativity significantly increased the probability of retweeting, although the effect size of negativity was slightly larger (Stieglitz & Dang-Xuan, 2012). In later research, they and their colleagues focused on only influentials during another state election in the same year in Germany and showed that emotionality and appraisal of political parties or politicians within their posts resulted in a higher number of retweets

(Dang-Xuan, Stieglitz, Wladarsch, & Neuberger, 2013). In contrast, Hoang and his colleagues investigating political tweets during the 2012 U.S. presidential campaign found that neutral tweets are more likely to be retweeted. However, they also report that the retweeting behavior of users who ever retweeted emotion-filled messages was significantly shaped by both their positivity and negativity. This means that the retweeting activity is affected by the sentiment of tweets only in the case of a special segment of users (2013). Attempting to resolve conflicting findings regarding the influence of sentiments on being retweeted, Hansen and his colleagues have demonstrated that the type of tweeted content moderates the effects of the sentiment on retweets. Interestingly, while the virality of news pieces was shaped by negativity, non-news tweets were affected more by positivity. As the authors put it, this suggests: "Sweet talk your friends or serve bad news to the public" (Hansen, Arvidsson, Nielsen, Colleoni, & Etter, 2011, p. 12). However, when interpreting these results, it is important to remember that Twitter differs from Facebook in many respects (features, norms, etc.), hence the sharing behavior on Twitter cannot be regarded as corresponding with the sharing behavior on Facebook (e.g., Bastos, 2015)

Little knowledge is available about the subject of the current article, that is, the virality of politicians' communication. Investigating a very specific sample, the most retweeted tweets of third-party presidential candidates during the 2012 U.S. campaign, Christiansen has shown that these tweets mostly focused on military, security, and human rights issues, and on the critiques of the two-party system and of corporate power (Christensen, 2013). However, given that the sample was very specific, these findings seem to be rather context-sensitive. Larsson examined the links between the content type of and reactions to Facebook posts on Norwegian party leaders' Facebook pages and has found that the mean number of shares was higher in the case of critical posts. However, this post type was very rarely used by the party leaders examined, and almost half of all critical posts were by one leader, who was generally the most reacted politician in the sample (Larsson, 2015). Therefore, it is not clear whether the high number of shares of critical posts was due to content type or the general viral potential and the popularity of the leader who predominantly used it. Samuel-Azran and his colleagues have investigated the effects of Aristotelian rhetorical tools on Facebook reactions on five Israeli leading politicians' Facebook pages. The results show that posts using logos (logic-based appeals) are significantly more likely to be shared than posts applying ethos (highlighting the speaker's credibility and trustworthiness), but the mean differences are not significant between ethos and pathos (emotional messages) or between logos and pathos. However, the dilemma is the same as in the case of Larsson's study: logos was a hardly used rhetorical tool and 62% of posts applying logos were posted by only one politician (Samuel-Azran, Yarchi, & Wolfsfeld, 2015). Many more content aspects were taken into account in Gerodimos and Justinussen's study than in earlier works, but their investigations were confined to only one Facebook page: Barack Obama's pages during the 2012 presidential election. The findings are that posts with policy statements, especially the policy area of education, as well as posts using any Aristotelian rhetorical devices were more likely to be shared. Interestingly, posts with positive acclaims were also shared more than other posts. At the same time, posts containing facts, statistics, or a video were significantly less likely to be shared on Obama's page (Gerodimos & Justinussen, 2015). The paper preceding this present work applies an even wider empirical approach with not a small number of prominent politicians' pages analyzed, but a total of 7,048 posts[3] from 183 single-member district candidates during the 2014 Hungarian general election campaign. In addition, the effects of 31 different content variables on Facebook reaction types (likes, comments, shares) have been tested on this sample. The findings suggest that the number of shares is significantly triggered by the text, video, share from external resources, and image macro appearing in the post, as well as the mobilization content calling to vote or containing some campaign material. However, the two strongest predictors are an explicit call for sharing and negativity. At the same time, campaign accounts, accomplishment reports, and general information are significantly less likely to be shared (Bene, 2017a).

This work is a follow-up to the latter study. That article offered a general picture about what content factors influence the number of shares. However, virality is hard to capture only by general patterns, because it is about extraordinariness. Though much of the aforementioned study talked about virality, it usually measured only the number of shares or retweets. The two concepts, however, are not the same, even if they are strongly connected. Numbers of shares are very unevenly distributed among political content, and viral posts mean highly shared content. Although highly shared posts count as extreme cases in the investigation of numbers of shares, they are the most typical cases in the investigation of virality. Therefore, for understanding virality, it is not enough to consider regular posts. We should get a handle on irregular content that cannot be captured by quantitative investigation because it has to be removed from data analysis as outliers. Highly shared posts are irregular content, and are truly important in order to understand virality, thus their distinct investigation may be fruitful. For this goal, a mixed-method approach is applied, using both quantitative and qualitative tools. Qualitative approaches are hardly ever used in this field. The only exception I know is Christiansen's above discussed article, which also investigates the most shared (retweeted) content, but it focuses only on topics on a very specific sample (Christensen, 2013). To sum up, this leads to the first research question as follows:

RQ1: What makes the most shared posts so viral? What is this content like?

Moreover, an important aspect of virality, namely, the way users share posts, is totally ignored within the literature. It is important however, because it is clear that going viral on Facebook does not mean a simple message transmission. It is more of an interactive process between various actors (Zhang & Vos, 2015), where users may interpret, comment on, criticize, or reframe the originally transmitted message, and thereby may distort it. This is recognized both by the political science literature and practitioners (see Stromer-Galley, 2014), yet it has not been empirically studied. In addition, it is crucial to know what happened to the post after it is disconnected from its original contexts. Is it any effect within personal networks? Is it able to generate further engagement by friends of sharers reacting to it? A well-grounded picture about virality can only be obtained as long as we gain knowledge about how posts are shared by users from politicians' Facebook pages. All in all, these interests are reflected in the second research question as follows:

RQ2: What happens to viral posts after they are disconnected from their original context?

RQ2.1: How do users share the viral content?

RQ 2.2: How do members of personal networks react to them?

Methods

To address the first research question about the virality of posts, two data sets are used. The first database (total sample—TS) contains all Facebook posts of three most voted candidates having Facebook pages from all single-member districts posted during the last two weeks of the 2014 Hungarian general election campaign. This means a total of 7,294 posts from 184 candidates (see Bene, 2017a). In this research, this data set serves as the population of posts from which viral posts are selected and as a comparative data set during the analysis. The second data set used as the subject of the analysis consists of the viral posts (VP) during the campaign, picked from TS. Virality depends on certain factors beyond content, which is the focus of this research. For example, in nonpolitical contexts, Liu and his colleagues have found that retweeting is shaped by source trustworthiness, expertise, and attractiveness (Liu, Liu, & Li, 2012), while other research has indicated that it is influenced by the number of followers and followees, as well as the age of the account (Suh, Hong, Pirolli, & Chi, 2010). Consequently, these findings suggest that Facebook pages have a viral potential that strongly affects the virality of their posts regardless of their content. As this research focuses on content aspects of virality, this viral potential must be controlled. Therefore, those posts have been selected from TS into the VP data set whose numbers of shares are much higher than the mean number of shares per post of the poster candidates. These are the posts whose standardized residuals are higher than 2.58 in a regression model where the individual post's number of shares is the dependent variable and the mean number of shares belonging to the candidates' given posts published is the independent variable. This means a total of 25 available posts from 20 candidates. Note that these are not the most shared posts during the whole campaign, but the posts whose number of shares cannot be explained by a given candidate's general popularity or their "viral potential." These are the most typical cases of content virality.

Table 1 shows the general characteristics of selected posts.The sample is dominated by politicians of the left-wing oppositional party coalition (*Kormányváltás*), while only a fifth of VP are published by government party politicians (*Fidesz*), and three posts belong to politicians of the radical right oppositional party (*Jobbik*). Most posts' number of shares ranges between 79 and 508, with only one post exceeding this. Endre Rózsa's post was shared 5,460 times, making it the most frequently shared post of the total sample during the campaign. The timing of posts does not seem to influence their success. However, slightly more viral content was posted during the first third of the whole period (10) than during the second (7) or the last (8) third.

In both data sets, posts are coded based on their content. Variables are grouped into four sets. By structural features, I mean whether a post contains some text, picture, video, shared content, image macro,[4] or emoticon. Two variables are associated with emotional tones. A post is coded as positive if it contains one of the following elements: applause, honor, reporting success, or inaugurations. A post is recorded as negative if it contains a critique, attack, or expressed pity or regret. The third variable set is the character of the post. Information posts contained one of the following elements: accounts of the candidate's acts or public utterances; the candidate's own opinions; pledges; presentation of earlier accomplishments; general information not directly connected to the candidate; or notification of upcoming events without calls for participation. Mobilization is coded if it contains an explicit call for voting or participation in an off-line event or shared campaign material. The engagement variable means an explicit call for Facebook action (like, comment, share, or question). Personalization is coded if a post contained something personal about the candidates: presentation of their family, personal interests, life beyond politics, or local patriotic

Table 1. General Characteristics of Selected Posts.

No.	Name	Share	Mean share	Stand. resid.	No. of posts[1]	Party	Day[2]
1	Benke László	112	3.96	3.60	80	Jobbik	12
2	Kiss László	82	7.1	2.72	30	Kormányváltás	10
3	Szabó Szabolcs	508	34.34	3.56	57	Kormányváltás	5
4	Zsigó Róbert	133	16.8	2.71	25	Fidesz	7
5	Teket Melinda	88	8.31	2.73	68	Kormányváltás	3
6	Teket Melinda	98	8.31	2.92	68	Kormányváltás	4
7	Simonka György	178	8.32	4.14	96	Fidesz	15
8	Nagy-Korsa Judit	119	9.37	3.18	52	Kormányváltás	3
9	Tállai András	116	3.08	3.76	87	Fidesz	4
10	Komáromi Zoltán	204	6.51	4.70	55	Kormányváltás	14
11	Pallás György	418	17.10	5.21	41	Kormányváltás	6
12	Szabó Zsolt	147	11.8	3.35	51	Fidesz	1
13	Korózs Lajos	106	10.98	2.82	64	Kormányváltás	12
14	Rózsa Endre	5460	71.17	4.70	81	Kormányváltás	1
15	Kiss Zsolt	155	6.42	4.04	66	Kormányváltás	14
16	Szabó Imre	173	15	3.36	117	Kormányváltás	2
17	Szabó Imre	232	15	3.98	117	Kormányváltás	3
18	Szabó Imre	144	15	3	117	Kormányváltás	8
19	Szabó Imre	213	15	3.79	117	Kormányváltás	10
20	Szabó Imre	163	15	3.24	117	Kormányváltás	11
21	Nyíri Márton	317	13.34	4.97	32	Jobbik	14
22	Seszták Miklós	80	5.46	2.81	69	Fidesz	7
23	Földi István	79	6.12	2.74	74	Jobbik	6
24	Helmeczy László	101	11.38	2.70	50	Kormányváltás	14
25	Scheiring Gábor	103	9.27	2.92	44	Kormányváltás	1

[1]The number of all posts posted by candidate during the two weeks. [2]Day when content posted. Day 1 is March 23, 2014, and day 15 is April 6, 2014, the election day.

sentiment. The last character variable is humor, and content is coded as such if it is intended to be humorous. The last variable set concerns the orientation of the posts, which could be local and/or national. The posts are not pushed exclusively into one or another category; all variables are treated as possible elements of posts, and posts are coded according to whether they contain any of these elements or not (see Bene, 2017a)[5].

To answer the first research question about virality, I investigate the general features of the selected posts in two steps. As a first step the viral posts' (VP) data set is contrasted with TS based on the coded elements in order to find features that (a) are common among selected posts and (b) appear in selected posts to a larger extent than in the TS. After identifying the most noteworthy features of selected posts, in the second step the way the most important elements were used in these posts is qualitatively investigated.

To answer the second research question about what happens to viral posts after they are disconnected from their original context, another data set was created containing all publicly available shares of posts in the VP data set. About half of the shares (47%) were publicly available and thereby have become subjects of the analysis. Only one post (No. 15) had much fewer publicly available shares than 50%. Unfortunately, two posts (No. 14 and No. 19) were no longer accessible when data were coded for the second phase of the research. All in all, the data contained a total of 1,822 shares of 23 VP. It is recorded for all shares whether they contained any individual contribution, that is, some text added by the user and the number of likes, comments, and shares it received. In addition, all individual contributions were separately collected for further qualitative investigation. During the analysis, shares are examined as a whole, but variances between posts in terms of their shares are also investigated, contrasting them with their content elements.

Table 2. Comparison of Viral Posts and Total Sample Based on the Elements of the Posts.

Element		% (*N*) among VP	% among TS
Structural features	Text	80% (20)	65%
	Picture	40% (10)	61%
	Video	16% (4)	14%
	Image macro	28% (7)	5%
	Share	20% (5)	33%
	Emoticon	8% (2)	7%
Emotional tone	Negative	76% (19)	16%
	Positive	0	13%
Character	Information	72% (18)	70%
	Mobilization	40% (10)	40%
	Engagement	24% (6)	3.5%
	Personalization	8% (2)	3.7%
	Humor	4% (1)	2.4%
Orientation	Local	48% (12)	55.7%
	National	48% (12)	42.7%
N		25	7,294

Results

Comparison with the total sample

First, the elements of the VP are investigated and compared with TS.

The first rows in Table 2 show the structural features of posts.It seems that most posts contain some text, more often than posts in TS. Only five posts do not use any text: two of them are only videos, the other three are image macros, campaign material, and shares themselves. Many posts include pictures, but posts in TS apply pictures more often than VP. At the same time, image macros appear more frequently than in general, with 28% of the posts applying them. It is important that there is no post with text only among VP, although they are rare in TS as well (3%). Text is always used with pictures, image macros, videos, or shares. Only one post uses all three of these features: No. 5 applies text, picture, and share at the same time. Emoticons and videos are rarely used in these posts similarly to the TS, while share is more often applied in general than among VP. In addition, the average word number is higher (50.6) than in TS (35.5). Thus, it seems that the viral posts are more talkative.

The most striking common feature of the viral posts is revealed when examining their emotional tone. In the total sample, most posts are neither negative nor positive, and the two opposite tones appear in a similar degree. In contrast, viral content is predominantly negative, and there are no positive posts in this circle. Nineteen out of 25 posts are filled with negative emotions and only six posts, or a fourth of all of them, are neutral. This is in sharp contrast with TS where more than two thirds of posts were neither positive nor negative.

When it comes to the character of the viral posts, no noticeable deviation from TS appears. Most posts contain information, and call for off-line action is also prevalent. Call for Facebook action appears only

Table 3. Comparison of Viral Posts and the Total Sample Based on Used Information Elements.

Element		% (*N*) among VP	% among TS
Information	Account	12% (3)	36.6%
	Opinion	48% (12)	15.7%
	Pledge	0	5.6%
	Accomplishment	0	1.4%
	General info	16% (4)	15%
	Future event	4% (1)	4.7%

in six posts but this frequency is higher than in TS. Use of personalized elements or humor is exceptional—in the same way as in the total sample.

The information element is a rather wide category in this research; hence, it is worth taking a look at what kind of information is applied in VP. Table 3 shows that the information used differs significantly from its use in TS. In VP information is more often the candidates' personal opinion, which is used less frequently in general. In TS giving a simple account is the dominant information type, which is hardly ever used by VP.

Considering the orientation of posts, there is no remarkable deviation from the TS. Though in general locally oriented posts appear slightly more often than nationally oriented ones, local and national focuses are present in the same degree in the TS and VP.

This overview demonstrates that the most striking common feature of VP is using negativity. Besides, they often use texts with pictures or image macros, and offer information, mainly personal opinion, or call for off-line action. These posts include texts, image macros, negativity, a call for Facebook action, and opinions more frequently than posts in the TS. Interestingly, personalization and humor do not appear to be conducive to virality.

However, these common features are not independent of each other. For example, all posts containing personal opinion are negative, and only six out of the 19 negative posts did not include an opinion element. Four of them provided only general information about negative incidences, another two in turn aimed to mobilize followers with content filled with negative emotions but without adding any personal opinion. Image macros are also all negative: they are an often-used tool for expressing negativity. Almost all calls for Facebook action are filled with negative emotions; only one post with an engagement element is neutral. Given that negativity seems to be the most important common feature of VP and is strongly related to other special features (opinion content, image macros, engagement), it is reasonable to more closely investigate the appearance of this element.

The use of negativity

First, I examine the general characteristics of negative posts. Only three negative posts do not contain any text: one informative image macro, one informative share, and a video reporting an event. Texts are most often used with image macros (seven times) or pictures (five times), but in three posts texts are presented along with shared content and once with a video. Out of the negative posts, there are twelve opinions, four general information pieces and three accounts. Five posts contain a call for Facebook action, and a call for off-line action appears in five posts as well. There are more negative posts focusing on national (eleven) than on local issues (seven).

Negative posts most often deal with corruption (seven posts), but there are also moral critiques about the opponents' political worldview, especially focusing on the lack of solidarity (four posts). Three posts are aimed at alleged election fraud and two criticize the opponents' economic performance as incumbent. Three posts use general negativity without any specific focus. Consequently, most negative posts applied some moral critique focusing on some injustice and the opponents' personal morality rather than substantive or performance-oriented criticism. It is noteworthy that no policy critique is present within these negative posts.

As for the target of negativity, thirteen posts are directed at specific persons, but three of them appear in a generalized form where the targeted person (the PM) represents a collective agent (the government). Four posts are against specific parties, and two criticize a generalized "they." No negative post focuses on a specific situation, issue, or policy without naming some enemies. It is not a surprise that all corruption-focused posts name specific persons, even if in one of them the named person represents a collective agent. All four posts about concrete worldview criticisms also target special persons, while in the two performance-oriented posts the persons were presented in a generalized form. Interestingly, only in one post does a not negatively presented specific person appear, thereby offering a way for a positive connection to the post. In this case the injustice is illustrated by a man who suffered it—as a symbol who could be sympathized with. This post is remarkable, as it is the most frequently shared one in the TS (No. 14).

Moral counterpoints, however, appear in only three posts. These counterpoints are usually collective substances (nation, political community) or values. Interestingly, only the right-wing critiques (*Jobbik, Fidesz*) use moral counterpoints; negative posts of left-wing antigovernment candidates only apply criticism without any positive counterpoint. The dominant emotion in negative posts is anger and outrage, while moral criticisms also involve disgust. These are high-arousal negative emotions (see Russell & Barrett, 1999) whose viral character is highlighted by Berger and Milkman (2012) as well.

As a rhetorical tool, left-wing antigovernment candidates often use statistics and data to illustrate the injustice presented. Pathos is a rhetorical device by *Jobbik* (two posts) and *Fidesz* (one post) candidates using negativity. It is there to support the moral counterpoint against the subject of their critiques. They all apply quotes for this purpose. Left-wing highly shared negative content does not contain a pathos element or quotes.

Nonnegative viral posts

Only six posts have no negative elements. Two of them are without any text, including only a video or campaign material. In three posts, the text appears with some campaign material, and in one post with a video. Out of the six posts, four focus on mobilization: two by calling on people to vote, and another two asking them to attend an off-line event. The other two posts are not explicitly political: one promotes a family day event sponsored by the given candidate and the other one is a video about a local fountain without any text, voice, or any person appearing in it, even if the given candidate inaugurated it the previous day as the local mayor. Although these posts are indeed nonpolitical themselves, the context is certainly not devoid of politics. Overall, nonnegative viral posts are mainly pure mobilization or seemingly nonpolitical posts.

Sharing viral posts

Interestingly, users share these posts mostly without making their own contribution. It is striking that only 8% of the shares contain some text written by the user. Considering individual posts, we see that the highest proportion is only 20% (No. 5). Thus, it seems true for all posts that shares are predominantly without any individual contribution.

When examining the small number of shares where users add some text, it turns out that these contributions are usually short and never contradict the original posts. In these cases, users generally express their agreement with the content of the posts. These expressions are mainly emotion-filled individual statements and simple reinforcements rather than rational arguments or personal opinions about the issue. When it comes to negative posts, these individual contributions reflect anger and outrage, and frequently employ exclamation marks and capital letters. If posts do not offer positive counterpoints in their content, their shares do not contain positive identification either. This means that they do not praise or express their identification with the candidate who posted the negative content or argued for a standpoint, they only criticize the subjects or the objects of negative posts. In contrast, positive identification appears in the shares of those negative posts that contain positive counterpoints, as well as in the shares of nonnegative posts. In addition, individual contributions quite often have a mobilization purpose, calling their friends for off-line action (voting or attending an off-line event). Call for off-line action appears in shares of both negative and nonnegative posts.

VP are not only shared mainly without individual contributions, but the users' friends hardly ever react to the shares. In this sample, 52% of all shares triggered absolutely no reaction from users' networks, and only 8% of them got at least five reactions in terms of likes, comments, and shares. Consequently, the great majority of the friends of users who shared candidates' posts were completely unconcerned with this political content: they ignored these posts or at least did not interact with them publicly. However, there are certainly some variations between individual viral posts in the sample. The main differences appear in likes: posts' mean number of likes per share range between 0.16 and 4, and shares without likes range between 36% and 85%. When it comes to comment and share, the range is smaller: in case of all posts but one (No. 11), four out of five shares got absolutely no comment; this is the same in the case of all but two posts in terms of shares (No. 6 and 24). Only 57 out of 1,822 shares received at least three comments, a result which shows that political debates or deliberation do not usually evolve from these shares.

VP are sometimes shared by highly followed Facebook pages or other politicians' personal accounts and these shares often generate extremely high reactivity. The ten most liked, as well as five out of the ten most frequent shares, were posted by Facebook pages or were politicians' personal accounts. Hence, the mean value belonging to individual posts has to be treated with caution, because it is highly distorted by extreme cases. As most posts have extremely low numbers of reactions,[6] if any at all, when examining individual differences, it makes more sense to investigate what proportion of shares receive no likes, comments, or shares at all rather than their mean values.

Investigating the effects of posts' content on individual variations in terms of shares and their reactions, the posts have been compared based on certain frequent features. When it comes to individual contributions to shares, there are no remarkable variations between different post types. Users add their own text to the shares in a similar degree regardless of whether the posts shared are negative or not, contain image macros, pictures, or a candidate's personal opinion or not. Slight differences can be detected when posts include a call for off-line action: these posts are slightly less frequently supplemented with an individual contribution (7%) than posts without it (10%). Considering reactions to shares, the different types of original posts differ mostly in the likes that their shares get. Shared negative posts (62% of shares without likes), posts without pictures (63%), with a personal opinion (64%), or without a call for off-line action (66%) stay without likes more frequently than shares of nonnegative posts (48%), posts with pictures (52%), or posts without a personal opinion (54%) or with a call for off-line action (48%). When it comes to comments, there are no remarkable differences. However, it can be seen that shares of posts without image macros (91% of shares without re-shares compared with 98% of shares of posts with image macros), without a picture (89% compared with 99%) or without a call for action (90% compared with 98%) are more frequently shared by friends of users.

An important aspect of virality is whether the shares of original posts generate further shares. This viral content rarely gains significant numbers of extra shares from their primary shares. When posts are taken out of their original context, they usually stop spreading further: the friends of users who shared candidates' posts rarely share that content further. However, there are some exceptions, but these are usually owed to highly followed pages or other politicians' accounts. Candidates' posts are sometimes shared by prominent Facebook pages with large numbers of followers, and these shares may generate high numbers of extra shares for candidates. Consequently, while ordinary users' shares may generate few extra shares for candidates, prominent Facebook pages can help in getting viral.

Discussion

Overall, the results show that the most common feature of viral posts is negativity. A large majority of the content is clearly negative, attacking political opponents. Although the prominence of negativity in social media political communication has already been demonstrated (Bene, 2017a, 2017b; Hansen et al., 2011), the literature about political virality is highly mixed regarding the role of sentiments. Several researchers have suggested that emotionality is what really matters as opposed to its valance: both negative and positive emotions could boost virality (see, e.g., Berger & Milkman, 2012; Stieglitz & Dang-Xuan, 2012;). In this research, among the viral posts the extreme dominance of negativity has been revealed, but there is no positive content appearing.

Among the possible reasons for the prominence of negativity in Facebook virality may be personalized political identities and extended networks. Bennett argues that political identities have increasingly been personalized (2012) and this process is strengthened by social media, which enable users to selectively connect to different issues, causes, or opinions and express these connections in front of a wide personal public. Political content that involves little identification burden may be more appreciated in this context because it could be used for performing individual, personalized identities without fitting people into homogenized collective identity blocks (see Bennett & Segerberg, 2012). Arguably, positive content involves a heavier identification burden than negative content: it is easier to be against something than for something. Incentives for avoiding the identification burden are further increased by "collapsed contexts" (Marwick & Boyd, 2011) and the dominance of weak ties (Vraga et al., 2015) in social media platforms. This urges users to present an image in their social media communication that they could undertake in wide and often heterogeneous social contexts (Diehl, Weeks, & De Zúñiga, 2015) separated off-line, but "collapsed" on Facebook.

However, beyond highlighting the dominance of negativity, this research offers some important findings regarding how negativity is applied in viral posts. The dominant negative emotions are high-arousal ones such as anger and outrage, and usually involve moral critiques, especially accusing opponents of corruption. Negative posts are usually targeted: they name a specific individual or collective opponents. However, moral counterpoints rarely appear in these negative viral posts and they are applied mainly by right-wing (*Fidesz* and *Jobbik*) politicians. There are no posts with policy critiques among our cases, and only in two posts do accomplishment critiques appear. The use of negativity is usually connected to other special features of these posts: all posts with personal opinions and image macros are negative. Although personal opinion is a rarely used element in the TS and has no significant effect on the number of shares (see Bene, 2017a), the highly shared negative content is very often personal opinions at the same time (see Bastos, 2015).

The small numbers of nonnegative posts are usually mobilization-targeted: all but one urges followers to act off-line, for example, to vote for the candidates or attend off-line events. This result shows that users not only express or perform themselves in front of their networks, but they also sometimes try to influence or persuade their friends. Sharing mobilization posts is certainly an expression and identity performance at the same time, but for these goals, candidates provide much more suitable content. Consequently, those who share mobilization posts probably aim to exert some political influence within their network. This intention is reflected in some individual contributions to shared posts, and not only in the shares of mobilization posts, but also of negative, nonmobilization posts. Personalization and humor are not present in the viral content, even though previous research has found them important in social media political communication (see Enli & Skogerbø, 2013; Vraga et al., 2015).

Interestingly, most shares stay without individual contributions. In nine out of ten cases, users share the content themselves. They only mediate candidates' Facebook posts rather than using them to express their own political selves in front of their friends in a substantive way. The small numbers of individual contributions are usually very short and always consistent with the original content. These are usually brief but heated expressions of negative emotional impressions about the subject or object of the posts (anger, indignation) or calling friends for off-line action. Users hardly ever share these posts in order to express their own distinct opinions or argue rationally for or against something. In addition, these shared posts receive hardly any reactions from members of personal networks; Facebook friends usually ignore this political content. Only the highly followed pages or personal accounts belonging to politicians seem to be exceptions to this rule: they could significantly increase the visibility or even the number of shares of the original posts.

Overall, the present results contradict some general assumptions and findings about Facebook political communication. One of these assumptions is that the politicians' biggest challenge in social media communication is controlling the message, because it is disseminated and commented on by ordinary citizens who could distort its original purposive content (see Stromer-Galley, 2014). These results show that citizens usually disseminate the candidates' message without distortion. Even in those rare cases when they add some of their own comments to the shares, they are short, supportive, and do not change the original message. Because their Facebook friends generally ignore these shares, they do not distort messages either. In addition, some findings reveal the conflict potential of political content on social media, deterring many users from posting about politics (see Vraga et al., 2015). In our cases, political posts did not induce conflicts between Facebook friends, because they usually simply ignored them. Naturally, the reverse normative expectation regarding the deliberative potential of talking about politics on social media is not fulfilled either. Only 5% of shares—including shares of highly followed pages—received at least two comments, which is a minimal condition of rational debate. Another assumption is that politicians' followers who, at the same time, communicate about politics on Facebook are influentials or opinion leaders of their personal networks (see Karlsen, 2015). As long as reactivity is considered an indicator of friends' attention, thereby being an influential or opinion leader (see Dang-Xuan et al., 2013), these results refute this assumption as well.

Last, the findings show the important role prominent pages or accounts play in achieving virality. Although ordinary users' shares hardly ever generate extra shares for the original content, the shares of prominent pages or accounts may boost virality. A reason for this may be that pages with many followers could transmit the original message to a wider public that would not otherwise see it. Another possible reason could be that as these pages are well familiar with their audiences and their needs, they can present the message in a way that is popular with followers. However, out of the highly re-shared pages' shares in our sample, only one contains some individual contribution; the others only shared the content without any substantive comments. Nonetheless, this implies that an important strategy for achieving virality could be reaching elite actors, thereby tailoring the message for their Facebook communication.

Conclusion

This work has investigated those viral posts from candidates that received extremely large numbers of shares during the 2014 Hungarian general election campaign. These posts could be regarded as typical cases of virality. The posts were picked from a database of 7,294 posts from 184 candidates. Their numbers of shares cannot be simply explained by the given candidate's general popularity and "viral potential." The main purpose of the research is to understand why and how this content could be so highly shared. For this, the content characteristics of the posts and the way they had been shared were examined.

Overall, these results have advanced our knowledge about virality in politics. Extreme cases are a crucial dimension of virality but have not been examined so far. In addition, no study has investigated the interactive dimension of virality, that is, how and how effectively viral content is shared. Furthermore, a more fine-grained picture is provided about negativity in social media political communication, which seems to be one of its most important features.

The greatest limitation of this study is its context-boundedness. In the lack of similar studies, it is hard to distinguish which findings are due to a specific political context and which ones may be specific features of Facebook political communication. Obviously, the political context and culture shape the way politicians communicate and the particular political content that can go viral and attract attention both online and off-line. For example, whereas Gerodimos and Justinussen found the viral character of the policy statement on Obama's page in his 2012 election campaign, this research shows that in the 2014 Hungarian elections policy questions were not at all present among the most viral content. To overcome this limitation, more case studies of political virality in many different contexts, as well as comparative investigations, should be conducted. Moreover, candidates' posts during campaigns are only one area of political virality. Virality should also be investigated in other political periods and for other actors. When it comes to the investigation of shares, the use of privacy settings poses another limitation of the study. Because only half the shares were available and thereby the subject of analysis, we know nothing about users who shared the message applying privacy settings. Furthermore, two posts were unavailable during the second phase of the analysis, including the most viral post of the total sample (No. 14). In addition, the present study has focused mainly on the content aspect of virality. Both earlier studies of information diffusion and social media virality studies have demonstrated that other factors such as the impact of key actors on the diffusion process and the demographic and network composition of the community also exert influence on the patterns of political information spreading. The study has controlled the candidates' viral potential and has investigated the effects of the sharer users and pages but other factors are still beyond the scope of the study.

As a theoretical consequence, scholars should consider whether it makes sense to talk about the viralization of politics. Whereas mass media political communication is about making media outlets communicate and trying to affect it, social media political communication is about making ordinary citizens communicate and trying to affect them and their reports. The former requires adapting to mass media logics, a process captured by the mediatization of politics approach (see Strömbäck, 2008). Does that mean that the latter requires adapting to the "networked media logic" (Klinger & Svensson, 2015) and/or a kind of logic of citizen political communication? Future theoretical and empirical studies should address these questions and related issues.

Notes

1. Mérték Médiaelemző Műhely, 2015. http://mertek.eu/sites/default/files/reports/politikaitajekozodas.pdf (accessed July 15, 2016).
2. Although sharing is the most important device in achieving visibility, likes and comments can also increase it to a certain degree, hence they are also part of virality. However, this research focuses only on sharing as the central element of virality.
3. After data cleaning, the total sample consisted of 7,294 posts.
4. Image macro is defined as a picture with some text on it, excluding official campaign materials (where the party or candidate's name appears).
5. Krippendorf's alpha intracoder reliability was measured in 109 posts. Alpha value of structural features = .95; of emotional tone = .87; of character variables = .91; of orientation variables = .82. These values are considered to be high (Hayes & Krippendorff, 2007).
6. 5% got at least five likes, 1% got at least five comments and 0.6% at least five shares.

Funding

This work was supported by the Hungarian Scientific Research Fund (OTKA) (legal successor of National Research, Development and Innovation Office [NKFIH]) [Grant agreement number 112323].

References

Bastos, M. T. (2015). Shares, pins, and tweets: News readership from daily papers to social media. *Journalism Studies, 16*(3), 305–325. doi:10.1080/1461670X.2014.891857

Bene, M. (2017a). Go viral on the Facebook! Interactions between candidates and followers on Facebook during the Hungarian general election campaign of 2014. *Information, Communication & Society, 20*(4), 513–529. doi:10.1080/1369118X.2016.1198411

Bene, M. (2017b). Influenced by Peers: Facebook as an information source for young people. *Social Media + Society, 3* (2). doi:10.1177/2056305117716273

Bennett, W. L. (2012). The personalization of politics: Political identity, social media, and changing patterns of participation. *The ANNALS of the American Academy of Political and Social Science, 644*(1), 20–39. doi:10.1177/0002716212451428

Bennett, W. L., & Segerberg, A. (2012). The logic of connective action: Digital media and the personalization of contentious politics. *Information, Communication & Society, 15*(5), 739–768. doi:10.1080/1369118X.2012.670661

Berger, J., & Milkman, K. L. (2012). What makes online content viral? *Journal of Marketing Research, 49*(2), 192–205. doi:10.1509/jmr.10.0353

Bond, R., Fariss, C., Jones, J., Kramer, A., Marlow, C., Settle, J., & Fowler, J. (2012). A 61-million-person experiment in social influence and political mobilization. *Nature, 489*, 295–298. doi:10.1038/nature11421

Boyd, D. (2014). *It's complicated: The social life of networked teens.* New Haven, CT: Yale University Press.

Budd, R. W., MacLean, M. S., & Barnes, A. M. (1966). Regularities in the diffusion of two major news events. *Journalism & Mass Communication Quarterly, 43*(2), 221–230.

Christensen, C. (2013). Wave-riding and hashtag-jumping: Twitter, minority 'third parties' and the 2012 US elections. *Information, Communication & Society, 16*(5), 646–666. doi:10.1080/1369118X.2013.783609

Coleman, J., Katz, E., & Menzel, H. (1957). The diffusion of an innovation among physicians. *Sociometry, 20*(4), 253–270. doi:10.2307/2785979

Costera Meijer, I., & Groot Kormelink, T. (2015). Checking, sharing, clicking and linking: Changing patterns of news use between 2004 and 2014. *Digital Journalism, 3*(5), 664–679. doi:10.1080/21670811.2014.937149

Dang-Xuan, L., Stieglitz, S., Wladarsch, J., & Neuberger, C. (2013). An investigation of influentials and the role of sentiment in political communication on Twitter during election periods. *Information, Communication & Society, 16*(5), 795–825. doi:10.1080/1369118X.2013.783608

Diehl, T., Weeks, B. E., & De Zúñiga, H. G. (2015). Political persuasion on social media: Tracing direct and indirect effects of news use and social interaction. *New Media & Society.* Advance online publication. doi:10.1177/1461444815616224

Enli, G. S., & Skogerbø, E. (2013). Personalized campaigns in party-centred politics: Twitter and Facebook as arenas for political communication. *Information, Communication & Society, 16*(5), 757–774. doi:10.1080/1369118X.2013.782330

Gerodimos, R., & Justinussen, J. (2015). Obama's 2012 Facebook campaign: Political communication in the age of the like button. *Journal of Information Technology & Politics, 12*(2), 113–132. doi:10.1080/19331681.2014.982266

Greenberg, B. S. (1964). Person-to-person communication in the diffusion of news events. *Journalism and Mass Communication Quarterly, 41*(4), 489.

Hansen, L. K., Arvidsson, A., Nielsen, F. Å., Colleoni, E., & Etter, M. (2011). Good friends, bad news—Affect and virality in Twitter. In J. J. Park, L. T. Yang, & C. Lee (Eds.), *Future Information Technology* (pp. 34–43). Springer Berlin Heidelberg.

Hayes, A. F., & Krippendorff, K. (2007). Answering the call for a standard reliability measure for coding data. *Communication Methods and Measures, 1*(1), 77–89. doi:10.1080/19312450709336664

Heimbach, I., & Hinz, O. (2016). The impact of content sentiment and emotionality on content virality. *International Journal of Research in Marketing, 33*(3), 695–701. doi:10.1016/j.ijresmar.2016.02.004

Hill, R. J., & Bonjean, C. M. (1964). News diffusion: A test of the regularity hypothesis. *Journalism & Mass Communication Quarterly, 41*(3), 336–342.

Hoang, T. A., Cohen, W. W., Lim, E. P., Pierce, D., & Redlawsk, D. P. (2013, August). Politics, sharing and emotion in microblogs. In *Proceedings of the 2013 IEEE/ACM International Conference on Advances in Social Networks Analysis and Mining* (pp. 282–289). ACM.

Holbrook, T. M., & McClurg, S. D. (2005). The mobilization of core supporters: Campaigns, turnout, and electoral composition in United States presidential elections. *American Journal of Political Science, 49*(4), 689–703. doi:10.1111/j.1540-5907.2005.00149.x

Huckfeldt, R. R., & Sprague, J. (1995). *Citizens, politics and social communication: Information and influence in an election campaign.* Cambridge, England: Cambridge University Press.

John, N. A. (2013). Sharing and Web 2.0: The emergence of a keyword. *New Media & Society, 15*(2), 167–182. doi:10.1177/1461444812450684

Jurvetson, S., & Draper, T. (1997). *Viral marketing.* Netscape M files.

Karlsen, R. (2015). Followers are opinion leaders: The role of people in the flow of political communication on and beyond social networking sites. *European Journal of Communication, 30*(3), 301–318. doi:10.1177/0267323115577305

Katz, E., & Lazarsfeld, P. F. (1955). *Personal influence: The part played by people in the flow of mass communications.* New York, NY: The Free Press.

Klinger, U., & Svensson, J. (2015). The emergence of network media logic in political communication: A theoretical approach. *New Media & Society, 17*(8), 1241–1257. doi:10.1177/1461444814522952

Larsson, A. O. (2015). Pandering, protesting, engaging. Norwegian party leaders on Facebook during the 2013 "Short campaign." *Information, Communication & Society, 18*(4), 459–473. doi:10.1080/1369118X.2014.967269

Larsson, A. O. (2016). "I shared the news today, oh boy": News provision and interaction on Facebook. *Journalism Studies.* Advance online publication. 1–19. doi:10.1080/1461670X.2016.1154797

Liu, Z., Liu, L., & Li, H. (2012). Determinants of information retweeting in microblogging. *Internet Research, 22*(4), 443–466. doi:10.1108/10662241211250980

Marichal, J. (2013). Political Facebook groups: Micro-activism and the digital front stage. *First Monday, 18,* 12. doi:10.5210/fm

Marwick, A. E., & Boyd, D. (2011). I tweet honestly, I tweet passionately: Twitter users, context collapse, and the imagined audience. *New Media & Society, 13*(1), 114–133. doi:10.1177/1461444810365313

Messing, S., & Westwood, S. J. (2014). Selective exposure in the age of social media: Endorsements trump partisan source affiliation when selecting news online. *Communication Research, 41,* 1042–1063. doi:10.1177/0093650212466406

Mutz, D. C. (2006). *Hearing the other side: Deliberative versus participatory democracy.* Cambridge, England: Cambridge University Press.

Nahon, K., Hemsely, J., Walker, S., & Hussain, M. (2011). Fifteen minutes of fame: The power of blogs in the lifecycle of viral political information. *Policy & Internet, 3*(1), 1–28. doi:10.2202/1944-2866.1108

Nielsen, R. K., & Vaccari, C. (2013). Do people "like" politicians on Facebook? Not really. Large-scale direct candidate-to-voter online communication as an outlier phenomenon. *International Journal of Communication, 7,* 24.

Pew Research Center. (2016a). *The modern news consumer.* Pew Research Center.

Pew Research Center. (2016b). *News use across social media platforms 2016.* Pew Research Center.

Rogers, E. M. (1962). *Diffusion of innovations.* New York, NY: Free Press of Glencoe.

Russell, J. A., & Barrett, L. F. (1999). Core affect, prototypical emotional episodes, and other things called emotion: Dissecting the elephant. *Journal of Personality and Social Psychology, 76*(5), 805. doi:10.1037/0022-3514.76.5.805

Samuel-Azran, T., Yarchi, M., & Wolfsfeld, G. (2015). Aristotelian rhetoric and Facebook success in Israel's 2013 election campaign. *Online Information Review, 39* (2), 149–162. doi:10.1108/OIR-11-2014-0279

Stieglitz, S., & Dang-Xuan, L. (2012). Political communication and influence through microblogging–An empirical analysis of sentiment in Twitter messages and retweet behavior. In *System Science (HICSS), 2012 45th Hawaii International Conference on IEEE* (pp. 3500–3509).

Strömbäck, J. (2008). Four phases of mediatization: An analysis of the mediatization of politics. *International*

Journal of Press/Politics, 13(3), 228–246. doi:10.1177/1940161208319097

Stromer-Galley, J. (2014). *Presidential campaigning in the Internet age*. New York, NY: Oxford University Press.

Suh, B., Hong, L., Pirolli, P., & Chi, E. H. (2010, August). Want to be retweeted? Large scale analytics on factors impacting retweet in Twitter network. In *Social Computing (socialcom), 2010 IEEE Second International Conference on* IEEE (pp. 177–184). The Institute of Electrical and Electronics Engineers, Inc. Location: Los Alamitos, California; Washington, Tokyo.

Turcotte, J., York, C., Irving, J., Scholl, R. M., & Pingree, R. J. (2015). News recommendations from social media opinion leaders: Effects on media trust and information seeking. *Journal of Computer-Mediated Communication, 20*(5), 520–535. doi:10.1111/jcc4.12127

Valeriani, A., & Vaccari, C. (2015). Accidental exposure to politics on social media as online participation equalizer in Germany, Italy, and the United Kingdom. *New Media & Society*. Advance online publication. doi:10.1177/1461444815616223

Vraga, E. K., Thorson, K., Kligler-Vilenchik, N., & Gee, E. (2015). How individual sensitivities to disagreement shape youth political expression on Facebook. *Computers in Human Behavior, 45*, 281–289. doi:10.1016/j.chb.2014.12.025

Wojcieszak, M. E., & Mutz, D. C. (2009). Online groups and political discourse: Do online discussion spaces facilitate exposure to political disagreement? *Journal of Communication, 59*(1), 40–56. doi:10.1111/j.1460-2466.2008.01403.x

Zhang, B., & Vos, M. (2015). How and why some issues spread fast in social media. *Online Journal of Communication and Media Technologies, 5*(1), 90.

Personalization of Politics Between Television and the Internet: Leader Effects in the 2013 Italian Parliamentary Election

Diego Garzia

ABSTRACT

This paper provides an empirical assessment of the relationship between media exposure and leader effects on voting through an analysis of Italy—an ideal case for the study of the personalization of politics and its connection with political communication. The results show the dominance of leader effects among voters strongly exposed to television and a somewhat differentiated impact on Internauts. By looking at leader effects across different audiences, this paper elaborates on the missing link between electoral research and political communication, and it eventually speaks to the broader question of how important media is for the outcome of contemporary democratic elections.

Introduction

In recent years, a growing amount of academic research has been devoted to the increasingly tighter relationship between personality and politics (for a review, see: McAllister, 2007). According to Rahat and Sheafer (2007), the process of *personalization* of politics entails that "the political weight of the individual actor in the political process increases over time, while the centrality of the political group (i.e., political party) declines" (Rahat & Sheafer, 2007, p. 65). In a similar vein, both Karvonen (2010, p. 4) and Swanson and Mancini (1996, p. 10) put forward the notion that individual politicians have become more prominent at the expense of parties, ideologies, and substantive political issues.

The growing importance of individuals in the political process has been put under scrutiny under multiple perspectives by political scientists. Previous research on the topic can nonetheless be summarized into three major categories, dealing in turn with political institutions (i.e., parties and electoral systems), political communication, and citizens' voting behavior (Karvonen, 2010). Available research shows that over the last three decades there has been a marked shift toward more personalized electoral systems (Renwick & Pilet, 2016). Institutional analyses have also stressed the growing importance of leaders within their own parties (Poguntke & Webb, 2005). The increasing centrality of political leaders in contemporary postbureaucratic parties has been shown to bear strong effects on patterns of political and electoral competition in turn. Previous research provides evidence that the transformation undergone by political parties in the last decades has fostered the role of individual leaders in driving voters' feelings of closeness to the party and, eventually, their voting behavior (Garzia, 2012, 2013a; Lobo, 2008). Also political communication research devoted a strong interest to the process of personalization. Analyses of modern election campaigns emphasized the increased visibility of political leaders at the expense of the respective parties (Kriesi, 2012; Mazzoleni & Schulz, 1999; Swanson & Mancini, 1996). Yet, not much is known about the relationship between changing patterns of political communication and the

Previous versions of this article have been presented at the ITANES/SISE Workshop in memory of Aldo Di Virgilio (Bologna, February 2016), the WPSA Annual Meeting (San Diego, March 2016), the EUI Political Behavior Colloquium (Fiesole, April 2016), the ECPR General Conference (Prague, September 2016), the Internet, Policy and Politics Conference (Oxford, September 2016), the SPSA Annual Conference (St. Gallen, January 2017), the MPSA Annual Conference (Chicago, April 2017), as well as at the Jack W. Peltason Center for the Study of Democracy's Departmental Seminar (Irvine, April 2017). Amongst the large number of people that I would like to thank for their support, useful comments and suggestions throughout the last two years, I will single out Paolo Bellucci, Neil Bendle, Daniel Bochsler, Russell Dalton, Andrea De Angelis, Catherine Dong, Marta Fraile, Carol Galais, Bernie Grofman, Sharon Haleva-Amir, Enrique Hernandez, Jeff Kopstein, Hanspeter Kriesi, Elie Michel, Davide Morisi, Anand Shastri (best discussant ever), Frederico Ferreira da Silva, Tiago Silva, Alex Trechsel, Stefaan Walgrave and Marty Wattenberg. Needless to say, all the unavoidable mistakes still present remain only mine.

electoral effect of party leader evaluations at the individual level. In particular, the role played by television as a vehicle of personalization in voting behavior, as well as the relationship between online-based political communication and the personalization trend have been by and large neglected by the previous scholarship on the topic.

This paper aims at filling these gaps through a case study of the Italian parliamentary election of February 2013. As a matter of fact, Italy provides an ideal case for the study of the personalization of politics and its relationship with political communication (Campus, 2010). Initially unfolded in the early 1990s as a result of party system breakdown and the simultaneous "entrance in the field" of media tycoon Silvio Berlusconi, personalization has heavily characterized the last two decades of Italian politics. In spite of their pivotal role in both party structures (Calise, 2000) and political communication (Mazzoleni, 1996), only a few studies investigated systematically the impact of party leaders on Italians' electoral behavior (Bellucci, Garzia, & Lewis-Beck, 2015; Garzia, 2013b; Venturino, 2000). A previous longitudinal study found relatively strong evidence of the link between the progressive personalization of party structures and increasing leader effects on voting behavior (Garzia & Viotti, 2011). In contrast, the relationship between media change and personalization in voting behavior has never been systematically measured. Within this context, the 2013 election stands as a potentially crucial point. Eventually, the historical dominance of television as the main source of political information for the electorate at large is counterbalanced by the emergence of the Internet (Bentivegna and Ceccarini, 2013). This development is paralleled by the massive instant success of Beppe Grillo's Internet-based Five Star Movement at the expense of "traditional" parties. The extent to which these two phenomena relate to each other, however, is currently a matter of debate (Barisione, Catellani, & Garzia, 2014). By looking at the electoral effect of political leaders across different audiences, this paper elaborates on what has been the missing link in electoral research on party leader effects, while also speaking to the broader question of how important the media is for the outcome of contemporary democratic elections.

The paper is structured as follows. The next section reviews the few available works from the international literature dealing with the connection between exposure to old and new media and leader effects on voting. The following sections present the case study, the data set and the operational measures in turn. The analysis investigates the importance of leaders in the voting calculus across voters' varying degrees of television exposure and political activity on the Internet. The results, showing the dominance of leader effects among voters strongly exposed to television and a somewhat differentiated impact on Internauts, are tested for their robustness across a wide range of model specifications and alternative operationalizations of dependent and independent variables. The final section discusses the major implications of the findings and concludes with an agenda for future research in the field.

Personalization of politics between television and the Internet

There is no doubt that the changing structure of mass communications in the second half of the 20th century has been central in emphasizing the role of political leaders at the expense of parties, making the latter "more dependent in their communications with voters on the essentially visual and personality-based medium of television" (Mughan, 2000, p. 129). The link between television and the personalization of politics has been repeatedly put forward (Druckman, 2003; Lenz & Lawson, 2011; Postman, 2006; Sartori, 1989). Because of its power to present images, it is easier for television to communicate political information through "individual" objects rather than abstract entities such as parties or ideologies (Hayes, 2009). By calling attention to some features of political competition while ignoring others, television news influences "the standards by which governments, presidents, and candidates for public office are judged" (Iyengar & Kinder, 1987, p. 63). News attention does not only affect the way in which candidates and leading politicians are judged. As a matter of fact, it also increases their perceived importance (Miller & Krosnick, 2000). In this sense, the inner logic of televised political communication—along with the rise of the medium itself as the chief source of political information for the predominant majority of citizens —has been "blamed" for the growing relevance of personality evaluations in voters' choice over the last decades. Yet, the link between patterns of televised political information and the determinants of voting behavior has received only limited attention in the empirical literature so far.

Currently available research in this domain pertains mostly to the American case. McLeod, Glynn, and McDonald (1983) analyzed post-election survey data from the 1980 U.S. presidential election, and found that voters heavily exposed to television were the most likely to rely on candidate image characteristics while casting their vote. Keeter's (1987) longitudinal analysis of the period 1952–1980 supports McLeod et al.'s findings, concluding that "television has facilitated and encouraged vote choices based upon the personal qualities of candidates" (Keeter, 1987, p. 344). Similar findings are reported by Holian and Prysby (2014) in their recent analysis of candidate character traits in U.S. presidential elections.

Unlike their American counterparts, European scholars have only recently started addressing these issues. Among the few available works on the topic, Mughan's (2000) study of British elections stands as the first systematic contribution, and it supports the idea that higher degrees of exposure to televised political information correspond to an increasing influence of party leader evaluations on vote choice. These conclusions, however, are only partially supported by Rico's (2014) analysis of three Spanish elections and Elmelund-Præstekær and Hopmann's (2012) study of Danish local elections. More convincing evidence in support of the link between television and personalization is offered by Takens, Kleinnijenhuis, van Hoof, and van Atteveldt (2015) in their analysis of the 2010 Dutch parliamentary election.[1]

In line with the aforementioned literature, the first research question tackled in this paper can be formulated as follows: *Is personality-based voting fostered by heavy exposure to television?*

As it currently stands, the extant literature on the personalization of politics seems to have overlooked the momentous transformations that occurred on the media landscape due to the advent of the Internet. Notwithstanding the dramatic changes in the way in which online political information is produced and digested by the electorate (Sudulich, Wall, & Baccini, 2015) there is only scattered evidence about the relationship between Internet usage and the determinants of electoral choice. At first, the growth of the Internet and social media has sparked interest in its impact on increasing political engagement and participation, either directly, for example, encouraging them to participate, or indirectly, for example, providing citizens with the necessary information to participate (Norris, 2000). Indeed, consumption of political information on the Internet has been shown to bear a positive impact on broadly defined patterns of political engagement (for a review, see Boulianne, 2009) as well as more specific patterns of electoral participation (Bond et al., 2012; Tolbert & McNeal, 2003).

When it comes to the relationship between exposure to political information on the Internet and individual-level patterns of voting behavior, the scant available literature fails to carry unequivocal indications. On the one hand, one notes that the interactive possibilities offered by Web 2.0 (and, most notably, by social media) now allow voters to "follow" politicians' activities on a daily basis. In a similar fashion, politicians themselves have now the possibility to bypass the role of parties as political intermediaries through social media channels. On the other hand, however, it has been shown that "online election news seekers are ... more likely to look to policy issues to determine their vote choice" (Gibson & McAllister, 2006, p. 256). What matters the most, for the purposes of this study, is that their higher propensity to vote based on issues is paralleled by a weakening impact of personality evaluation in the voting calculus. Holian and Prysby (2014) analyze the link between consumption of political information on the Internet and the attitudinal determinants of vote choice based on national election study data from the 2012 U.S. presidential election. Their results support the idea that online news seekers are systematically less likely to base their candidate choice on personality evaluations as compared to television viewers.

So far, European scholarship on the topic has concentrated on individual's exposure to specific informational sources, with a growing interest in so-called Voting Advice Applications (VAAs). The existing literature supports the notions that VAAs foster turnout (Garzia, De Angelis, & Pianzola, 2014; Gemenis & Rosema, 2014) and "prime" issues at the expense of personality evaluations in the individual voting calculus (Walgrave, Van Aelst, & Nuytemans, 2008). Besides this emerging strand of scholarship, however, the European case highlights the virtual absence of systematic studies connecting voters' exposure to Internet-based political information and leader effects on voting.

Due to the lack of systematic empirical evidence on the topic, the second research question that this paper will tackle is inevitably exploratory in character, and it unfolds as follows: *How does Internet-based political information impact the role of personality evaluations in voting behavior?*

The 2013 Italian parliamentary election

Italy represents a crucial case for the mediatization of politics and its links with the processes of party transformation and electoral change. In this respect, the collapse of the old *partitocrazia* in the early 1990s stands as a key point of departure for the wide-ranging political developments that unfolded throughout the last two decades. The disappearance of virtually all the parties that populated Italian politics since the end of WW2 produced the most appropriate conditions for new competitors to enter the field. In 1994, media tycoon Silvio Berlusconi established his own personal party, *Forza Italia*. His entrance in the political arena prompted to a large extent the process of personalization of Italian politics (Campus & Pasquino, 2006). As a man who personally owned a media empire, and being himself highly adept in the language of television, Berlusconi would soon set a standard for personal campaigning with no comparable precedents in modern mass democracies (Calise, 2005). Indeed, the unforeseeable triumph of *Forza Italia* in the 1994 election made the other parties increasingly dependent on television, for it immediately seemed clear that "no party could remain in the contest without heavy use of mass communication channels" (Mazzoleni, 1996, p. 200). This process of transformation found its climax during the 2008 campaign, when the political supply reached unparalleled levels of personalization due to the choice of the main center-left party, *Partito Democratico*, to center its electoral strategy on the figure of its leader and prime-ministerial candidate, Walter Veltroni (Barisione, Catellani, & Garzia, 2013).

This party-led development unfolded in parallel with the progressive expansion of television as the main source of political information for the Italian electorate. Whereas in 1990 "only" two thirds of the electorate resorted primarily to television for political information, in less than 20 years this proportion went up to reaching almost four voters out of five (see Figure 1). Notwithstanding the inherent limitations of a cross-sectional case study when it comes to long-term processes such as the personalization of politics, there are good reasons to believe that the 2013 Italian election provides a number of ideal conditions for the study of the determinants of voting behavior in a changing media environment: (a) because it corresponds to the first instance of decline of television (i.e., minus 7% between 2008 and 2013) and (b) most important to the purposes

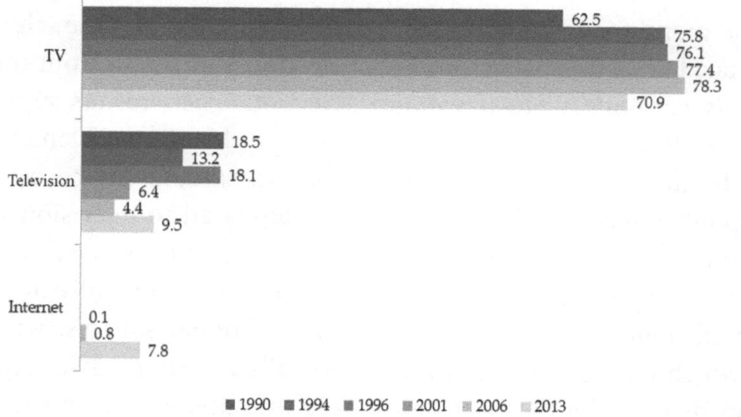

Figure 1. Italian voters' main source of political information (1990–2013).
Source: ITANES Series (1990–2013)

of this paper, because television's decline is paralleled by the entrance of the Internet into the game—now representing the major source of political information to almost 8% of eligible voters (the figure being 10% across those who did actually cast a vote).

The aforementioned changes in patterns of media consumption relate in fascinating ways to the outcome of an election that witnessed the massive decline of traditional parties at the advantage of a brand-new (and by then almost entirely Internet-based) political movement. Albeit with a much smaller margin than forecast, the winning coalition was the center-left led by Pier Luigi Bersani, with 29.6% of the valid votes, while Berlusconi's center-right coalition gained 29.2% of the votes. In other words, the two "traditional" coalitions obtained less than 60% of the valid votes together (as compared to 84% in 2008 and 99% in 2006). The biggest surprise was Beppe Grillo's *Movimento 5 Stelle* (Five Star Movement) with 25.6% of the votes, which made it the third political force in the country as well as the most electorally successful newcomer of Italian political history (Biorcio, 2013). Although an analysis of the organizational features of Grillo's movement lies beyond the scope of this article, it is worth remembering that—unlike its traditional counterparts—the Five Star Movement originates as a by-product of Grillo's personal blog and still relies to a large extent on the Web as its key organizational resource (for an extensive discussion, see Bordignon & Ceccarini, 2013).

Data and measures

The empirical analysis that follows will rely on the 2013 Italian National Election Study (ITANES) postelectoral data set. This is a nationally representative multistage sample conducted through face-to-face interviews/CAPI.[2] The dependent variable of the analysis is vote choice. Due to the central position granted to electoral coalitions by the current Italian electoral law, the analysis will focus on *coalition* rather than *party* choice throughout the analysis. In the light of the election results, which saw the three major coalitions awarded more than 80% of the popular vote, I will model voting as a fourfold choice between Bersani's center-left coalition, Berlusconi's center-right coalition, Grillo's Five Star Movement, and minor parties/coalitions.[3]

When it comes to measuring respondents' media exposure, the available literature has suggested numerous possibilities, each of which carries methodological advantages as well as substantive drawbacks. Apparently, the most straightforward way to measure respondents' exposure to televised political information in the context of a survey would consist of asking them to self-assess the amount of time spent watching the news. However, Prior (2009) compared survey estimates with Nielsen estimates, and found severe overreporting of news exposure on behalf of survey respondents. According to Prior, error occurs at the estimation stage rather than as a product of social desirability bias. Against this background, he thus proposes to concentrate on the exposure to message reception, ideally through political knowledge indicators (see also Price & Zaller, 1993). As he admits, however, this approach "does not help us study the effect of exposure" (Prior, 2009, p. 139). Moreover, political knowledge indicators are much less common in traditional election study data sets compared to media exposure indicators. For instance, the comparative analysis by Gidengil (2011) resorts—by necessity—to mere television exposure insofar as it represents the only comparable measure available in her cross-national election study data set.

Although suboptimal, mere television exposure can be thought to approximate actual information exposure because (a) we know that news watching increases proportionally to television watching (Wonneberger, Schoenbach, & van Meurs, 2011) and (b) a measure of mere television exposure is also able to subsume, to at least some extent, the amount of information gathered as a result of accidental exposure. According to *passive learning* theories, the simple availability of information produces learning (Zukin & Snyder, 1984). In this sense, "even broadcast viewers who prefer entertainment programs absorb at least basic political knowledge when they happen to tune in when only news is on" (Prior, 2005, p. 579).

In light of all the aforementioned considerations, I will segment ITANES respondents on the basis of their self-reported amount of television hours per day. To better understand the pervasiveness of television in Italian households during the

2013 election, it suffices to say that only 5% of respondents in the sample declare to have watched less than 30 minutes of television per day. The median respondent watched between two and three hours, while over a quarter of the sample watched between three and six hours.

As no comparable measure for Internet usage is available in the ITANES data set, the analysis will resort to the battery on political activity on the Internet, ranging from lighter forms of activity such as watching video content to more substantive ones such as attending (in person) political events that have been organized online (see full list in Table 1). The data presented in the table provides some interesting patterns. First of all, it is interesting to observe that, among all possible political activities on the Web, voters resorted mostly to "watching video content"—that is, typically, old media content online. Second, and somehow surprisingly given the relatively lenient selection of items in the battery, the proportion of respondents having performed *at least* one of these activities online does not rise much above one quarter.

Table 2 presents the cross tabulation of these two variables, with columns partitioning respondents by levels of daily exposure to television (low = less than three hours per day; high = three or more hours per day) and rows partitioning them by patterns of political activity on the Internet (yes = performed at least one of the activities in the battery; no = did not perform any online political activity). [4] This coding scheme has the advantage of isolating in an almost perfect way the two audiences of interest, with 25% of respondents reporting heavy exposure to television and no political activity on the Internet, 23% with comparatively lower exposure to television but politically active on the Internet, and only a negligible proportion (around 4%) of respondents heavily exposed to television and politically active on the Internet at the same time.

Table 1. Patterns of Political Activity on the Internet.

	%
Watched video content about the campaign	17.7
Visited political Web site	16.2
Visited political social network profile	14.2
Shared content about the campaign	12.2
Participated in online political discussions	8.6
Participated in an event organized online	6.2
Performed (at least) one of the above	*28.7*

Table 2. Television Exposure and Patterns of Political Activity on the Internet.

Web \ TV exposure	Low	High	Total
No	47.9%	23.4%	71.3%
(*N*)	(722)	(353)	(1,075)
Yes	24.9%	3.8%	28.7%
(*N*)	(375)	(58)	(433)
Total	72.8%	27.2%	100%
(*N*)	(1,097)	(411)	(1,508)

Moving to the measurement of voters' evaluation of leaders, the analysis will rely on politically relevant *personality traits.*[5] A wide body of available works supports the idea that the traits used to evaluate politicians are limited in number and tend to load onto a few general categories (Bittner, 2011). The ITANES series conforms to the close-ended trait battery developed in 1980 by the American National Election Study (Kinder, Abelson, & Fiske, 1979). Respondents are thus asked whether they perceive each of the major coalition's leader to be *competent, honest, empathic*, and a *strong leader*. According to the data presented in Table 3, the respective coalitions' leaders differ sharply in terms of perceived personality characteristics. Especially noteworthy are the rather low values relative to Berlusconi's honesty (only 19% of respondents consider him a honest politician), Bersani's leadership strength (36%), and Grillo's competence (40%). In order to assess the overall impact of leaders' personality on respondents' electoral calculus, their evaluation of coalition leaders will be measured through an additive personality trait index ranging, for each individual respondent, from "0" (leader is credited with no single characteristic) to "1" (leader is credited with all four characteristics).[6] Mean values of the additive personality trait index show that both Bersani and Grillo enjoy a substantial advantage vis-à-vis the long-term center-right leader Berlusconi.

If broken down by respondents' patterns of media consumption, mean values of the index provide a few key findings. Although respondents' evaluation of center-left leader Bersani does not seem to differ across levels of television consumption and patterns of political activity on the Internet, both Berlusconi and Grillo appear to enjoy a strong competitive advantage across heavy television viewers and political Internauts, respectively.

Table 3. Leaders' Personality Traits and Overall Score on the Additive Personality Trait Index.

	Bersani Center-left coalition	Berlusconi Center-right coalition	Grillo Five Star Movement
Leadership	.36	.81	.68
Competence	.73	.61	.40
Honesty	.68	.19	.61
Empathy	.58	.39	.68
Additive personality trait index			
All respondents	.59	.49	.59
By level of TV consumption			
Low	.59	.47*	.60
High	.59	.56*	.56
By political activity on the Web			
Politically inactive	.58	.50	.54*
Politically active	.61	.47	.70*

Note. Asterisks signal that the *t* test of paired means is significant at the .001 level (two-tailed).

Analysis

In order to assess the impact of voters' evaluation of party leaders' personality on their patterns of vote choice, I make use of logistic regression. Modeling strategy and the comprehensive set of covariates included in the analysis rely on the *valence politics* literature (Clarke et al., 2004). The composite modeling strategy relates to the different assumptions involved in modeling the choice to vote for incumbent and opposition parties, respectively. Insofar as voting for the incumbent party vis-à-vis any of its opposition rivals can be considered a fundamental electoral decision of its own, the first column of Table 4 reports the results of a binomial logistic regression, which pits center-left voting versus voting for any of the other coalitions. The second and third columns report the results of a multinomial logistic regression, which provide more detailed information about the factors driving voters to cast a ballot for opposition parties (in this case, center-left voting is used as the reference category). Controls include respondents' long-term ideological orientations (measured though self-placement on the left–right scale), their retrospective assessment of the state of the economy in the country, and whether the coalition voted for is considered the best at solving the most important issue in the country, plus controls (i.e., region of residence and frequency of church attendance). Age, gender, and educational level are also included, in order to control for sociodemographic differences between heavy television viewers and political Internauts (descriptive statistics for all independent variables included in the analysis are presented in Appendix B).

Table 4 provides a detailed report of the performance of the various variables in predicting a vote for each of the main coalitions. As all table entries are measured on a 1-point scale, coefficients are comparable in magnitude. The results clearly highlight the dominance of the leader's evaluations as driver of his respective coalition choice.

The dominance of coalition leaders as drivers of vote choice in the 2013 election is further highlighted in Figure 2, where the estimated effect of leader evaluations is summarized by means of the predicted probability of casting a vote for a given coalition moving from the minimum to the maximum value of the predictor of interest (with all other variables included in the model set at their mean value). The effect of leader evaluations appears relatively stronger for the Five Star Movement, with voters crediting Beppe Grilo with the highest score on the trait index, being 59% more likely to vote for his party compared to those assigning him the lowest score on the trait index. Lower figures can be credited to Bersani (49% increase in predicted probability to vote for the center-left coalition moving from a completely negative to a completely positive evaluation of its leader) and Berlusconi (32% increase). The importance of leader evaluations emerges even more clearly by comparing them with the explanatory power of the second-best predictor included in the model, that is, perceived competence at the most important issue. Although the latter is only slightly less important in the case of the Five Star Movement, it is worth noting that competence is outnumbered by leader evaluations with ratios ranging between 2:1 (center-left coalition voting) and 4:1 (center-right coalition voting).

After having assessed the dominance of leaders in the respondents' voting calculus, the analysis now turns to answering the central questions of this paper, focusing on the relationship between leader effects and patterns of television exposure and political activity on the Internet in turn. To do so, I follow the analytical strategy employed by

Table 4. The Determinants of Vote Choice in the Italian Election of 2013.

	Vote		
	Center-left coalition (Bersani)	Center-right coalition (Berlusconi)	Five Star Movement (Grillo)
Coalition leaders			
Pierlugi Bersani	**2.76*****	−3.11***	−3.27***
	(.44)	(.65)	(.53)
Silvio Berlusconi	−.81	**4.01*****	.27
	(.43)	**(.75)**	(.55)
Beppe Grillo	−1.41***	.81	**3.85*****
	(.38)	(.59)	**(.58)**
Ideology (Ref.: No L-R Self-Placement)			
Center-left	1.28**	−.66	−1.31**
	(.41)	(.80)	(.47)
Center-right	−.74	2.62***	.10
	(.47)	(.77)	(.54)
Best coalition at most important issue			
Center-left coalition	1.23***	−1.98*	−1.27**
	(.32)	(.83)	(.41)
Center-right coalition	−1.61**	1.57*	.39
	(.62)	(.73)	(.81)
Five Star Movement	−2.04***	.11	2.26***
	(.42)	(.83)	(.46)
Other	−.53	−.56	−.36
	(.32)	(.56)	(.43)
Retrospective economic evaluations	−.31	.64	.36
	(.84)	(1.19)	(.99)
Region of residence			
North-West	.37	.07	−.54
	(.34)	(.54)	(.41)
North-East	.69	−1.36*	−.72
	(.43)	(.66)	(.50)
Red Belt	0.70*	−.27	−1.11**
	(.34)	(.56)	(.43)
Center	.17	−.61	−.25
	(.40)	(.68)	(.46)
Church attendance	−1.41**	1.22	1.10
	(.46)	(.75)	(.57)
Constant	−.64	−2.21*	−1.47
	(.64)	(1.08)	(.82)
Pseudo *R*-Squared	.48	.50	
Log-likelihood	−247.52	−452.83	
N	704	704	

Notes. First column's coefficient are from a binomial logit (centre-left vs. all other coalition voting). Centre-right coalition and Five Star Movement analysis is a multinomial logit with centre-left coalition as the reference category. Other party voting is included in the multinomial logit analysis but coefficients are not displayed in table Age, gender and educational level are included in all models. Coefficients are not shown.

***$p \leq .001$. **$p \leq .01$. *$p \leq .05$.

Holian and Prysby (2014) in their analysis of leader effects by levels of media exposure. That is, I replicate the analysis presented in Table 4 on split samples (i.e., low *vs.* high levels of television consumption, and politically inactive on the Internet *vs.* politically active on the Internet). As logistic coefficients from split-sample estimations are not straightforwardly comparable in magnitude, I only report the changes in predicted probabilities of coalition voting moving from the minimum to the maximum value of each leaders' personality trait index while keeping all other variables in the model set at their means.

Findings from Figure 3 are strongly in line with expectations. The effect of coalition leader evaluations on voting is systematically stronger for those heavily exposed to television. This is especially the case for voters of Berlusconi's coalition, who appear to rely on their evaluation of the leader twice as much if heavily exposed to television as compared to those reporting comparatively lower patterns of television exposure. This finding comes by and large as no surprise, given the much higher popularity of Berlusconi across heavy TV viewers (see Table 3). Ratios of leader effects across television viewership groups are less spectacular in the cases of Grillo's movement as well as Bersani's coalition, but they witness nonetheless the stronger importance of leader evaluations for those voters more heavily exposed to television.[7]

Findings from the Internet analysis are presented in Figure 4. Politically active citizens voting for *established* parties would seem to pay less attention to leaders' personality within their voting calculus. This appears to be especially the case for voters of the center-right coalition. According to the results of the simulation stemming from the multinomial regression analysis, the coalition leader's evaluation turns even insignificant across the group of politically active on the Internet. Though this is not the case for center-left voters, one notes nonetheless that coalition leader Bersani matters roughly twice as much for those *not* active on the Internet. The most interesting finding of this analysis, however, comes from the case of Five Star Movement voters. Here, party leader Grillo would appear to matter *more* for those politically active on the Web.

Taken together, these findings suggest an interesting interpretation by which leader effects do not depend on the main source of information per sé. Their magnitude would seem to rather interact with

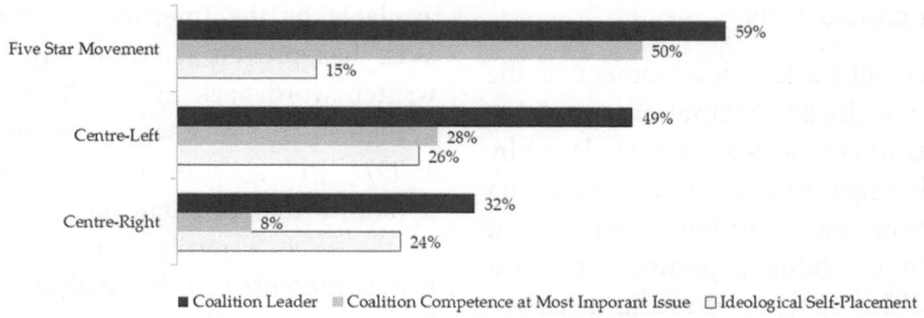

Figure 2. Predicted probability of coalition voting by key independent variables.

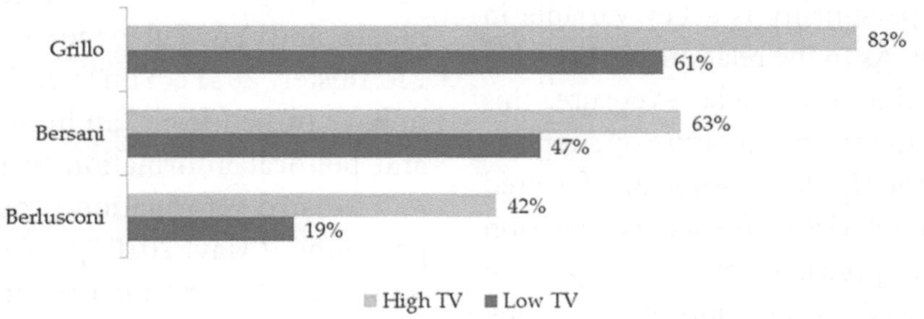

Figure 3. Predicted probability of coalition voting by evaluation of the respective leader and level of television exposure.

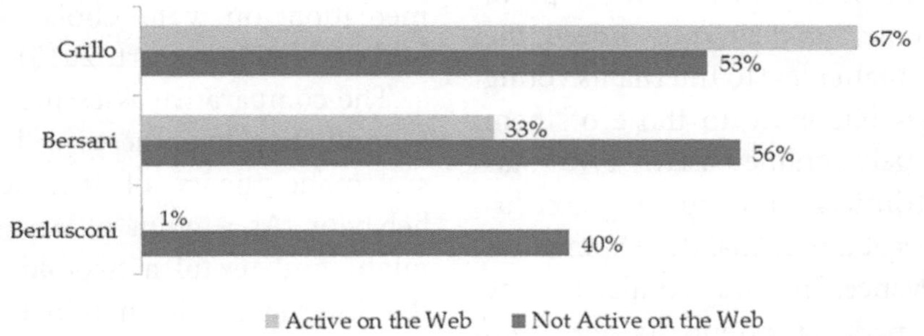

Figure 4. Predicted probability of coalition voting by evaluation of the respective leader and political activity on the Internet.

the characteristics of the political offer and their respective interaction with old as well as new media. Leaders of more traditional political formations that rely mostly on television for political communication matter more to those voters heavily exposed to television. In turn, their lack of appeal to political Internauts might explain their smaller importance within their voting calculus, and account in turn for the strong effect of Beppe Grillo on this segment of voters.

Robustness

To test the robustness of these findings to model specification and variable measurement, I performed extensive tests. First, I tested a different operationalization of the dependent variable with party votes in place of coalition votes (Table A.1 in Appendix A). Second, I tested a different measurement of coalition leaders' evaluation by replacing the additive personality trait index with leaders' thermometer scores (Table A.2). Third, I reran all models with a threefold segmentation of exposure to television (i.e., low, medium, and high exposure; Table A.3). Fourth, I tested the robustness of the results against different measurements of political activity on the Internet, by excluding one activity at a time from the index (Table A.4).[8] In all but one instance, the results of the robustness tests confirmed those presented in Figures 3 and 4.[9]

Discussion and conclusions

This paper looked into a key development of the democratic process—the personalization of politics. Whereas previous works tackled the role played by party change in driving the personalization of voting behavior across time, this contribution focused on the part played by individual exposure to political information on different types of media in conditioning leader effects on voting. The analysis of the determinants of vote choice in the 2013 Italian election confirms the notion that individuals' evaluation of political leaders' personality is a key variable in their voting equation. As to the relationship between leader effects on voting and media exposure, this paper contributes to the extant literature by supporting the idea that leader effects are somehow fostered by heavy exposure to television. Insofar as television is (at least partly) responsible for the heightened importance of party leader evaluations in the voting calculus, what is the intervening role of the Internet? The answer that can be derived from our empirical results is twofold, and it depends on the type of parties for which people cast their vote. Indeed, the leader would seem to matter less to Internauts voting for traditional parties but more to those of them voting for the (largely online-based) Five Star Movement. This intrinsically unsurprising conclusion hints nonetheless at a potential development of utmost political relevance. In a way similar to how Berlusconi gathered personal popularity and electoral influence through television, forcing all his political competitors to surrender to his media logic accordingly, Grillo might be paving the way for traditional parties and their respective leaders to "invade" the online arena. The political communication of former Italian Prime Minister Matteo Renzi has been proved to be a telling example in this respect (Bordignon, 2014). In turn, this supports a fascinating idea by which rather than depersonalizing politics, the Internet itself might provide parties and leaders with a new arena to actually foster patterns of political personalization.

In view of the rapid spread of the Internet as the most important (and at times only) source of political information for Western electorates, further research in this domain is in urgent need—also taking into account the wide range of formats through which political information is made available by the Internet. On the one hand, the Web has proven its capability of "bringing the written word back in" as all newspapers become available—free of charge—to every user (Morris, 1999). In a similar vein, personality-based dynamics that originate in television have found in the Web a fertile ground. According to the results presented in this analysis, most of the political activity on the Internet consists in watching video content. Although candidates and political leaders' video content is widely present—and increasingly so—on the Internet through social media and YouTube video channels (Gibson & McAllister, 2011), YouTube itself has been shown to have turned from "an innovative source of news and political information to one more hospitable to mediated information produced by media corporations" (May, 2010, p. 501). At the same time, however, the interactive possibilities of social media have highlighted the possibility for voters to connect horizontally, thus reviving classic theories of social influence and interpersonal intermediation on vote choice (Miller, Bobkowski, Maliniak, & Rapoport, 2015).[10]

The comparative assessment of—not necessarily—conflicting hypotheses will help move toward a systematic theory of Internet effects on voting behavior. As a point of departure, such a theory might find useful a twofold conceptualization of the Internet's informational features, pitting *old media online* (i.e., newspapers and television broadcasters) against *new media online* (e.g., social media) as a way to isolate their potentially different impacts on voting. The theoretical development will certainly benefit from a more comparative focus, with research also taking into account less peculiar party systems (for instance, where television is not by and large "owned" by one of the main political actors and the Internet is not "home" of the organizational structure of another) and contexts (for instance, countries where television is a less powerful source of political information and/or the Internet is a more powerful source).[11]

Finally, the results presented in this paper call for explicitly longitudinal analyses able to take into account the intervening role of party transformation in the process of progressive personalization of elections. Thirty years ago, Meyrowitz (1985) made clear the practical impossibility of assessing the impact of old (as well as new) media in isolation with all other (political) variables. Whereas previous works have documented the relationship between the "fourth information revolution" and the transformation of party organizations (Bimber, 2003; Mancini, 2015), the initial results presented here highlight the crucial need to integrate theories from both political communication and party research into a "shared research agenda" for future analyses of electoral change at the individual level.

Notes

1. So far, only one study by Gidengil (2011) tackled the issue in a comparative perspective—albeit with inconclusive results due to the acknowledged limitations within the available data.
2. From a methodological point of view, sticking to survey data alone implies opting (along the lines of virtually all existing research on the topic) for an "attentiveness" approach. This approach carries some drawbacks as compared to a "linkage" approach, most notably, the inability to connect the actual content of media coverage to individual patterns of voting behavior. However, the "linkage" approach comes with problems too. According to Dobrzynska et al. (2003, p. 29), the major limitation of this approach refers to the fact that it "does not address the bottom line question, that is, how much effect the media do exert on voters' final choice." Given the foremost interest of this paper in the very same bottom-line question, I thus decided to resort to the "attentiveness" approach, yet keeping in mind its inherent limitations when it comes to interpretation and generalization of the empirical findings.
3. Because the analysis deals with the determinants of vote choice, I will leave aside respondents who abstained as well as those who picked the 'did not vote,' 'do not know,' or 'no answer' response options. In turn, this lowers the number of cases included in the analysis down to $N = 950$.
4. The choice to sum up all the items from the Internet activity battery into a single additive scale is supported by the results of a factor analysis (all items load heavily onto the same factor; Cronbach's Alpha for the additive index equals .84). I further tested different versions of the index by excluding one activity at a time, each time obtaining the very same results.
5. The use of personality traits in place of thermometer score evaluations relies on the idea set forth by Fiorina (1981) that the thermometer might also be capturing factors such as retrospective judgments, party influence, issue positions, and so on.
6. Respondents have been asked to rate each political leader on the four traits on a 4-point scale ranging from "not at all" to "very much." Each variable has then been rescaled: "0" stands for a negative attitude (i.e., "not at all" and "not very much") while "1" stands for a positive attitude (i.e., "fairly much" and "very much").
7. Previous contributions highlighted that Grillo's popularity, already high among Internauts, grew exponentially among television viewers throughout the 2013 campaign as a result of the progressive *hybridization* of the Italian media system (Barisione et al., 2014).
8. Unfortunately, it was not possible to estimate the effect of coalition leader evaluations on single-activity-based subgroups of Internauts due to the very low number of cases.
9. When testing the model on party rather than coalition choice, Berlusconi appeared somewhat *less* important to respondents heavily exposed to television.
10. Bentivegna and Ceccarini (2013) show that the figure for political discussion during the 2013 election campaign was 66% among citizens who used the Internet to get political information compared to 45% for all others.
11. It is worth highlighting that Italy ranks fourth in the world—and first among Western European countries —when it comes to average daily television viewing time per person (http://www.statista.com/statistics/276748/average-daily-tv-viewing-time-per-person-in-selected-countries/ [last accessed: 07/16/2017]). At the same time, Italy also ranks way below the EU27 average with regard to the frequency of Internet use (http://ec.europa.eu/eurostat/statistics-explained/index.php/File:Internet_use_and_frequency_of_use_by_individuals,_2013_(%25_of_individuals).png)

References

Barisione, M., Catellani, P., & Garzia, D. (2013). Alla ricerca di un leader. In ITANES (Ed.), *Voto amaro. Disincanto e crisi economica nelle elezioni del 2013*. Bologna, Italy: Il Mulino pp. 147–157

Barisione, M., Catellani, P., & Garzia, D. (2014). Tra Facebook ei TG. Esposizione mediale e percezione dei leader nella campagna elettorale italiana del 2013. *Comunicazione Politica*, 15(1), 187–210.

Bellucci, P., Garzia, D., & Lewis-Beck, M. (2015). Issues and leaders as vote determinants. The case of Italy. *Party Politics*, *21*(2), 272–283. doi:10.1177/1354068812472583

Bentivegna, S., & Ceccarini, L. (2013). Web, giovani e voto. In ITANES (Ed.), *Voto amaro. Disincanto e crisi economica nelle elezioni del 2013*. Bologna, Italy: Il Mulino pp. 193–204

Bimber, B. (2003). *Information and American democracy: Technology in the evolution of political power*. Cambridge, England: Cambridge University Press.

Biorcio, R. (2013). La sfida del Movimento 5 stelle. In ITANES (Ed.), *Voto amaro. Disincanto e crisi economica nelle elezioni del 2013*. Bologna, Itlay: Il Mulino. pp. 107–119

Bittner, A. (2011). *Platform or personality? The role of party leaders in elections*. Oxford, England: Oxford University Press.

Bond, R., Fariss, C., Jones, J., Kramer, A., Marlow, C., Settle, J., & Fowler, J. (2012). A 61-million-person experiment in social influence and political mobilization. *Nature, 489*, 295–298. doi:10.1038/nature11421

Bordignon, F. (2014). Matteo Renzi: A "Leftist Berlusconi" for the Italian Democratic Party? *South European Society and Politics*, 19(1), 1–23. doi:10.1080/13608746.2014.887240

Bordignon, F., & Ceccarini, L. (2013). Five stars and a cricket. Beppe Grillo shakes Italian politics. *South European Society and Politics, 18*(4), 427–449. doi:10.1080/13608746.2013.775720

Boulianne, S. (2009). Does Internet use affect engagement? A meta-analysis of research. *Political Communication, 26*(2), 193–211. doi:10.1080/10584600902854363

Calise, M. (2000). *Il partito personale*. Rome/Bari, Italy: Laterza.

Calise, M. (2005). Presidentialization: Italian style. In T. Poguntke & P. Webb (Eds.), *The presidentialization of politics: A comparative study of modern democracies*. Oxford, England: Oxford University Press.

Campus, D. (2010). Mediatization and personalization of politics in Italy and France: The cases of Berlusconi and Sarkozy. *The International Journal of Press/Politics, 15*(2), 219–235. doi:10.1177/1940161209358762

Campus, D., & Pasquino, G. (2006). Leadership in Italy: The changing role of leaders in elections and in government. *Journal of Contemporary European Studies*, 14(1), 25–40. doi:10.1080/14782800600617912

Clarke, H., Sanders, D., Stewart, M. and Whiteley, P., (2004). *Political Choice in Britain*. Oxford: Oxford University Press.

Dobrzynska, A., Blais, A., & Nadeau, R. (2003). Do the media have a direct impact on the vote? The case of the 1997 Canadian election. *International Journal of Public Opinion Research*, 15(1), 27–43. doi:10.1093/ijpor/15.1.27

Druckman, J. (2003). The power of television images: The first Kennedy-Nixon debate revisited. *Journal of Politics, 65* (2), 559–571. doi:10.1111/1468-2508.t01-1-00015

Elmelund-Præstekær, C., & Hopmann, D. (2012). Does television personalise voting behaviour? Studying the effects of media exposure on voting for candidates or parties. *Scandinavian Political Studies*, 35(2), 117–140. doi:10.1111/scps.2012.35.issue-2

Fiorina, M. (1981). *Retrospective voting in American national elections*. New Haven: Yale University Press.

Garzia, D. (2012). Party and leader effects in parliamentary elections: Towards a reassessment. *Politics*, 32(3), 175–185. doi:10.1111/j.1467-9256.2012.01443.x

Garzia, D. (2013a). The rise of party/leader identification in Western Europe. *Political Research Quarterly*, 66(3), 533–544. doi:10.1177/1065912912463122

Garzia, D. (2013b). Can candidates' image win elections? A counterfactual assessment of leader effects in the second Italian Republic. *Journal of Political Marketing*, 12(4), 348–361. doi:10.1080/15377857.2013.837303

Garzia, D., De Angelis, A., & Pianzola, J. (2014). The impact of VAAs on electoral participation. In D. Garzia & S. Marschall (Eds.), *Matching voters with parties and candidates*. Colchester, England: ECPR Press. pp. 105–114

Garzia, D., & Viotti, F. (2011). Leader, identità di partito e voto in Italia, 1990–2008. *Rivista Italiana Di Scienza Politica*, 41(3), 411–432.

Gemenis, K., & Rosema, M. (2014). Voting advice applications and electoral turnout. *Electoral Studies, 36*, 281–289. doi:10.1016/j.electstud.2014.06.010

Gibson, R., & McAllister, I. (2006). Does cyber-campaigning win votes? Online communication in the 2004 Australian election. *Journal of Elections, Public Opinion and Parties*, 16(3), 243–263. doi:10.1080/13689880600950527

Gibson, R., & McAllister, I. (2011). Do online election campaigns win votes? The 2007 Australian "YouTube" election. *Political Communication*, 28(2), 227–244. doi:10.1080/10584609.2011.568042

Gidengil, E. (2011). Voter characteristics and leader effects. In K. Aarts, A. Blais, & H. Schmitt (Eds.), *Political leaders and democratic elections*. Oxford, England: Oxford University Press.

Hayes, D. (2009). Has television personalized voting behavior? *Political Behavior*, 31(2), 231–260. doi:10.1007/s11109-008-9070-0

Holian, D., & Prysby, C. (2014). *Candidate character traits in presidential elections*. Abingdon, England: Routledge.

Iyengar, S., & Kinder, D. (1987). *News that matters. Television and American opinion*. Chicago, IL: University of Chicago Press.

Karvonen, L. (2010). *The personalisation of politics. A study of parliamentary democracies*. Colchester, England: ECPR Press.

Keeter, S. (1987). The illusion of intimacy: Television and the role of candidate personal qualities in voter choice. *Public Opinion Quarterly*, 51(3), 344–358. doi:10.1086/269040

Kinder, D., Abelson, R., & Fiske, S. (1979). *Developmental research on candidate instrumentation: Results and recommendations*. Report submitted to the Institute for Social Research, University of Michigan.

Kriesi, H. (2012). Personalization of national election campaigns. *Party Politics*, 18(6), 825–844. doi:10.1177/1354068810389643

Lenz, G., & Lawson, C. (2011). Looking the part: Television leads less informed citizens to vote based on candidates' appearance. *American Journal of Political Science*, 55(3), 574–589. doi:10.1111/ajps.2011.55.issue-3

Lobo, M. (2008). Parties and leader effects: Impact of leaders in the vote for different types of parties. *Party Politics*, 14 (3), 281–298. doi:10.1177/1354068807088123

Mancini, P. (2015). *Il Post-Partito*. Bologna, Italy: Il Mulino.

May, A. (2010). Who tube? How YouTube's news and politics space is going mainstream. *The International Journal of Press/Politics*, 15(4), 499–511. doi:10.1177/1940161210382861

Mazzoleni, G. (1996). Patterns and effects of recent change in electoral campaigning in Italy. In D. Swanson & P. Mancini (Eds.), *Politics, media and modern democracy. An international study of innovations in electoral campaigning and their consequences*. Westport, CT: Praeger. pp. 193–206

Mazzoleni, G., & Schulz, W. (1999). "Mediatization" of politics: A challenge for democracy? *Political Communication*, 16(3), 247–261. doi:10.1080/105846099198613

McAllister, I. (2007). The personalization of politics. In R. Dalton & H.-D. Klingemann (Eds.), *The Oxford handbook of political behaviour*. Oxford, England: Oxford University Press. pp. 88–106

McLeod, J., Glynn, C., & McDonald, D. (1983). Issues and images: The influence of media reliance in voting decisions. *Communication Research*, 10(1), 37–58. doi:10.1177/009365083010001002

Meyrowitz, J. (1985). *No sense of place: The impact of electronic media on social behavior*. Oxford, England: Oxford University Press.

Miller, J., & Krosnick, J. (2000). News media impact on the ingredients of presidential evaluations: Politically knowledgeable citizens are guided by a trusted source. *American Journal of Political Science*, 44(2), 301–315. doi:10.2307/2669312

Miller, P., Bobkowski, P., Maliniak, D., & Rapoport, R. (2015). Talking politics on Facebook: Network centrality and political discussion practices in social media. *Political Research Quarterly*. Advance online publication. doi:10.1177/1065912915580135

Morris, D. (1999). *Vote.com: How big-money lobbyists and the media are losing their influence, and the Internet is giving power to the people*. Los Angeles, CA: Renaissance Books.

Mughan, A. (2000). *Media and the presidentialization of parliamentary elections*. Basingstoke, England: Palgrave Macmillan.

Norris, P. (2000). *A virtuous circle. Political communication in post-industrial societies*. Cambridge, England: Cambridge University Press.

Poguntke, T., & Webb, P. (Eds.). (2005). *The presidentialization of politics. A comparative study of modern democracies*. Oxford, England: Oxford University Press.

Postman, N. (2006). *Amusing ourselves to death: Public discourse in the age of show business*. London: Penguin.

Price, V., & Zaller, J. (1993). Who gets the news? Alternative measures of news reception and their implications for research. *Public Opinion Quarterly*, 57(2), 133–164. doi:10.1086/269363

Prior, M. (2005). News vs. entertainment: How increasing media choice widens gaps in political knowledge and turnout. *American Journal of Political Science*, 49(3), 577–592. doi:10.1111/ajps.2005.49.issue-3

Prior, M. (2009). The immensely inflated news audience: Assessing bias in self-reported news exposure. *Public Opinion Quarterly*, 73(1), 130–143. doi:10.1093/poq/nfp002

Rahat, G., & Sheafer, T. (2007). The personalization(s) of politics: Israel, 1949–2003. *Political Communication*, 24 (1), 65–80. doi:10.1080/10584600601128739

Renwick, A., & Pilet, J.-B. (2016). *Faces on the ballot: The personalization of electoral systems in Europe*. Oxford, England: Oxford University Press.

Rico, G. (2014). Political sophistication and media consumption as factors of personalization. In M. Lobo & J. Curtice (Eds.), *Personality politics? The role of leader evaluations in democratic elections*. Oxford, England: Oxford University Press.

Sartori, G. (1989). Video-power. *Government and Opposition*, 24(1), 39–53. doi:10.1111/j.1477-7053.1989.tb00106.x

Sudulich, L., Wall, M., & Baccini, L. (2015). Wired voters: The effects of Internet use on voters' electoral uncertainty. British Journal of Political Science, 45(4), 853–881.

Swanson, D., & Mancini, P. (Eds.). (1996). *Politics, media, and modern democracy. An international study of innovations in electoral campaigning and their consequences*. Westport, CT: Praeger.

Takens, J., Kleinnijenhuis, J., Van Hoof, A., & Van Atteveldt, W. (2015). Party leaders in the media and voting behaviour. Priming rather than learning or projection. *Political Communication*, 32, 249–267. doi:10.1080/10584609.2014.944319

Tolbert, C., & McNeal, R. (2003). Unraveling the effects of the Internet on political participation? *Political Research Quarterly*, 56(2), 175–185. doi:10.1177/106591290305600206

Venturino, F. (2000). La personalizzazione della politica italiana. Il ruolo dei leader nelle elezioni del 1996. *Rivista Italiana Di Scienza Politica*, 20(2), 295–328.

Walgrave, S., Van Aelst, P., & Nuytemans, M. (2008). "Do the vote test": The electoral effects of a popular vote advice application at the 2004 Belgian elections. *Acta Politica*, 43 (1), 50–70. doi:10.1057/palgrave.ap.5500209

Wonneberger, A., Schoenbach, K., & Van Meurs, L. (2011). Interest in news and politics—Or situational determinants? Why people watch the news. *Journal of Broadcasting & Electronic Media*, 55(3), 325–343. doi:10.1080/08838151.2011.597466

Zukin, C., & Snyder, R. (1984). Passive learning: When the media environment is the message. *Public Opinion Quarterly*, 48(3), 629–638. doi:10.1086/268864

Appendix A. Detailed estimation procedure for robustness tests

Table A.1. Different Operationalization of the Dependent Variable (Party Rather Than Coalition Votes).

	Partito Democratico (PD)	Popolo delle Libertá (PdL)	Five Star Movement
Level of TV exposure			
Low	36%	16%	55%
High	46%	7%	84%
Politically active on the Web			
Low	46%	36%	48%
High	22%	n.s.	63%

Table A.2. Different Operationalization of Leader Evaluations (Thermometer Rather Than Trait Index).

	Center-left coalition	Center-right coalition	Five Star Movement
Level of TV exposure			
Low	79%	79%	95%
High	98%	99%	96%
Politically active on the Web			
Low	89%	86%	94%
High	70%	77%	98%

Table A.3. Three Categories of TV Viewership (% of Respondents in the Sample in Parentheses).

	Center-left coalition	Center-right coalition	Five Star Movement
Low (43.4%)	39%	58%	63%
Medium (29.2%)	n.s.	23%	42%
High (27.2%)	68%	26%	83%

Table A.4. One-by-One Exclusion of Items From the Measurement of Political Activity on the Internet.

	Center-left coalition		Center-right coalition		Five Star Movement	
	Min.	Max.	Min.	Max.	Min.	Max.
Not active on the Internet	[55%	57%]	[36%	42%]	[52%	54%]
Active on the Internet	[29%	35%]	[n.s.	n.s.]	[64%	70%]

Appendix B. Descriptive statistics of independent variables included in the regression analysis

	N	Min.	Max.	Mean	St. Dev.
Coalition leaders trait index					
Pierluigi Bersani (center-left)	868	0	1	0.63	0.33
Silvio Berlusconi (center-right)	896	0	1	0.48	0.33
Beppe Grillo (Five Star Movement)	746	0	1	0.62	0.36
Ideology					
No self-placement	950	0	1	0.09	0.29
Center-left	950	0	1	0.58	0.49
Center-right	950	0	1	0.33	0.47
Best coalition at most important issue					
Center-left	950	0	1	0.25	0.43
Center-right	950	0	1	0.13	0.34
Five Star Movement	950	0	1	0.14	0.35
Other	950	0	1	0.14	0.35
Retrospective economic evaluations	950	0	1	0.11	0.15
Age category					
18–24	950	0	1	0.09	0.29
25–34	950	0	1	0.14	0.35
35–44	950	0	1	0.15	0.35
45–54	950	0	1	0.19	0.39
55–64	950	0	1	0.20	0.40
65+	950	0	1	0.23	0.42
Gender (female)	950	0	1	0.49	0.50
Educational level	950	0	1	0.43	0.25
Region of residence					
North-West	950	0	1	0.27	0.44
North-East	950	0	1	0.13	0.34
Red Belt	950	0	1	0.21	0.40
Center	950	0	1	0.15	0.36
South	950	0	1	0.24	0.43
Frequency of church attendance	950	0	1	0.35	0.27

Index

Note: Page numbers in *italics* refer to figures
Page numbers in **bold** refer to tables
Page numbers followed by 'n' refer to notes